Integrated 1 Mathematics

Study Guide

This Study Guide includes a section for every section in the textbook. Each Study Guide section contains an illustrated list of Key Terms, worked-out Samples, and practice exercises, including Review/Preview questions. Each Study Guide unit contains a Unit Review consisting of a Unit Check-Up and a Spiral Review of all previous units. Answers are provided in a separate Answer Key.

McDougal Littell/Houghton Mifflin

Evanston, Illinois

Boston   Dallas   Phoenix

Acknowledgments
The authors wish to thank Chuck Kruger, Mathematics Teacher, Eden Valley-Watkins High School, Eden Valley, Minnesota, for his valuable contributions to this Study Guide.

p. 195
A Scientific Approach to Distance Running, by David L. Costill. Courtesy of Track & Field News, Mountain View, California, USA.

ISBN: 0-395-64435-6

23456789 - PO - 98 97 96 95

Contents

Unit 1   **Page**

Section 1-1   Communicating with Diagrams   1
Section 1-2   Investigating Patterns   4
Section 1-3   Patterns with Powers   7
Section 1-4   Writing and Evaluating Expressions   11
Section 1-5   Modeling the Distributive Property   13
Section 1-6   Working Together on Congruent Polygons   16
Section 1-7   Exploring Quadrilaterals and Symmetry   19
Unit 1 Review   23

Unit 2   **Page**

Section 2-1   Numbers and Estimates   25
Section 2-2   Using Negative Numbers   28
Section 2-3   Exploring Scientific Notation   31
Section 2-4   Estimating Measures: Length and Area   34
Section 2-5   Exploring Angle Relationships   38
Section 2-6   Expressions for Measures   43
Section 2-7   Solving Equations: Balancing   45
Section 2-8   Solving Equations: Undoing   48
Section 2-9   Square Roots and Cube Roots   50
Unit 2 Review   53

Unit 3   **Page**

Section 3-1   Using Matrices and Graphs   55
Section 3-2   Mean, Median, and Mode   60
Section 3-3   Inequalities and Intervals   62
Section 3-4   Histograms and Stem-and-Leaf Plots   64
Section 3-5   Box-and-Whisker Plots   68
Section 3-6   Choosing a Data Display   71
Section 3-7   Analyzing Misleading Graphs   75
Unit 3 Review   78

Unit 4   Page

Section 4-1   Coordinates for Locations   80
Section 4-2   Introduction to Coordinate Geometry   84
Section 4-3   Translations   88
Section 4-4   Rotations   91
Section 4-5   Scatter Plots   95
Section 4-6   Graphs and Functions   99
Section 4-7   Functions and Equations   103
Unit 4 Review   107

Unit 5   Page

Section 5-1   Modeling Problem Situations   109
Section 5-2   Opposites and the Distributive Property   113
Section 5-3   Variables on Both Sides   116
Section 5-4   Inequalities with One Variable   119
Section 5-5   Rewriting Equations and Formulas   122
Section 5-6   Using Reciprocals   124
Section 5-7   Area Formulas   127
Section 5-8   Systems of Equations in Geometry   133
Unit 5 Review   135

Unit 6   Page

Section 6-1   Ratios and Rates   137
Section 6-2   Investigating Probability   140
Section 6-3   Solving Proportions   144
Section 6-4   Sampling and Making Predictions   147
Section 6-5   Similar Polygons   150
Section 6-6   Dilations   154
Section 6-7   Sine and Cosine Ratios   157
Unit 6 Review   160

Unit 7   Page

Section 7-1   Direct Variation, Slope, and Tangent   162
Section 7-2   A Direct Variation Model   165
Section 7-3   Circumference and Arc Length   170
Section 7-4   Direct Variation with $y = kx$ 173
Section 7-5   Using Dimensional Analysis   176
Section 7-6   Areas of Circles and Sectors   179
Unit 7 Review   182

Unit 8   Page

Section 8-1	Linear Growth and Decay	184
Section 8-2	Linear Combinations	188
Section 8-3	Horizontal and Vertical Lines	192
Section 8-4	Writing Equations for Lines	195
Section 8-5	Graphing Systems of Linear Equations	198
Section 8-6	Graphing Linear Inequalities	201
Section 8-7	Systems of Linear Inequalities	204
Unit 8 Review		207

Unit 9   Page

Section 9-1	The Pythagorean Theorem and Reasoning	209
Section 9-2	Investigating Properties of Square Roots	213
Section 9-3	If-Then Statements and Converses	216
Section 9-4	Geometric Probability	220
Section 9-5	Surface Area of Space Figures	223
Section 9-6	Volumes of Prisms and Cylinders	228
Section 9-7	Volumes of Pyramids and Cones	232
Section 9-8	Similar Figures: Area and Volume	235
Unit 9 Review		239

Unit 10   Page

Section 10-1	Reflections	241
Section 10-2	Transforming Parabolas	245
Section 10-3	Factors and Intercepts	249
Section 10-4	Working with Powers	252
Section 10-5	Factored Form and x-Intercepts	255
Section 10-6	Expanded Form and Line of Symmetry	258
Section 10-7	Using Factors to Sketch $y = x^2 + bx + c$	261
Section 10-8	Solving Quadratic Equations	264
Unit 10 Review		267

Communicating with Diagrams

FOCUS

Make statements about information presented in tables, graphs, and concept maps.

Many road signs convey information by using symbols rather than words.

KEY TERMS

Concept map (p. 5)
a visual summary that helps you remember the connections between ideas

EXAMPLE / ILLUSTRATION

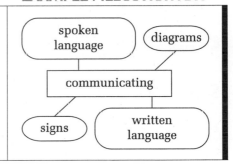

UNDERSTANDING THE MAIN IDEAS

Concept maps

A concept map is a way of organizing and summarizing what you know about a concept or process. A concept map does not have a set format; it can take a variety of forms, depending on the ideas being summarized.

Sample 1

This concept map summarizes some information about geometric figures you may have studied.

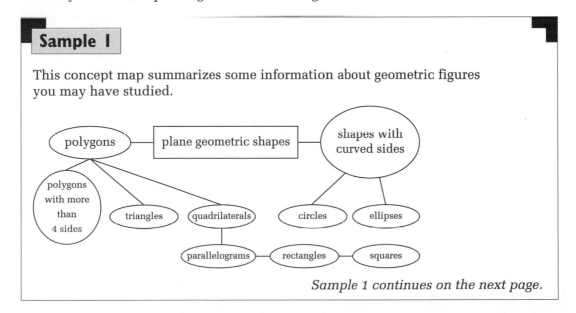

Sample 1 continues on the next page.

---

a. What are the two main types of figures shown in the concept map?
b. What three major categories are shown for polygons?
c. Where would you put eight-sided polygons on the map?

1. Use the elements listed below to make a concept map.
   - mathematical statements
   - equations
   - inequalities
   - formulas
   - $1 + 2 = 3$
   - $x + 5 = 8$

   - $A = \pi r^2$
   - $P = 2l + 2w$
   - $6y = 18$
   - $x < 5$
   - $4 + 7 \le y$
   - $3 \cdot 5 > 10$

Tables and graphs

A table shows data numerically. A graph shows data in a visual format.
Both tables and graphs can be useful for making comparisons of data.
However, sometimes a table is more precise than a graph.

Sample 2

The table and graph below show the 1995 enrollment figures for
Jordan High School.

1995 Jordan High School Enrollment		
Class	Number of girls	Number of boys
Freshman	80	90
Sophomore	94	84
Junior	70	80
Senior	70	56

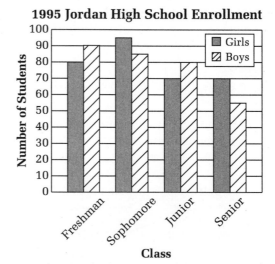

1995 Jordan High School Enrollment

a. What are two things you can learn from the table?
b. What are two things you can learn from the graph?
c. Write a question that is more easily answered from the table than from
   the graph.
d. Write a question that is more easily answered from the graph than from
   the table.

Sample Response

a. In each of the freshman, sophomore, and junior classes, the difference between the number of boys and girls is the same, 10. The number of girls is the same for the junior and senior classes.

b. The total number of students is greatest in the sophomore class. The total number of students is lowest in the senior class.

c. One possible question is "How many fewer boys are in the senior class than in the sophomore class?".

d. One possible question is "In which class is the difference between the numbers of boys and girls greatest?".

2. Use the table below to make a double-bar graph.

Michael Jordan's Seven-in-a-Row		
Year	Field Goals	Free Throws
1986–87	1098	833
1987–88	1069	723
1988–89	966	674
1989–90	1034	593
1990–91	990	571
1991–92	943	491
1992–93	992	476

Review PREVIEW

Find the perimeter of each rectangle. *(Toolbox Skill 17)*

3.
1.9
1.9 1.9
1.9

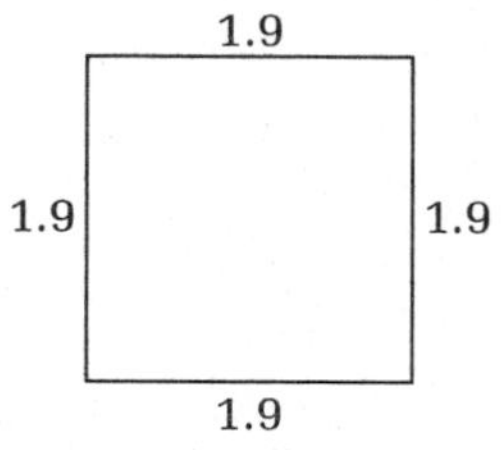

4.
10
3 3
10

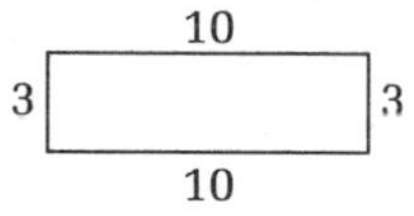

5.
8 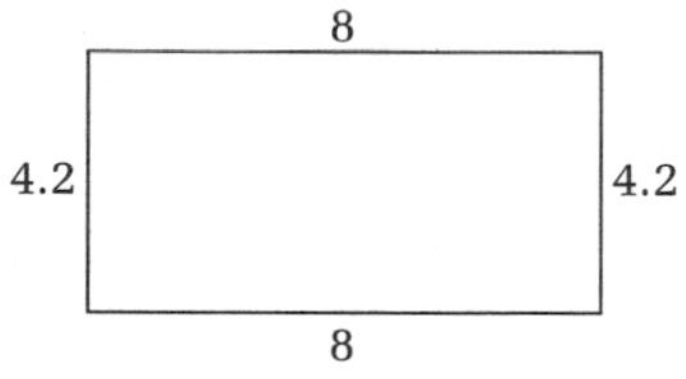
4.2 4.2
8

INTEGRATED MATHEMATICS 1 Study Guide

FOCUS

Describe patterns using tables and variable expressions. Evaluate variable expressions.

> " The sea awoke at midnight from its <u>sleep</u>,   <u>a</u>
>   And round the pebbly beaches far and <u>wide</u>   <u>b</u>
>   I heard the first wave of the rising <u>tide</u>   <u>b</u>
>   Rush onward with uninterrupted <u>sweep</u>;   <u>a</u>
>   A voice out of the silence of the <u>deep</u>,   <u>a</u>
>   A sound mysteriously <u>multiplied</u>   <u>b</u>
>   As of a cataract from the mountain's <u>side</u>   <u>b</u>
>   Or roar of winds upon a wooded <u>steep</u>.   <u>a</u>
>
>   So comes to us at times, from the <u>unknown</u>   <u>c</u>
>   And inaccessible solitudes of <u>being</u>,   <u>d</u>
>   The rushing of the sea-tides of the <u>soul</u>;   <u>e</u>
>   And inspirations that we deem our <u>own</u>,   <u>c</u>
>   Are some divine foreshadowing and <u>foreseeing</u>   <u>d</u>
>   Of things beyond our reason or <u>control</u>. "   <u>e</u>
>
> <u>The Sound of the Sea</u>, by Henry Wadsworth Longfellow

A sonnet is an example of poetry with structure and pattern containing fourteen lines, usually written in rhymed iambic pentameter. This Italian, or Petrarchan, sonnet consists of an octave (eight-line stanza) and a sestet (six-line stanza). Often the octave rhyming pattern is <u>abbaabba</u> and the sestet rhyming pattern is <u>cdecde</u>.

KEY TERMS | **EXAMPLE / ILLUSTRATION**

KEY TERMS	EXAMPLE / ILLUSTRATION
Variable (p. 10) a letter used to represent one or more numbers	In the expression $2x + 3y$, the variables are x and y.
Variable expression (p. 10) a mathematical expression that contains numbers, variables, and symbols for operations	$3n$ and $a - 5$ are variable expressions.
Evaluate (p. 12) to find the value of a variable expression by computing the result when each variable is replaced by a number	To evaluate $6n + 2$ when $n = 6$, replace n by 6: $6(6) + 2 = 38$.
Substitute (p. 12) to replace a variable in an expression by a number	To evaluate $1.5x$ when $x = 3, 4,$ and 5, substitute each number for x and find the result: $1.5(3) = 4.5$; $1.5(4) = 6$; $1.5(5) = 7.5$.

UNDERSTANDING THE MAIN IDEAS

Variable expressions

Writing a variable expression is a useful way to summarize the pattern that can be found in a table. The table on the next page shows the relationship between the length of the side of a square and its perimeter.

Side length	1	2	3	4	...	s
Perimeter	4	8	12	16	...	$4s$

Sample 1

A car is traveling at an average speed of 45 mi/h. Write a variable expression for the distance traveled in h hours.

Sample Response

Notice the pattern.

45(1) ⟵ In 1 hour, the distance traveled is 45 miles.
45(2) ⟵ In 2 hours, the distance traveled is 90 miles.
45h ⟵ In h hours, the distance traveled is 45h miles.

1. Draw Shapes 4 and 5 in the pattern below. Make a table of the perimeters of the shapes. Then write a variable expression for the perimeter of Shape n.

Shape 1   **Shape 2**   **Shape 3**

Write a variable expression for each phrase.

2. twice the length l plus twice the width w

3. the number of items n times the price p

4. the number of students s divided by the number of classes c

Evaluating variable expressions

You evaluate a variable expression by substituting a number for each variable and then performing the operations given in the expression.

Sample 2

Evaluate 3.14d for each value of d.
  a. 6   **b.** 10   **c.** 15

Sample Response

  a. 3.14d **b.** 3.14d **c.** 3.14d
  3.14(6)   3.14(10)   3.14(15)
  18.84   31.4   47.1

INTEGRATED MATHEMATICS 1 **Study Guide**   5

5. Evaluate $\dfrac{p}{2 \cdot 2}$ for each value of p.

    a. 1   **b.** 25   **c.** 2000

Evaluate each variable expression for $x = 3$ and $y = 30$.

6. $x + y$ **7.** xy **8.** $\dfrac{y}{x}$ **9.** $\dfrac{1}{3}y - x$

Review **PREVIEW**

Use the excerpt about the public debt. *(Section 1-1)*

The public debt has been increasing steadily for the past 30 years. The amount owed by each citizen of the United States was about $1800 in 1970, more than double that amount in 1980, and more than triple the 1980 amount in 1990.

10. Which bar graph shows the information from the excerpt?

  a.   **Debt per U.S. Citizen**

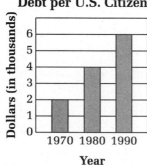

  b.   **Debt per U.S. Citizen**

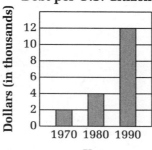

  c.   **Debt per U.S. Citizen**

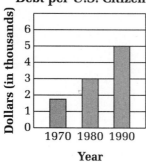

Calculate each repeated multiplication.

11. $(1.2)(1.2)(1.2)$ **12.** $6 \cdot 6 \cdot 6 \cdot 6$ **13.** $4 \cdot 4 \cdot 4 \cdot 4 \cdot 4$

1-3 Patterns with Powers

FOCUS

Use exponents to express repeated multiplication. Make conjectures.

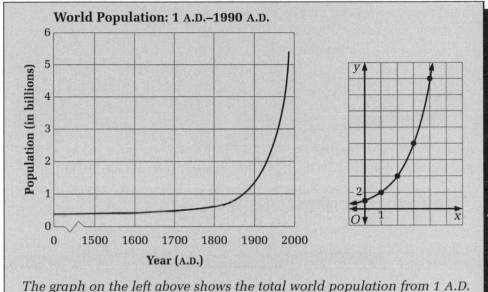

World Population: 1 A.D.–1990 A.D.

The graph on the left above shows the total world population from 1 A.D. to 1990 A.D. Notice the similarities to the graph at the right. Because of these similarities, world population experts state that our world population is growing exponentially.

KEY TERMS

EXAMPLE / ILLUSTRATION

KEY TERMS	EXAMPLE / ILLUSTRATION
Factor (p. 19) each of a group of numbers that are multiplied together	There are 4 factors in the product $8 \cdot 8 \cdot 8 \cdot 8$.
Power (p. 19) an expression indicating how many times a number is multiplied by itself	10^3 (third power of ten)
Base (p. 19) the repeated factor in a power	The base of the power above is 10.
Exponent (p. 19) the number of times the base appears as a factor in a power	The exponent of the power above is 3.
Conjecture (p. 21) a guess based on past experiences	For any two numbers a and b, $ab > a$ and $ab > b$.
Counterexample (p. 22) an example that shows that a statement is false	Counterexample for the conjecture above: Let $a = 10$ and $b = 0.5$, then $ab = (10)(0.5) = 5$, and since $5 < 10$, $ab < a$.

UNDERSTANDING THE MAIN IDEAS

Writing products as powers

When the same number is repeated as a factor, it is convenient to write the product as a power of that number. For example, instead of writing

$$5 \cdot 5 \cdot 5 \cdot 5 \cdot 5 \cdot 5 \cdot 5 \cdot 5 \cdot 5 \cdot 5,$$

it is easier to write 5^{10}. In the power 5^{10}, 5 is the base and 10 is the exponent.

Sample 1

Write using exponents.

a. eight cubed   **b.** ten to the sixth   **c.** two squared

Sample Response

a. 8^3 **b.** 10^6 **c.** 2^2

Write each product as a power.

1. $12 \cdot 12 \cdot 12 \cdot 12 \cdot 12$ **2.** $25 \cdot 25 \cdot 25 \cdot 25$

3. $16 \cdot 16 \cdot 16$ **4.** $9 \cdot 9 \cdot 9 \cdot 9 \cdot 9 \cdot 9$

Write using exponents.

5. four to the fifth   **6.** ten to the sixth

7. six to the eighth   **8.** twelve to the third

Evaluating powers of variables

You can use a variable as the base of a power. When you evaluate a power of a variable for a given number, you substitute the number for the variable and then find the product. For example, when $a = 3$, you evaluate a^4 by substituting 3 for a and then simplifying 3^4.

Sample 2

Write an expression for the area covered by the tiles shown. Then evaluate the expression when $x = 6$.

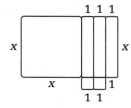

Sample Response

The tiles have areas x^2, x, x, x, 1, and 1. The total area covered by the tiles is $x^2 + 3x + 2$ square units.

Evaluate $x^2 + 3x + 2$ when $x = 6$.

$x^2 + 3x + 2$
$6^2 + 3 \cdot 6 + 2$ ⟵ Substitute 6 for x.
$36 + 18 + 2$
56

The tiles cover 56 square units when $x = 6$.

Evaluate each expression for $x = 5$.

9. x^3 **10.** $x^2 + x$ **11.** $x^2 + 2x + 7$

12. $2x^2$ **13.** $3x^2 + 4x + 1$ **14.** $2x^2 + 5x + 9$

Conjectures and counterexamples

A conjecture is an "educated" guess, that is, a guess based on past experiences. A conjecture in mathematics is a generalization based on specific examples. It can sometimes be difficult to show that a conjecture is true, but it is often easy to show that one is false. To disprove a conjecture, just one counterexample is needed.

Sample 3

Use the pattern shown below to make a conjecture about the value of 10^n.

$10^6 = 1{,}000{,}000$
$10^5 = 100{,}000$
$10^4 = 10{,}000$
$10^3 = 1{,}000$
$10^2 = 100$
$10^1 = 10$
$10^0 = ?$

Sample Response

Notice that 10^6 has six zeros, 10^5 has five zeros, 10^4 has four zeros, 10^3 has three zeros, 10^2 has two zeros, and 10^1 has one zero. If the pattern of zeros continues, 10^0 has no zeros, so $10^0 = 1$.

Write as a power of 10.

15. $10^{10} \cdot 10^2$ **16.** $10^5 \cdot 10$ **17.** $\frac{10^5}{10}$

18. $\frac{10^{12}}{10^5}$ **19.** $\frac{10^7}{10^4}$ **20.** $10^8 \cdot 10^6$

Sample 4

Observation: If the three angles of a triangle are equal, then the sides are all the same length.

Conjecture: If the four angles of a quadrilateral are equal, then the sides are all the same length.

Find a counterexample.

Sample Response

The rectangle shown has four right angles, but the sides are not all the same length.

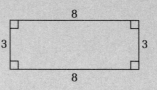

21. Consider some examples and make a conjecture about the number of zeros there will be in 100^6.

22. Give a counterexample for this conjecture: When you divide two numbers, the answer is always less than the number you are dividing.

Review **PREVIEW**

Computer disks are sold in large packages of 25 and small packages of 10. *(Section 1-2)*

23. **a.** Write a variable expression for the number of disks in *l* large packages.
    b. Write a variable expression for the number of disks in *s* small packages.
    c. Evaluate the expressions in parts (a) and (b) for *l* = 5 and *s* = 10.

24. A type of concept map, called a Venn diagram, is shown at the right. Write three sentences about polygons based on this concept map. *(Section 1-1)*

25. Find the sum of these numbers: 16, 16, 52. *(Toolbox Skill 1)*

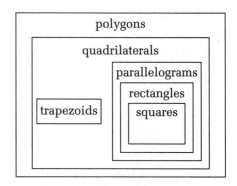

Writing and Evaluating Expressions

Use the order of operations to evaluate expressions.

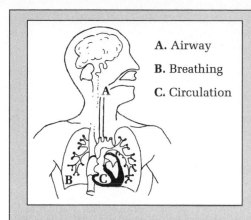

A. Airway

B. Breathing

C. Circulation

The ABCs of Basic Life Support is a memory device that is used to ensure the proper order of the steps of basic life support. It is estimated that many lives would be saved if these steps would be started immediately when individuals stop breathing due to cardiac arrest or other injuries.

KEY TERMS	EXAMPLE / ILLUSTRATION
Order of operations (p. 26) a set of agreed-upon rules used to evaluate an expression	$2 \cdot 6 + (4^3 - 9 \div 3)$ $2 \cdot 6 + (64 - 9 \div 3)$ $2 \cdot 6 + (64 - 3)$ $2 \cdot 6 + 61$ $12 + 61$ 73

UNDERSTANDING THE MAIN IDEAS

Order of operations

Mathematicians have established rules for simplifying mathematical expressions that are used by people and by machines so that an expression has just one correct value. This set of rules is called the *order of operations*, and it must be used to evaluate an expression that contains several operations.

Parentheses	← Simplify expressions inside parentheses in the order given in the following steps.
Exponents	← Calculate any powers.
Multiplication and **D**ivision	← Do these as they appear from left to right.
Addition and **S**ubtraction	← Do these as they appear from left to right.

Sample 1

Calculate according to the order of operations.

$45 - 12 \div 3 \cdot 6 + 2^3$

Sample Response

$45 - 12 \div 3 \cdot 6 + 2^3$
$45 - 12 \div 3 \cdot 6 + 8$ ←— Calculate the power first.
$45 - 4 \cdot 6 + 8$ ←— Do the division (it appears before the multiplication).
$45 - 24 + 8$ ←— Do the multiplication.
$21 + 8$ ←— Do the subtraction (it appears before the addition).
29 ←— Do the addition.

Sample 2

Calculate according to the order of operations.

$45 - (12 \div 3 \cdot 6 + 2^3)$

Compare with the result of Sample 1. Do the parentheses make a difference?

Sample Response

$45 - (12 \div 3 \cdot 6 + 2^3)$
$45 - (12 \div 3 \cdot 6 + 8)$ ←— Inside the parentheses, calculate the power first.
$45 - (4 \cdot 6 + 8)$ ←— Inside the parentheses, do the division.
$45 - (24 + 8)$ ←— Inside the parentheses, do the multiplication.
$45 - 32$ ←— Inside the parentheses, do the addition.
13 ←— Do the subtraction.

Yes, the parentheses change the value of the expression.

Calculate according to the order of operations.

1. $7 - 2 \cdot 3$ **2.** $16 \div 2 \cdot 3$ **3.** $2^3 - (8 - 4 \div 2)$

4. $(6 \cdot 3 - 2) + 4^2$ **5.** $9 \cdot 5 \div 5 - 3^2$ **6.** $36 \div 6^2 \cdot 100$

Review

Show each conjecture is false by finding a counterexample. *(Section 1-3)*

7. $x^3 + x^2 = x^5$ **8.** $x^3 \cdot x^2 = x^6$

For Exercises 9–11, tell whether each word phrase can be represented by the variable expression 8c. Write *Yes* or *No*. *(Section 1-2)*

9. 8 more than c cats

10. 8 items that cost c cents apiece

11. the cost per item for 8 items that cost c cents total

12. a. Evaluate the expressions $5(2 + x)$ and $2 + 5x$ for three values of x.
   b. For each expression, what operations did you use? in what order?
   c. Which expression is larger? Why? *(Section 1-2)*

Modeling the Distributive Property

FOCUS

Use the distributive property to simplify calculations, rewrite expressions, and combine like terms.

For an art project, a teacher supplies each of 20 students with sheets of colored construction paper. Each student is to have 5 sheets of blue paper, 6 sheets of red paper, and 4 sheets of white paper. If the teacher chooses to distribute the paper one color at a time, he would distribute $20 \cdot 5 + 20 \cdot 6 + 20 \cdot 4$ *sheets of paper. Or the teacher could make up sets of papers consisting of 5 blue, 6 red, and 4 white sheets which could be distributed all at once to each student. In this case, he would distribute* $20(5 + 6 + 4)$ *sheets of paper.*

KEY TERMS

EXAMPLE / ILLUSTRATION

Distributive property (p. 31) the property which says that for all numbers a, b, and c: $a(b + c) = ab + ac$ and $a(b - c) = ab - ac$	$6(2 + 3) = 6 \cdot 2 + 6 \cdot 3$ $3(x + 1) = 3 \cdot x + 3 \cdot 1$
Term (p. 33) a number, a variable, or a product of numbers and variables in a mathematical expression	The terms of the expression $x^2 + 2x + 5$ are x^2, $2x$, and 5.
Coefficient (p. 33) the numerical part of a variable term	The coefficient of the term $2x$ is 2.
Like terms (p. 33) terms with the same variable part	$3x^2y + 3xy + xy^2 + 5x^2y$ ⌐———— like terms ————⌐

UNDERSTANDING THE MAIN IDEAS

Using the distributive property

The distributive property allows you to think about products that involve sums or differences in two ways. You can think of $7(50 - 1)$ as the product of 7 and 49 or you can think of it as the difference $7 \cdot 50 - 7 \cdot 1$, or $350 - 7$. In general, for all numbers a, b, and c, $a(b + c) = ab + ac$ and $a(b - c) = ab - ac$.

Sample 1

Find each product.
  a. $12(99)$ **b.** $7(x - 5)$ **c.** $2\pi(r^2 + rh)$

Sample Response

a. Think of 99 as 100 − 1 and use the distributive property.

$$12(99) = 12(100 - 1)$$
$$= 12(100) - 12(1)$$
$$= 1200 - 12$$
$$= 1188$$

b. $7(x - 5) = 7x - 7 \cdot 5$ ⟵ Use the distributive property.
$$= 7x - 35$$

c. $2\pi(r^2 + rh) = 2\pi r^2 + 2\pi rh$ ⟵ Use the distributive property.

Find each product using mental math.

1. 8(298)
2. $5\left(6\frac{2}{5}\right)$
3. 4(725)

Use the distributive property to find each sum or difference mentally.

4. $639 \cdot 2 + 639 \cdot 8$
5. $249 \cdot 60 - 49 \cdot 60$

Use the distributive property to rewrite each expression without parentheses.

6. $-5(x + 5)$
7. $\frac{1}{4}(8x^2 - 16y)$
8. $7(x + y)$

Combining like terms

Mathematical expressions can be added to form new expressions. When an expression is part of a sum, it is called a *term*. A term can be a number, also called a constant term, or a product of numbers and variables, called variable terms. The numerical part of a variable term is called the *coefficient*. If the variable part of two variable terms is the same, that is, the same variables raised to the same power, then they are called *like terms*. You can combine like terms by using the distributive property. When you simplify an expression you combine like terms.

Sample 2

Simplify $9x + (3 - x)4$.

Sample Response

$9x + (3 - x)4$
$9x + 12 - 4x$ ⟵ Use the distributive property.
$9x - 4x + 12$ ⟵ Group like terms together.
$5x + 12$ ⟵ Combine like terms.

Combine like terms. If not possible, explain why.

9. $4a + 5b + 3a$
10. $a^2 - b^2 + c^2$
11. $3(2 - x) + 5x + 1$

Evaluate when $x = 7$. *(Section 1-4)*

12. $x^2 + 3x + 2$ **13.** $2x^2 - 14$ **14.** $5x^2 - 7x + 7$

Write as a power of ten. *(Section 1-3)*

15. $10 \cdot 10 \cdot 10$ **16.** $10^4 \cdot 10^4$ **17.** $\dfrac{10^{10}}{10^5}$

Write two expressions for the perimeter of each figure, one with parentheses and one without parentheses. *(Section 1-2)*

18.
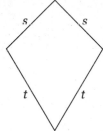

19.
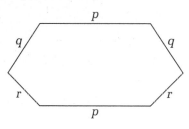

Working Together on Congruent Polygons

Create and
identify congruent
polygons.

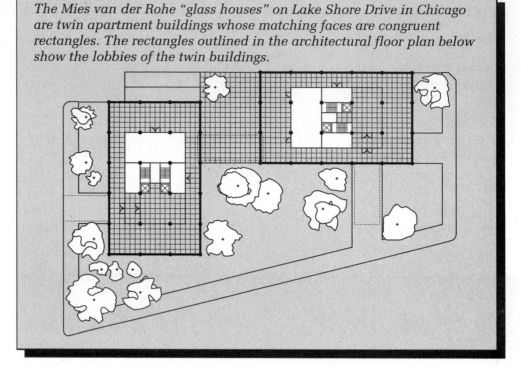

The Mies van der Rohe "glass houses" on Lake Shore Drive in Chicago are twin apartment buildings whose matching faces are congruent rectangles. The rectangles outlined in the architectural floor plan below show the lobbies of the twin buildings.

KEY TERMS

EXAMPLE / ILLUSTRATION

Congruent (p. 38) 　having the same size and shape (The symbol "≅" is read "is congruent to.")	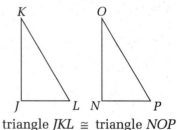 triangle *JKL* ≅ triangle *NOP*
Polygon (p. 39) 　a figure with straight sides, such as a triangle or a quadrilateral	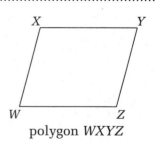 polygon *WXYZ*
Vertex (p. 40) 　a corner of a polygon (plural: *vertices*)	The vertices of quadrilateral *WXYZ* above are *W*, *X*, *Y*, and *Z*.
Side (p. 40) 　a part of a polygon defined by two consecutive vertices	Quadrilateral *WXYZ* above has sides *WX*, *XY*, *YZ*, and *WZ*.

UNDERSTANDING THE MAIN IDEAS

Congruent polygons

Congruent polygons are polygons that have the same size and the same
shape. When two polygons are congruent, they can be placed one on top
of the other so that their sides and vertices match exactly. Matching
sides and vertices of congruent polygons are called *corresponding parts.*

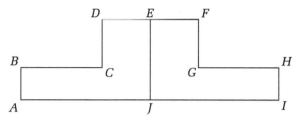

hexagon *ABCDEJ* ≅ hexagon *IHGFEJ*

A corresponds to *I*	side *AB* ≅ side *IH*
B corresponds to *H*	side *BC* ≅ side *HG*
C corresponds to *G*	side *CD* ≅ side *GF*
D corresponds to *F*	side *DE* ≅ side *FE*
E corresponds to *E*	side *EJ* ≅ side *EJ*
J corresponds to *J*	side *JA* ≅ side *JI*

Sample

Write a statement about congruent
triangles *ABD* and *CDB*. Then list
corresponding sides and
corresponding vertices.

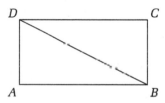

Sample Response

triangle *ABD* ≅ triangle *CDB*

corresponding sides
sides *AB* and *CD*
sides *BD* and *DB*
sides *AD* and *CB*

corresponding vertices
vertices *A* and *C*
vertices *B* and *D*
vertices *D* and *B*

For Exercises 1–3, name the congruent polygons. Then list three pairs of
corresponding sides.

1.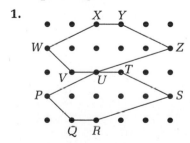

2.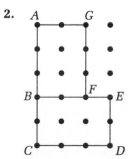

3.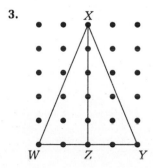

---

4. **Open-ended** Make a logo for a school team by using congruent polygons.

Rewrite without parentheses. *(Section 1-5)*

5. $(3x - 2)4$ 6. $5(a^2 - 6a - 7)$

Evaluate according to the order of operations. *(Section 1-4)*

7. $7 + 10 \div 2$ 8. $6 \cdot 8 - 5$

Write a variable expression for the perimeter of each polygon.
(Section 1-4)

9.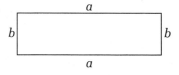

10.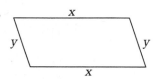

1-7 Exploring Quadrilaterals and Symmetry

FOCUS

Build quadrilaterals from congruent triangles and write expressions for their perimeters. Find lines of symmetry. Communicate ideas through writing.

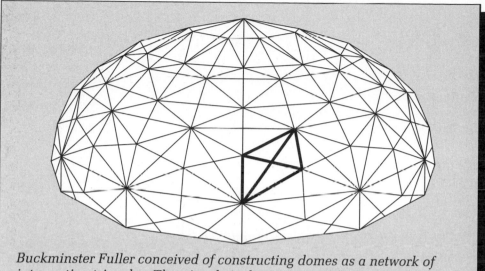

Buckminster Fuller conceived of constructing domes as a network of intersecting triangles. The triangle is the strongest geometric shape. Notice that groups of connected triangles form parallelograms.

KEY TERMS	EXAMPLE / ILLUSTRATION
Equilateral triangle (p. 44) a triangle with all three sides the same length	6 in. 6 in. 6 in.
Isosceles triangle (p. 44) a triangle with two sides the same length	3 cm 1 cm 3 cm
Scalene triangle (p. 44) a triangle with no sides the same length	7 m 3 m 5 m
Right triangle (p. 44) a triangle with one right angle	10 ft 6 ft 8 ft
Right angle (p. 44) an angle measuring 90°	In the triangle above, the angle between the 8 ft and 6 ft sides is a right angle.

Perpendicular sides (p. 44) sides of a polygon that meet at a right angle	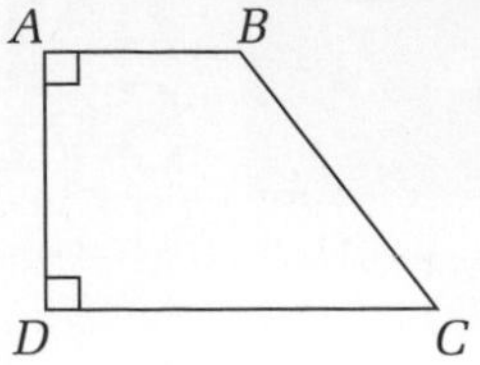 Sides AB and AD and sides CD and AD are perpendicular.
Parallel sides (p. 44) sides of a polygon that do not meet (and would never meet if extended indefinitely)	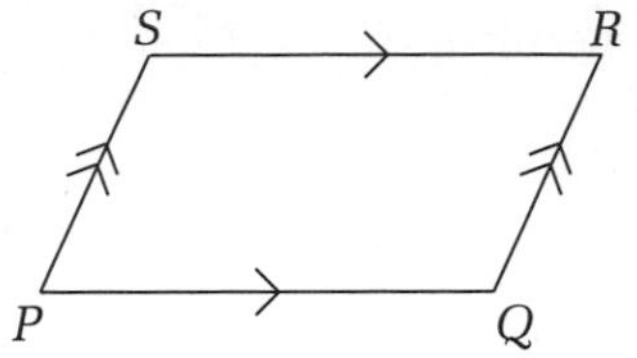 Sides SR and PQ are parallel. Sides PS and QR are parallel.
Parallelogram (p. 45) a quadrilateral with both pairs of opposite sides parallel	Quadrilateral $PQRS$ above is a parallelogram.
Kite (p. 45) a quadrilateral with two pairs of consecutive sides that are congruent	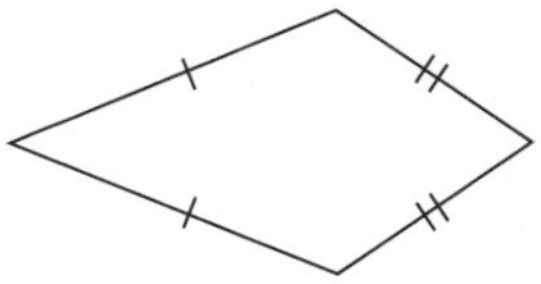
Rhombus (p. 45) a quadrilateral with all four sides congruent	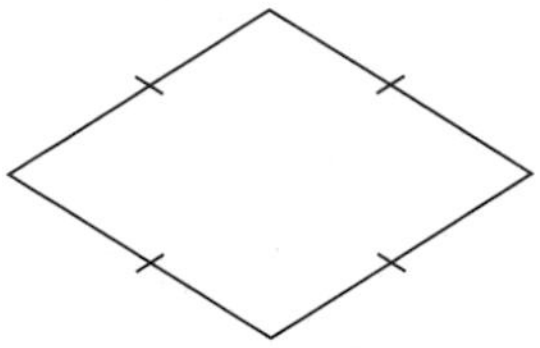
Symmetry (p. 45) a property of some polygons that makes it possible to fold them into matching halves	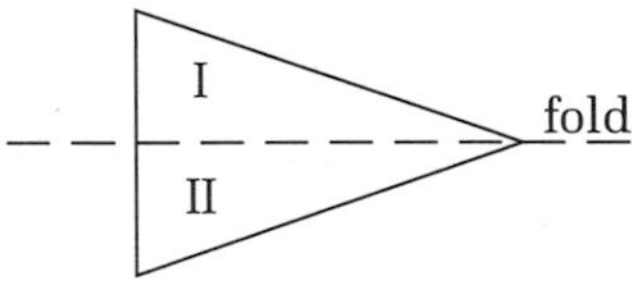 Region I matches region II.
Line of symmetry (p. 45) the "fold line" of a polygon that has symmetry	The fold line in the figure above is the line of symmetry for the triangle.

UNDERSTANDING THE MAIN IDEAS

Describing quadrilaterals

Different types of quadrilaterals are formed when two congruent triangles are positioned so that one pair of congruent sides coincide. Depending on whether the triangles are equilateral, isosceles, or scalene, the resulting quadrilaterals will be rhombuses, kites, parallelograms, rectangles, or squares.

Sample 1

What name best describes
the quadrilateral?

Sample Response

The right angle symbols and tick marks indicate that the quadrilateral is
a rectangle.

What name best describes each quadrilateral?

1. 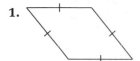   2.    3.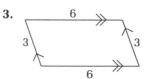

Symmetry

A polygon has symmetry if you can fold a copy of it in such a way that
the two parts fit exactly, with one half on top of the other. The fold line
is a line of symmetry for the polygon. A figure may have more than one
line of symmetry.

Sample 2

Draw the lines of symmetry for each polygon.

a.    b.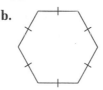

Sample Response

a. 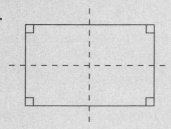   b.

INTEGRATED MATHEMATICS 1 **Study Guide**

Draw all lines of symmetry for each figure or write *no symmetry*.

4.  5. 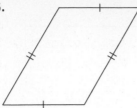 6.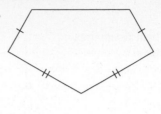

Review **PREVIEW**

7. Use a triangle and a copy of it to draw a quadrilateral. Label the vertices of the quadrilateral and name some congruent sides.   *(Section 1-6)*

Combine like terms.   *(Section 1-5)*

8. $x + y + y + z + x$ 9. $p + q + q + q + p$

Write each power of ten as a number and in words.   *(Section 1-3)*

10. 10^5 11. 10^{12} 12. 10^8 13. 10^1

Unit 1 Review

Complete these exercises for a review of Unit 1. If you have difficulty with a particular problem, review the indicated section.

1. Use the information given in the table below to make a bar graph. (*Section 1-1*)

Prime Time Television Viewing (Millions of People)							
Day	Mon.	Tues.	Wed.	Thur.	Fri.	Sat.	Sun.
Total persons	102.8	100.4	94.1	96.6	89.7	91.8	109.1

2. Would you use the table or the graph you made for Exercise 1 to find out how many more prime time television viewers there are on Saturday than on Friday? (*Section 1-1*)

3. Can you find out more quickly from the table or the graph from Exercise 1 that Sunday and Monday are the two top viewing days? (*Section 1-1*)

4. Write a variable expression for the number of quarters in d dollars. (*Section 1-2*)

For Exercises 5–7, evaluate each expression for $a = 6$ and $b = 10$. (*Section 1-2*)

5. ab 6. $2b - a$ 7. $0.5a + 0.5b$

8. Write $c \cdot c \cdot c \cdot c$ as a power. Then write how to say the power. (*Section 1-3*)

9. Write y to the eighth power using exponents. (*Section 1-3*)

10. Write $10^2 \cdot 10^5$ as a power of ten. (*Section 1-3*)

Calculate according to the order of operations. (*Section 1-4*)

11. $16 \div 4 - 3 + 5^2$ 12. $(8 + 6) \cdot 2 - 18$ 13. $4^3 - 4^2 \cdot 3$

Use the distributive property to rewrite each expression without parentheses. (*Section 1-5*)

14. $4(3x - y)$ 15. $0.5(6a + 2)$

Combine like terms. (*Section 1-5*)

16. $4 + 2(x - 3) + 5x$ 17. $3y^2 + 2y + 6y^2 + 5$

Name the congruent polygons. Then list three pairs of congruent sides. (*Section 1-6*)

18. 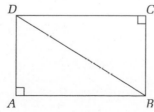 19.

20. a. Make two copies of △ABC. Make as many quadrilaterals as you can from the triangles.

b. What kinds of quadrilaterals did you make?

c. What are the perimeters of the quadrilaterals you made? *(Section 1-7)*

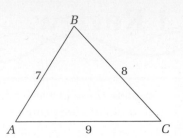

Write an expression for the area covered by each group of tiles. Evaluate each expression when *x* = 4.

1.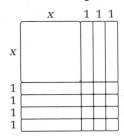
2.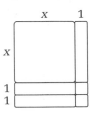

Write each fraction as a percent.

3. $\frac{3}{4}$ **4.** $\frac{3}{5}$ **5.** $\frac{2}{3}$ **6.** $\frac{12}{5}$

Evaluate each expression for *a* = 2, *b* = 3, and *c* = 5.

7. $2a + 4b - c$ **8.** $ab + 3c$ **9.** $a + bc$ **10.** $a(b + 2c)$

Simplify each expression.

11. $3(x - 7)$ **12.** $\frac{1}{2}(6a^2 + 12a)$ **13.** $3p^2 - 6pq - 2p^2 + 3pq$

Name the congruent triangles. Then list three pairs of corresponding sides.

14.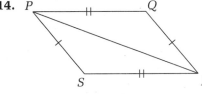
15.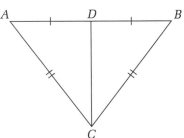

Write a variable expression for the perimeter of each polygon.

16.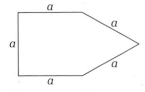
17.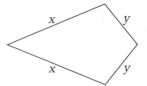

2-1 Numbers and Estimates

See different ways that numbers are used and tell whether an estimate of a population or distance is reasonable or likely.

The Department of Commerce, acting through its Fishery Management Councils, has the authority to regulate the number of days fishermen can go out to fish, to restrict certain areas to no fishing, and to prohibit the sale of troubled species of fish once the total allowable take is reached. These regulations and restrictions are based on estimates of the fish population derived from population sampling.

KEY TERMS

EXAMPLE / ILLUSTRATION

Continuous (p. 60) quantities that are measured	 The temperature of water as it is heated to boiling is a continuous quantity.
Discrete (p. 60) quantities that are counted	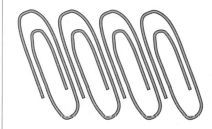 There are 4 paper clips shown. The number of items is a discrete quantity.

UNDERSTANDING THE MAIN IDEAS

Making estimates

Numbers are used for identifying, ordering, counting, and measuring. Numbers that are used for counting and measuring are often estimates— population estimates, distance estimates, and so on. Reasonable estimates can be based upon comparisons with given information or previously-learned facts.

INTEGRATED MATHEMATICS 1 Study Guide **25**

Sample 1

Estimate the number of apples in a bushel of apples.

Sample Response

From an almanac, a bushel is equal to 32 dry quarts. Estimating, a quart container will hold about 2 lb of apples and there are about 3 apples to a pound. Now multiply to estimate the number of apples in a bushel.

$$3 \quad \cdot \quad 2 \quad \cdot \quad 32 \quad = \quad 192$$

apples/lb   lb/qt   qt/bu

So, there are about 190 apples in a bushel.

Estimate whether each value is in the *hundreds, thousands, millions,* or *billions.*

1. the length in miles of the Mississippi River

2. the number of people who live in California

3. the weekly salary of a person who earns $25,000 per year

4. the population of the world in the year 2000

Estimating probabilities

When you estimate the probability of an event, you can use information about events that have already occurred. The probability of an event can be given as a number between 0 and 1 or as a percent between 0% and 100%.

Sample 2

Use a number anywhere along the scale shown below to estimate the probability that Americans will be driving cars powered by electricity within the next 10 years. Give a reason for your answer.

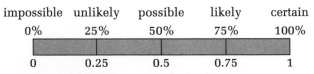

Sample Response

Using information about the experimentation currently being conducted by the auto industry and the need to reduce air pollution, a conservative estimate would be 50% or 0.5. A more optimistic estimate would be 75% or 0.75.

For Exercises 5–7, use a number anywhere along the scale shown in Sample 2 to estimate the probability of each event. Give a reason for your answer.

5. A hurricane will occur along the east coast of the United States sometime in September.

6. A live dinosaur will be found in the year 2010.

7. The Chicago White Sox will win the American League pennant in 1999.

Discrete and continuous quantities

Quantities that are measured, such as distances and temperatures, are continuous; they correspond to all the points on a number line. Quantities that are counted, such as objects or people, are discrete; they correspond to only the whole-number points on a number line.

Sample 3

Classify each quantity as *continuous* or *discrete*. Give a reason for your answer.

a. the number of people on an elevator

b. the height of the elevator above the ground

Sample Response

a. Discrete; the number is counted.

b. Continuous; the amount is measured.

Classify each quantity as *continuous* or *discrete*.

8. the number of people in a library

9. the amount of sugar being poured into a cup

10. the number of days in October

11. the temperature on October 16

 *Review* **PREVIEW**

For Exercises 12–15, write the prime factorization of each number.
(Toolbox Skill 7)

12. 52   **13.** 18   **14.** 64   **15.** 115

16. Graph the numbers -5, $-2\frac{1}{2}$, 0, $1\frac{1}{2}$, $2\frac{1}{2}$, and $3\frac{1}{2}$ on a number line. What do you notice about $-2\frac{1}{2}$ and $2\frac{1}{2}$? *(Toolbox Skill 2)*

2-2 Using Negative Numbers

FOCUS
Review how to do operations with negative numbers.

In a football game, when the ball carrier is tackled behind the line of scrimmage, the play will be tabulated as negative yardage—a loss of yardage.

KEY TERMS

EXAMPLE / ILLUSTRATION

KEY TERMS	EXAMPLE / ILLUSTRATION
Absolute value (p. 64) the distance a number is from zero on a number line	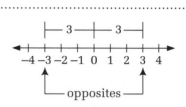
Opposites (p. 64) two numbers that are the same distance from zero on a number line, but on opposite sides of zero	

UNDERSTANDING THE MAIN IDEAS

Calculating with positive and negative numbers

The following rules apply when calculating with positive and negative numbers.

1. The sum of two positive numbers is positive.

2. The sum of two negative numbers is negative.

3. The sum of a positive and a negative number is positive if the positive number has the greater absolute value, negative if the negative number has the greater absolute value, and 0 if the numbers are opposites.

4. The difference of a positive and a negative number is found by adding the opposite of the number being subtracted and then using the sign rules for sums (rules 1–3) given above.

5. The product of two positive numbers is positive.

6. The product of two negative numbers is positive.

7. The product of a positive and a negative number is negative.

8. The sign rules given for products also apply to quotients.

Sample 1

Simplify. Tell which rule(s) given above are applied.

a. $27.3 + 6.7$ **b.** $-4.8 + (-2)$ **c.** $-7.5 + 3$

d. $15 - (-5)$ **e.** $-18 - 9.2$ **f.** $-8.1 - (-13.8)$

g. $(-6)(8)$ **h.** $(-1.5)(-2.5)$ **i.** $(17)(3)$

j. $130 \div (-5)$ **k.** $-74 \div 2$ **l.** $-92 \div (-4)$

Sample Response

a. 34; rule 1

b. –6.8; rule 2

c. –4.5; rule 3: $|-7.5| > |3|$

d. 15 + 5 = 20; rules 4 and 1

e. –18 + (–9.2) = –27.2; rules 4 and 2

f. –8.1 + 13.8 = 5.7; rules 4 and 3: $|13.8| > |-8.1|$

g. –48; rule 7

h. 3.75; rule 6

i. 51; rule 5

j. –26; rules 8 and 7

k. –37; rules 8 and 7

l. 23; rules 8 and 6

Simplify.

1. 16.3 + (–10.7)

2. –12.4 + 5.8

3. –9.5 – (–3.6)

4. –63 – 84

5. –7.1(–8)

6. –14.4 ÷ 3

Evaluating algebraic expressions involving negative numbers

The rules you learned earlier for evaluating expressions and using the order of operations can be applied when expressions involve negative numbers.

Sample 2

Evaluate each expression for the given values of the variables.

a. $-6c + d$ when $c = 4$ and $d = -8$

b. $x^2 - 4y$ when $x = -2$ and $y = 3$

c. $\frac{3a + 4b}{4}$ when $a = -12$ and $b = 1$

Sample Response

a. $-6c + d$

$-6(4) + (-8)$ ← Substitute 4 for c and –8 for d.

$-24 + (-8)$ ← Simplify.

-32

b. $x^2 - 4y$

$(-2)^2 - 4(3)$ ← Substitute –2 for x and 3 for y.

$4 - 12$ ← Simplify.

$4 + (-12)$

-8

c. $\frac{3a + 4b}{4}$

$\frac{3(-12) + 4(1)}{4}$ ← Substitute –12 for a and 1 for b.

$\frac{-36 + 4}{4}$ ← Simplify.

$\frac{-32}{4}$

-8

Evaluate each expression for the given values of the variables.

7. $3x^2 - 2xy + 3y^2$ when $x = 4$ and $y = -5$

8. $2m - 3n + 2mn$ when $m = -1.5$ and $n = -2$

9. $\dfrac{p}{q} - 7p + 8q$ when $p = 8$ and $q = -4$

Review **PREVIEW**

For Exercises 10–12, estimate whether each value is in the *hundreds*, *thousands*, *millions*, or *billions*. *(Section 2-1)*

10. the population of Canada

11. the number of people at a performance of a play

12. the distance from Seattle, Washington to Miami, Florida

13. Replace each __?__ with the correct term. *(Section 1-3)*

   In the power 10^{18}, 10 is the __?__ and 18 is the __?__ . The number 18 in 10^{18} tells you that 10 is used as a __?__ 18 times.

Write each expression as a power of ten. *(Section 1-3)*

14. $10^4 \cdot 10^{10}$ 15. $10^{15} \cdot 10^3$ 16. $\dfrac{10^{12}}{10^3}$ 17. $\dfrac{10^{28}}{10^7}$

FOCUS

Read and write numbers in scientific notation and recognize whether a result in scientific notation on a calculator is reasonable.

When you find the product $0.000068 \cdot 0.00082$ on a scientific calculator, the display will read $5.576\ -08$ or $5.576\ E-08$. The value displayed is the product given in the form of scientific notation used by your calculator. The paper-and-pencil equivalent is 5.576×10^{-8}.

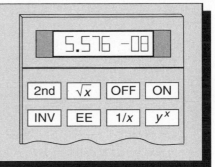

KEY TERMS

Scientific notation (p. 74)
    a number written as the product of a decimal that is greater than or equal to 1 and less than 10, and a power of 10

EXAMPLE / ILLUSTRATION

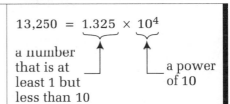

$$13{,}250 = 1.325 \times 10^4$$

a number that is at least 1 but less than 10   a power of 10

UNDERSTANDING THE MAIN IDEAS

Scientific notation

Scientific notation is a convenient shorthand for writing very large or small numbers. The numbers are written as the product of a decimal and a power of 10. If the number is a large number, the exponent of 10 is positive. If the number is small, the exponent is negative.

Sample 1

Write each number in scientific notation.
  a. 250,640,000   **b.** 0.000039

Sample Response

a. The leading digit is in the hundred millions place.

$$
\begin{aligned}
250{,}640{,}000 &= 2.5064 \text{ hundred millions} \\
&= 2.5064 \times 100{,}000{,}000 \\
&= 2.5064 \times 10^8
\end{aligned}
$$

b. The leading digit is in the hundred thousandths place.

$$
\begin{aligned}
0.000039 &= 3.9 \text{ hundred thousandths} \\
&= 3.9 \times 0.00001 \\
&= 3.9 \times \frac{1}{100{,}000} \\
&= 3.9 \times \frac{1}{10^5} \quad \longleftarrow \quad \frac{1}{10^n} = 10^{-n} \\
&= 3.9 \times 10^{-5}
\end{aligned}
$$

Sample 2

Write each number in decimal notation.

a. 3.35×10^8 **b.** 5.5×10^{-7}

Sample Response

a. $3.35 \times 10^8 = 3.35 \times 100{,}000{,}000$ ← Multiplying by 100,000,000 moves the decimal point right 8 places.

$= 335{,}000{,}000$

b. $5.5 \times 10^{-7} = 5.5 \times \dfrac{1}{10^7}$

$= 5.5 \times \dfrac{1}{10{,}000{,}000}$

$= 5.5 \times 0.0000001$ ← Multiplying by 0.0000001 moves the decimal point left 7 places.

$= 0.00000055$

Write each number in scientific notation.

1. 3425.7   **2.** 0.0206   **3.** 40,563

Write each number in decimal notation.

4. 1.3×10^{-5} **5.** 6.457×10^4 **6.** 7.3×10^{-1}

Scientific notation on a calculator

Calculations involving multiplication or division of very large or very small numbers result in displays on the calculator that are in scientific notation. You can use estimates in scientific notation to decide if the calculator result is reasonable.

Sample 3

In the situation presented in the box above the Key Term, the calculator display shows 5.576 −08 as the product of 0.000068 and 0.00082. Is the calculator result reasonable?

Sample Response

$0.000068 \cdot 0.00082 \approx 0.00007 \cdot 0.0008$ ← Round each decimal to the leading digit.

$\approx (7 \times 10^{-5}) \cdot (8 \times 10^{-4})$ ← Write each number in scientific notation.

$\approx (7 \times 8) \cdot (10^{-5} \times 10^{-4})$ ← Use the commutative and associative properties.

$\approx 56 \cdot 10^{-9}$ ← Use the product of powers rule.

$\approx (5.6 \times 10^1) \cdot 10^{-9}$ ← Write 56 in scientific notation.

$\approx 5.6 \cdot (10^1 \cdot 10^{-9})$ ← Use the associative property.

$\approx 5.6 \times 10^{-8}$ ← Use the product of powers rule.

The product found using estimates, 5.6×10^{-8}, is close to the calculator display, 5.576 −08. The calculator result is reasonable.

Simplify. Write each answer in scientific notation.

7. $220(6.4 \times 10^5)$ **8.** $45(7.2 \times 10^{-4})$ **9.** $\dfrac{3.8 \times 10^8}{160,000}$

Review **PREVIEW**

Simplify.   *(Section 2-2)*

10. $|-6.5|$ **11.** $-12 - 35$ **12.** $-7.6 + 3.3$ **13.** $-5 + 5(2 - 8)$

Replace each __?__ with the correct number.   *(Table of Measures)*

14. $4 \text{ yd} = \underline{\ ?\ } \text{ ft}$ **15.** $2 \text{ km} = \underline{\ ?\ } \text{ m}$ **16.** $23 \text{ mm} = \underline{\ ?\ } \text{ cm}$

INTEGRATED MATHEMATICS 1 Study Guide

Estimating Measures: Length and Area

FOCUS

Estimate lengths, distances on a map, and areas.

Professional painters multiply the perimeter of a room by its height to get an estimate of the total area of the walls of the room. This estimate helps them determine the number of gallons of paint they will need.

KEY TERMS	EXAMPLE / ILLUSTRATION
Line (p. 82) a geometric figure determined by two points that extends forever in two directions (The line through points A and B is denoted $\overleftrightarrow{AB}$.)	line AB, or $\overleftrightarrow{AB}$
Segment (p. 82) a part of a line that consists of two points on the line and all the points on the line between these two endpoints (The segment from point X to point Y is denoted $\overline{XY}$.)	segment XY, or $\overline{XY}$
Endpoint (pp. 82, 85) one of two points on a line that determines a segment	The endpoints of $\overline{XY}$ above are X and Y.
Length of a segment (p. 82) the distance between the endpoints of a segment (The length of $\overline{PQ}$ is denoted PQ.)	8 P Q The length of $\overline{PQ}$ is 8.
Midpoint (p. 82) the point on a segment that divides the segment in half	4 4 C M D M is the midpoint of $\overline{CD}$.

UNDERSTANDING THE MAIN IDEAS

Estimating distance and area on a map

The scale given on a map helps you estimate the distance between any two locations on the map. The scale also helps you estimate the area of any region on a map.

Use the map below to estimate the air distance from Chicago to Mexico City to the nearest hundred miles.

200 mi

Sample Response

Step 1 Copy the map scale repeatedly onto the edge of a sheet of paper. (Be sure the copies are laid end-to-end, without gaps between them.)

Step 2 Place your paper ruler on the map so that Chicago and Mexico City are located along the edge of the ruler. (Be sure that the beginning of your scale is located at either Chicago or Mexico City.) Count the number of 200-mi units between the two cities. There are about 8.5 of the units between the cities.

Sample Response continues on the next page.

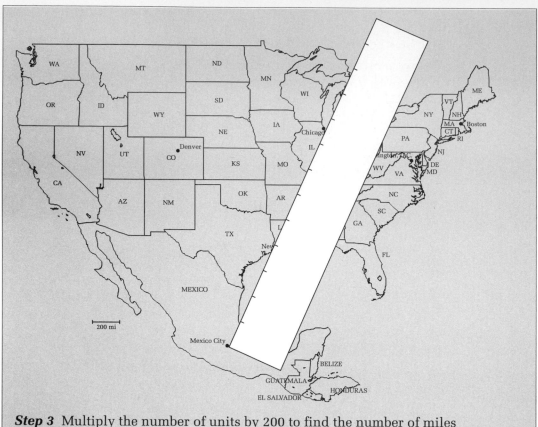

Step 3 Multiply the number of units by 200 to find the number of miles between the two cities: 8.5 • 200 = 1700.

The distance from Chicago to Mexico City is about 1700 mi.

Use the map and its scale given in Sample 1.

1. Estimate the distance from Washington, D.C., to Denver, CO.

2. Is 2000 mi a good estimate of the distance from Boston, MA, to New Orleans, LA? Why or why not?

3. Estimate the area of Wyoming.

Lines and lengths of segments

In geometry, there are symbols for points, lines, and segments.

Sample 2

Use the figure at the right.
a. Name a line shown in the diagram.
b. Name three segments shown in the diagram.
c. Find XY.
d. What is point M?

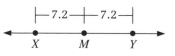

---

a. $\overleftrightarrow{XY}$, $\overleftrightarrow{XM}$, and $\overleftrightarrow{MY}$ are possible names for the line. (The order of the points may be reversed.)

b. $\overline{XM}$, $\overline{MY}$, and $\overline{XY}$ (The order of the points may be reversed.)

c. $7.2 + 7.2 = 14.4$

d. the midpoint of $\overline{XY}$

Polygon *ABCD* is a rectangle. *M* is the midpoint of $\overline{AB}$ and *N* is the midpoint of $\overline{BC}$. Find each measure.

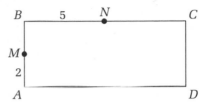

4. *MB*   5. *AD*

6. the perimeter of rectangle *ABCD*

Review **PREVIEW**

7. One angstrom is equal to 1×10^{-10} m. What is the length, in meters, of 7850 angstroms? Write your answer in scientific notation and in decimal notation. *(Section 2-3)*

Name each quadrilateral. *(Section 1-7)*

8.

9.

10.

2-5 Exploring Angle Relationships

FOCUS

Investigate and use the relationships among angles in circles, angles in triangles, and angles formed by intersecting lines.

To be a successful billiards player, one must have the necessary playing skills, the ability to handle pressure, and an understanding of angles.

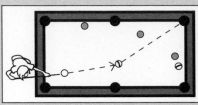

KEY TERMS	EXAMPLE / ILLUSTRATION
Ray (p. 85) a part of a line that extends forever in one direction	$S \longrightarrow T$ ray ST, or $\overrightarrow{ST}$
Angle (p. 85) the figure formed when two rays meet at a common endpoint	angle PQR or angle RQP, or $\angle PQR$ or $\angle RQP$
Vertex of an angle (p. 85) the common endpoint of the two rays that form an angle	The vertex of $\angle PQR$ above is the point Q.
Central angle of a circle (p. 85) an angle with its vertex at the center of a circle	central angle COD
Right angle (p. 86) an angle whose measure is 90°	$\angle JKM$ and $\angle LKM$ are both right angles.
Straight angle (p. 86) an angle whose measure is 180°	In the figure above, $\angle JKL$ is a straight angle.

Obtuse angle (p. 86)
an angle whose measure is between 90° and 180°

In the figure for right angle, ∠JKN is an obtuse angle.

Acute angle (p. 86)
an angle whose measure is between 0° and 90°

In the figure for right angle, ∠MKN and ∠NKL are both acute angles.

Complementary angles (p. 86)
two angles whose measures add up to 90°

In the figure for right angle, ∠MKN and ∠NKL are a pair of complementary angles.

Supplementary angles (p. 86)
two angles whose measures add up to 180°

In the figure for right angle, ∠JKN and ∠NKL are a pair of supplementary angles.

Congruent angles (p. 87)
angles with equal measures (The symbol ≅ means "is congruent to.")

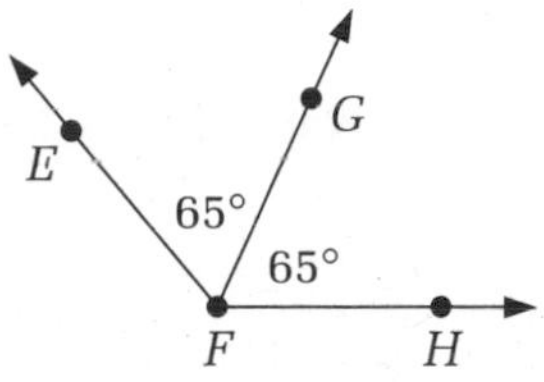

∠EFG ≅ ∠GFH

Vertical angles (p. 87)
two angles formed by intersecting lines and facing in opposite directions (Vertical angles have equal measures.)

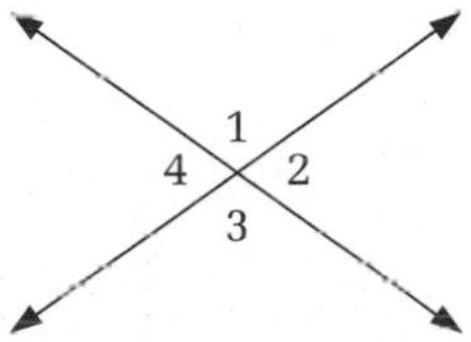

∠1 and ∠3 are vertical angles.
∠2 and ∠4 are vertical angles.

Acute triangle (p. 88)
a triangle with three acute angles

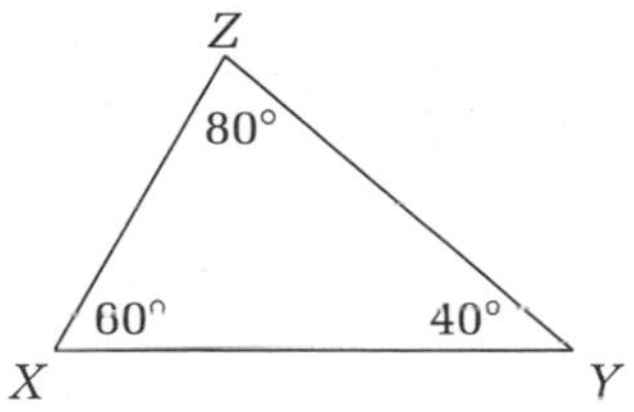

Obtuse triangle (p. 88)
a triangle with one obtuse angle

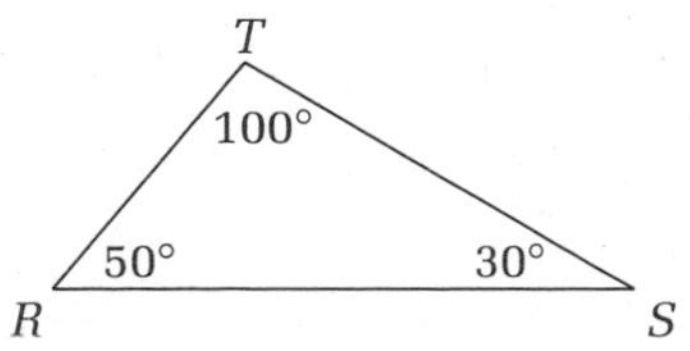

Right triangle (p. 88)
a triangle with one right angle

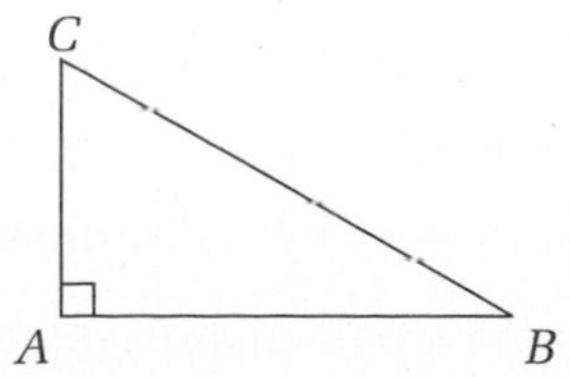

Naming and classifying angles

An angle is a geometric figure that is formed when two rays meet at a common endpoint. The common endpoint is the vertex of the angle. An angle is usually named by using a point on each ray and the vertex, with the letter for the vertex between the letters for the other two points. Angles are measured in degrees and are classified by their measures. An angle with its vertex at the center of a circle is a central angle of the circle. Pairs of angles are complementary if the sum of their measures is 90°. The sum of the measures of two supplementary angles is 180°.

Sample 1

Use the figure at the right.
a. What point is the vertex of the angles shown?
b. What rays form ∠VOY?
c. Name three central angles of the circle.
d. Name two right angles.
e. Name three acute angles.
f. Name two obtuse angles.
g. Which angle is a straight angle?
h. Name a pair of complementary angles.
i. Name a pair of supplementary angles.

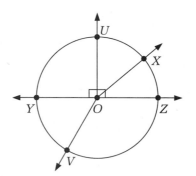

Sample Response

a. point O

b. $\overrightarrow{OV}$ and $\overrightarrow{OY}$

c. Answers may vary. Sample answers are given: ∠VOY, ∠YOU, and ∠XOZ.

d. ∠YOU and ∠UOZ

e. ∠XOZ, ∠VOY, and ∠UOX

f. Answers may vary. Sample answers are given: ∠YOX and ∠XOV.

g. ∠YOZ

h. ∠XOZ and ∠UOX

i. Answers may vary. A sample answer is given: ∠YOX and ∠XOZ.

Use the figure at the right for Exercises 1–6.

1. What rays form ∠TPU?

2. Name two acute angles.

3. Name three obtuse angles.

4. Name a pair of complementary angles.

5. Name a pair of supplementary angles.

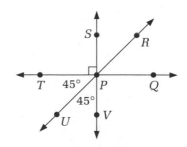

Special angle relationships

Angles with equal measures are congruent. The pairs of congruent angles formed by intersecting lines are called vertical angles. The sum of the measures of the three angles of a triangle is always 180°. A triangle with three acute angles is an acute triangle, a triangle with one right angle is a right triangle, and a triangle with one obtuse angle is an obtuse triangle.

Sample 2

Use the figure at the right.
a. What is the measure of ∠ACB?
b. What is the measure of ∠ACM?
c. Name an obtuse triangle.
d. Name two pairs of vertical angles.
e. ∠ACZ ≅ ___?___

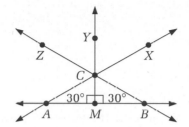

Sample Response

a. In △ABC, ∠ACB + 30 + 30 = 180; ∠ACB + 60 = 180;
   ∠ACB = 120°

b. In △ACM, ∠ACM + 30 + 90 = 180; ∠ACM + 120 = 180;
   ∠ACM = 60°

c. △ACB

d. Answers may vary. Sample answers are given: ∠ZCA and ∠XCB, ∠ZCX and ∠ACB.

e. Since ∠ACZ and ∠XCB are vertical angles, ∠ACZ ≅ ∠XCB.

For Exercises 6–9, write and solve an equation to find each unknown angle measure.

6.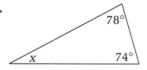

7.

8.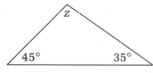

9.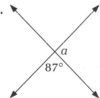

10. Classify each triangle in Exercises 6–8 as *right*, *acute*, or *obtuse*.

Review PREVIEW

Describe in words what each symbol means. *(Section 2-4)*

11. ∠A
12. ≅
13. $\overrightarrow{OP}$
14.

INTEGRATED MATHEMATICS 1 Study Guide

Name the property shown. *(Toolbox Skill 1)*

15. $(6 + 28) + 12 = 6 + (28 + 12)$

16. $32(12 + 8) = 32 \cdot 12 + 32 \cdot 8$

Simplify. *(Section 1-5)*

17. $(x - 5)7$

18. $5x^2 + 3 - 2x^2 - 8$

2-6 Expressions for Measures

FOCUS

Simplify
expressions for
measures of
geometric figures
by multiplying and
combining like
terms.

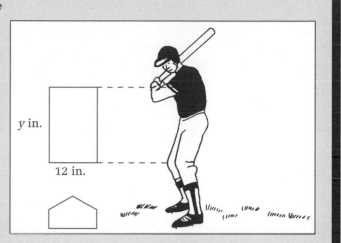

In baseball, the strike zone for a batter is a rectangular region 12 in. wide and y in. high, where y is the distance between the batter's armpits and knees. An expression for the area of the strike zone is 12y in.², where the value of y varies according to the batter's height and stance.

UNDERSTANDING THE MAIN IDEAS

Adding, multiplying, and simplifying variable expressions

Variable expressions can be used to represent the dimensions of geometric figures. In many geometric situations, you need to multiply and/or add these expressions and then simplify the resulting expression by combining like terms.

Sample

Write and simplify an expression for the perimeter and area of each rectangle.

a.

x
$2x$

b.
$y + 5$
y

c.
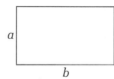
a
b

Sample Response

a. Perimeter $= 2(x) + 2(2x)$ ◄── Perimeter $= 2l + 2w$
$= 2x + 4x$
$= 6x$

Area $= (x)(2x)$ ◄── Area $= l \cdot w$
$= 2x^2$

Sample Response continues on the next page.

b. Perimeter $= 2(y) + 2(y + 5)$
$= 2y + 2y + 10$
$= 4y + 10$ ← Combine like terms.

Area $= (y)(y + 5)$
$= y^2 + 5y$ ← Use the distributive property.

c. Perimeter $= 2(a) + 2(b)$
$= 2a + 2b$

Area $= (a)(b)$
$= ab$

Simplify if possible. If not, explain why not.

1. $(12x)(12x)$

2. $(7m)(15n)$

3. $6c(14c^2)$

4. $5a + 7c + 2a + 5b - 6c$

5. $3x^2 + 2xy + 3y^2$

6. $5ab + 4bc + 6ab - 7bc$

7. $8x^3 - 3y^2 + 2xy + 12y^2$

 *Review* **PREVIEW**

8. Sketch a 30° angle. Describe how you estimated the size of the angle. *(Section 2-5)*

Model each expression using algebra tiles. *(Section 1-3)*

9. $3x$

10. $5 + x$

11. $4x + 2$

2-7 Solving Equations: Balancing

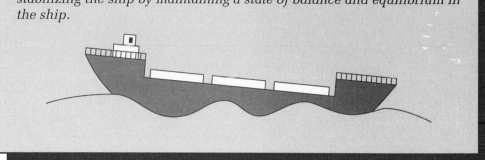

A cargo ship has ballast tanks to which water can be added or from which water can be removed. These ballast tanks serve the purpose of stabilizing the ship by maintaining a state of balance and equilibrium in the ship.

KEY TERMS

EXAMPLE / ILLUSTRATION

KEY TERMS	EXAMPLE / ILLUSTRATION
Equation (p. 99) a mathematical statement in which one expression equals another	$x - 2 = 5$
Solution (p. 99) a value of a variable that makes an equation true	7 is a solution to $x - 2 = 5$, since $7 - 2 = 5$.
Solving an equation (p. 99) the process of finding the solution to an equation	$x - 2 = 5$ $x - 2 + 2 = 5 + 2$ $x = 7$
Equivalent equations (p. 100) equations that have the same solution	$x = 7$ and $x - 2 = 5$ are equivalent equations.

UNDERSTANDING THE MAIN IDEAS

Solving equations by balancing

Equations can be solved by making changes to both sides until the variable is alone on one side and the solution is alone on the other side. In changing an equation as you solve it, you must keep the equation in balance. This balance is maintained if you perform the same operation on both sides of the equation.

> **Sample 1**
>
> Solve the equation $2x + 8 = 2$.

INTEGRATED MATHEMATICS 1 **Study Guide**

Solve.

1. $3x = 24$ **2.** $y + 5 = 14$ **3.** $a - 8 = 0$

4. $4x - 5 = 15$ **5.** $3x + 18 = 3$ **6.** $2 + 5x = 12$

Solving equations about geometric figures

You can write and solve equations to find unknown measures in geometric figures.

Sample 2

The perimeter of the parallelogram below is 70 in. Find the value of x.

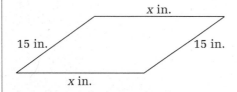

15 in.   *x* in.   15 in.

x in.

Sample Response

Write an equation for the perimeter.
$$2(x) + 2(15) = 70$$
$$2x + 30 = 70 \quad \longleftarrow \text{Simplify the left side.}$$
$$2x + 30 - 30 = 70 - 30 \quad \longleftarrow \text{Subtract 30 from } both \text{ sides.}$$
$$2x = 40$$
$$\frac{2x}{2} = \frac{40}{2} \quad \longleftarrow \text{Divide } both \text{ sides by 2.}$$
$$x = 20$$

The value of x is 20.

Write and solve an equation to find each unknown measure in each figure. (*Note:* **The sum of the measures of the angles of a quadrilateral is 360°.**)

7.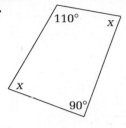

8.

9.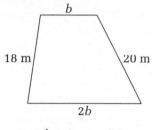

perimeter = 71 m

Review **PREVIEW**

Simplify if possible. If not, explain why not. *(Section 2-6)*

10. $-6(-8x^3)$

11. $4b^3 + 4b + b$

12. $8p^3 - 10pq - 5p^3 + 6p + 12pq$

Simplify. *(Section 2-2)*

13. $12 + (-7)$

14. $13 - (-8)$

15. $(7.2)(-5)$

16. $-30 \div (0.3)$

2-8 Solving Equations: Undoing

FOCUS

Use equations to solve a variety of real-life problems.

A version of the following puzzle problem can be found in many books about mathematics:

"*Some generous person likes to pick apples, but doesn't much enjoy eating them. So she picks a sackful of apples and then proceeds to give most of them away. Each person who receives apples gets a whole number of apples; no apples are cut. She does this in the following way: The first person she meets gets half the apples in the sack. The second person gets half the remaining apples. The third person gets half the remaining apples. And the fourth person gets half the remaining apples. The generous person has one apple left. How many apples were in the sack?* **"**

The puzzle can be solved by working backward, undoing the process of giving away the apples.

UNDERSTANDING THE MAIN IDEAS

Solving equations by undoing

Many problems in mathematics and in real-world applications of mathematics can be solved by first writing an equation and then finding the solution(s) of that equation. When you solve an equation, you can use the fact that subtracting is the inverse of adding and the fact that dividing is the inverse of multiplying.

Sample 1

The total cost for 3 lb of grapes and a 98¢ melon is $2.75. How much do the grapes cost per pound?

Sample Response

Write and solve an equation. Let g = the cost per pound for the grapes.
Then $3g$ = the cost of 3 pounds of grapes.

$3g + 0.98 = 2.75$ ⟵ cost of grapes + cost of melon = total cost

$3g + 0.98 - 0.98 = 2.75 - 0.98$ ⟵ Undo the addition of 0.98 by subtracting 0.98 from *both* sides.

$3g = 1.77$

$\dfrac{3g}{3} = \dfrac{1.77}{3}$ ⟵ Undo the multiplication by 3 by dividing *both* sides by 3.

$g = 0.59$

The grapes cost 59¢ per pound.

---

48 *INTEGRATED MATHEMATICS 1* **Study Guide** Copyright © by Houghton Mifflin Company. All rights reserved.

Sample 2

Ari's lunch cost her $4.80. This amount included the price of the lunch plus 5% sales tax and a tip of 15% of the price of the lunch. What was the price of the lunch?

Sample Response

Write and solve an equation. Let p = the price of the lunch. Then $0.05p$ = the amount for sales tax and $0.15p$ = the amount of the tip.

$p + 0.05p + 0.15p = 4.80$ ⟵ price of lunch + tax + tip = total amount

$1.20p = 4.80$ ⟵ Combine like terms; $p = 1p$.

$\dfrac{1.20p}{1.20} = \dfrac{4.80}{1.20}$ ⟵ Undo the multiplication by dividing both sides by 1.20.

$p = 4.00$

The price of the lunch was $4.00.

For Exercises 1–6, solve.

1. $4x - 7 = 45$

2. $-2y + 6 = 0$

3. $4n + 6n = 80$

4. $\dfrac{a}{5} = 75$

5. $\dfrac{x}{2} - 2.8 = 1.7$

6. $1.5b + 3.2b = 28.2$

7. **Open-ended** Write a problem situation that could be solved using the equation $15 + 3n = 60$.

Review **PREVIEW**

8. **a.** What equation does the diagram below illustrate? *(Section 2-7)*

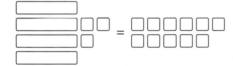

   b. Show how to solve for ▢ using the model in part (a).

Write each number in decimal notation. *(Section 2-3)*

9. 7.413×10^6

10. 1.39×10^{-4}

Replace each __?__ with the correct number. *(Section 1-3)*

11. $13^2 =$ __?__ • __?__ = __?__

12. $8^3 =$ __?__ • __?__ • __?__ = __?__

2-9 Square Roots and Cube Roots

FOCUS

Find square roots and cube roots and distinguish a rational number from an irrational number.

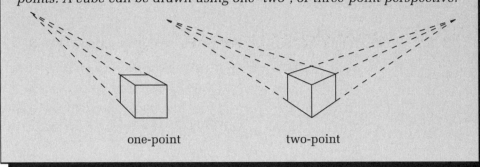

When artists and draftspersons draw cubes or other three-dimensional objects, they use perspective. When viewed from different perspectives, lines and planes that are actually parallel appear to meet at vanishing points. A cube can be drawn using one- two-, or three-point perspective.

one-point   two-point

KEY TERMS	EXAMPLE / ILLUSTRATION
Square root (p. 112) one of two equal factors of a number	Both 5 and −5 are square roots of 25.
Rational number (p. 113) a number that can be written as a quotient of two integers	Since $-0.5 = -\frac{1}{2} = \frac{-1}{2}$, −0.5 is a rational number.
Irrational number (p. 113) a number that cannot be written as a quotient of two integers	Since $\sqrt{2}$ cannot be written as a quotient of two integers, $\sqrt{2}$ is an irrational number.
Real number (p. 113) any rational or irrational number	π is an irrational number, so π is a real number.
Perfect square (p. 114) a number whose square roots are integers	$\sqrt{64} = \pm8$, so 64 is a perfect square.
Cube root (p. 114) one of three equal factors of a number	Since $3 \cdot 3 \cdot 3 = 27$, 3 is a cube root of 27.
Perfect cube (p. 114) a number whose cube root is an integer	$\sqrt[3]{125} = 5$, so 125 is a perfect cube.

UNDERSTANDING THE MAIN IDEAS

Squares, square roots, and types of numbers

The square root of a number is one of two equal factors of the number. A number that is equal to the product of two equal integer factors is a perfect square. Every positive number has both a positive and a negative square root.

The set of real numbers includes all the rational and irrational numbers. Rational numbers are numbers that can be written as the quotient of two integers. Irrational numbers are numbers that cannot be written as the quotient of two integers; their decimals are nonterminating and non-repeating. You can use known perfect squares to help you estimate the square roots of numbers that are not perfect squares.

Sample 1

Find the square roots of each number.

a. 0.01   **b.** 6.25   **c.** 121

Sample Response

a. 0.1 and −0.1   **b.** 2.5 and −2.5   **c.** 11 and −11

Find the square roots of each number.

1. $\dfrac{1}{49}$ **2.** 2.25   **3.** $\dfrac{169}{81}$

Tell whether each number is rational or irrational.

4. $8.\overline{6}$ **5.** $\sqrt{1.44}$ **6.** $-\sqrt{8}$

Estimate each square root within a range of two integers. Then use a calculator to find each square root to the nearest hundredth.

7. $\sqrt{12}$ **8.** $\sqrt{72}$ **9.** $\sqrt{90}$

Cube roots and solving equations involving square roots and cube roots

The cube root of a number is one of three equal factors of the number. A number that is equal to the product of three equal integer factors is a perfect cube. The symbol $\sqrt[3]{}$ stands for cube root. If you know the area of a square then you use the formula $A = s^2$ to find the length of each side. If you know the volume of a cube, then you use the formula $V = s^3$ to find the length of each edge.

Sample 2

Estimate $\sqrt[3]{5}$ between two integers. Then use a calculator to find $\sqrt[3]{5}$ to the nearest hundredth.

Sample Response

$$1 < 5 < 8$$
$$\sqrt[3]{1} < \sqrt[3]{5} < \sqrt[3]{8}$$
$$1 < \sqrt[3]{5} < 2$$

$\sqrt[3]{5}$ is between 1 and 2.

On a calculator, $\sqrt[3]{5} \approx 1.71$.

For Exercises 10–13, choose the letter of the point on the number line that matches each number.

10. $\sqrt[3]{9}$ **11.** $\sqrt[3]{100}$ **12.** $\sqrt{13}$ **13.** $\sqrt[3]{2}$

Each measurement is the area of a square. Find the length of a side of the square, to the nearest hundredth.

14. 75 ft^2 **15.** 150 cm^2

Each measurement is the volume of a cube. Find the length of an edge of the cube, to the nearest hundredth.

16. 512 in.^{3} **17.** 0.198 m^3

Review **PREVIEW**

For Exercises 18–20, solve. *(Section 2-8)*

18. $4a - 1.6 = 3.8$ **19.** $\frac{x}{5} + 3 = 9$ **20.** $20 = -5.4b + 3.8$

21. 15 is what percent of 75?
(Toolbox Skill 12)

22. Find 30% of 94.
(Toolbox Skill 14)

23. 85 is 40% of what number?
(Toolbox Skill 15)

24. Draw a bar graph for the data shown in the table at the right.
(Toolbox Skill 22)

Composition of the Earth's Crust	
Element	**Percentage**
Aluminum	8
Calcium	4
Iron	5
Magnesium	2
Oxygen	47
Potassium	3
Silicon	28
Sodium	3

Unit 2 Review

Complete these exercises for a review of Unit 2. If you have difficulty with a particular problem, review the indicated section.

1. Guess whether the number of printed letters, numbers, and other symbols on this page is in the *hundreds*, *thousands*, or *millions*. Then estimate the number. Describe your method. *(Section 2-1)*

2. **Open-ended** Estimate the distance from your home to the state capital. *(Section 2-1)*

3. Is your estimate for Exercise 2 *continuous* or *discrete*? *(Section 2-1)*

Simplify. *(Section 2-2)*

4. $-5.4 \div (-6)$ 5. $-18 + 7$ 6. $-12 - (-15)$ 7. $(-8)(1.5)$

Write each number in scientific notation. *(Section 2-3)*

8. 54,000,000   9. 0.000068

Write each number in decimal notation. *(Section 2-3)*

10. 7.462×10^3 11. 7.462×10^{-3}

Use the map of Alaska for Exercises 12 and 13. *(Section 2-4)*

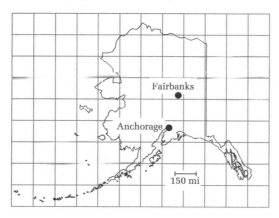

12. Estimate the distance from Anchorage to Fairbanks.

13. Estimate the area of Alaska in square miles.

Use the figure at the right for Exercises 14–16. *(Section 2-5)*

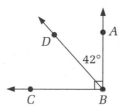

14. Name the rays shown.

15. Which angles are complementary?

16. What is the measure of $\angle CBD$?

For Exercises 17 and 18, simplify. *(Section 2-6)*

17. $x^3 - 5x^2 + x + 3x^3 + 9x$ 18. $6a^2 + 3ab - 2a^2 + 5b^2 - 5ab$

19. Write and simplify an expression for the volume of a box with dimensions x, $2x$, and $3x$. *(Section 2-6)*

Solve. *(Sections 2-7, 2-8)*

20. $6p - 7 = 41$ **21.** $8 + 3a = 29$ **22.** $45 = 3a + 6$

Write and solve an equation for each unknown value. *(Section 2-8)*

23. Andre bought a pen that cost $1.79 and 3 notebooks. The cost for all four items was $3.86. What was the price of each notebook?

24. Ms. Ramirez bought a 3-lb bag of oranges for $1.98. What was the price per pound for the oranges?

Estimate each number between two integers. Then use a calculator to find each root to the nearest hundredth. *(Section 2-9)*

25. $\sqrt{74}$ **26.** $\sqrt{133}$ **27.** $\sqrt[3]{50}$ **28.** $\sqrt[3]{180}$

Spiral Review *Units 1–2*

For Exercises 1–6, calculate according to the order of operations.

1. $6 \div 3 + 10$ **2.** $7 \cdot 13 - 3^3$ **3.** $5 + 5^2 \cdot 4$

4. $(7 - 1) \cdot 2 + 5$ **5.** $24 + (6 + 7) \cdot 2$ **6.** $24 + 6 + 7 \cdot 2$

7. Find 35% of 2500.

8. What percent is 54 of 50?

9. 15 is what percent of 90?

Draw all lines of symmetry for each figure.

10.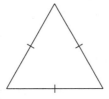

11.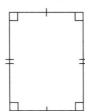

12.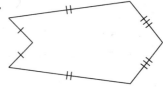

Simplify.

13. $(a - 3)2 - 3a$ **14.** $\frac{1}{2}(6x + 4) - 2$ **15.** $12 - 2(x + 5)$

Solve.

16. $4y - 3 = 57$ **17.** $6n + 8 = 32$ **18.** $42 = 3n$

Simplify.

19. $(-8)(-7)$ **20.** $13 - (-6)$ **21.** $48 \div (-3)$

Write and solve an equation to find each unknown angle measure.

22.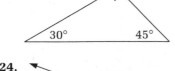

23.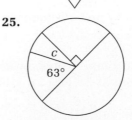

24.

25.

Using Matrices and Graphs

Some articles in newspapers and magazines present statistical (numerical) data pertinent to the topic being discussed. The writers and editors who prepare these articles for publication must decide on the format which best presents the data to the reader. With the extensive use of computers in the publishing industry today, the data can be displayed in a variety of table or graph formats.

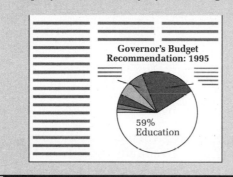

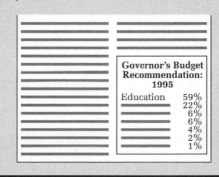

KEY TERMS

EXAMPLE / ILLUSTRATION

Matrix (p. 128)	
an arrangement of data in rows and columns	

Calories Burned per Hour

Exercise	Person's Weight	
	110 lb	**154 lb**
Exercycle	515	655
Aerobics	350	445
Walking	435	555
Swimming	330	420
Jogging	515	655

row of matrix   column of matrix

Dimensions of a matrix (p. 128)
the number of rows and columns, in that order, of a matrix

The dimensions of the matrix above are 5×2.

rows   columns

Spreadsheet (p. 129)
a computer-generated matrix

	A	B	C	D
1	2.50	4.10	3.40	10.00
2	2.10	3.00	4.50	9.60
3	2.00	4.00	5.00	11.00
4	6.60	11.10	12.90	30.60

Cell (p. 129)
the location for a piece of data in a spreadsheet

There are 16 cells in the spreadsheet above; the entry in cell C2 is 4.50.

UNDERSTANDING THE MAIN IDEAS

Matrices and graphs for understanding data

Information can be summarized in a matrix and can be displayed in a graph. A matrix consists of rows and columns of data; the dimensions of a matrix are indicated by specifying the number of rows and the number of columns, in that order. Graphs for displaying data can be bar graphs, line graphs, pictographs, and circle graphs. For exact numerical data, a matrix is more useful than a graph; for making comparisons and observing trends, a graph is usually more useful than a matrix.

Sample 1

Use the data in the matrix and the pictograph below. The data is from the 1990 United States Census.

Average Yearly Income in U.S. by Gender and Education

	Elementary School Graduate	High School Graduate	College, One or More Years
Males	$16,850	$25,900	$33,500
Females	$11,830	$17,400	$24,000

Average Yearly Income in U.S. by Gender and Education

Elementary School Graduate ♂ ♂ ♂ ♂ ♂ ☾
♀ ♀ ♀ ♀

High School Graduate ♂ ♂ ♂ ♂ ♂ ♂ ♂ ♂ ♂ ☾
♀ ♀ ♀ ♀ ♀ ♀

One or More Years of College ♂ ♂ ♂ ♂ ♂ ♂ ♂ ♂ ♂ ♂ ♂ ☽
♀ ♀ ♀ ♀ ♀ ♀ ♀ ♀

Key: ♂ = male, $3000
♀ = female, $3000

a. What are the dimensions of the matrix?

b. Which data display enables you to quickly compare income by gender in each education category?

c. Which data display would you use to determine how much more a male high school graduate is likely to earn than a male elementary school graduate?

d. Which data display quickly shows that higher salaries correspond to more education?

e. How can you use the data in the matrix to check the accuracy of the pictograph?

f. Is it a fair statement to say that in each education category, women earn about 70% of the amount that men earn?

For Exercises 1–4, use the table and the bar graph.

Book Sales at Collin's Bookcase						
Month	April	May	June	July	Aug.	Sept.
Total Sales	$6500	$7200	$8800	$9200	$8500	$8300

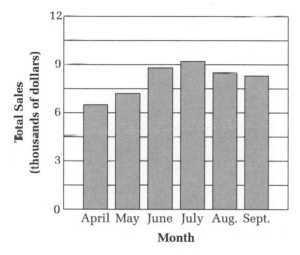

1. Would you use the graph or the table to determine the increase in total sales from May to June?

2. In which months was there a decrease in the total sales from the previous month?

3. Which months show an increase in total sales from the previous month?

4. *Open-ended* What prediction would you make for the month of October? Explain your reasoning.

Spreadsheets

Matrices can be created on a computer by using spreadsheet software. The data in spreadsheets can be used for calculations, which are carried out by using "hidden formulas." Spreadsheets use letters to name columns and numbers are used for rows. The labeling is the reverse of the labeling for the dimensions of a matrix; that is, the column is named first, and the row second. The location C5 is called cell C5 and is located in column C, row 5.

Sample 2

Use the spreadsheet below.

Sales Prices for 20% Off Sale

	A	B	C	D
1		**Regular price**	**Discount**	**Sale price**
2	T-shirt	10.50	2.10	8.40
3	Sweat shirt	18.50	3.70	14.80
4	Sweat pants	15.00	3.00	12.00
5	Cap	8.00	1.60	6.40
6	Jacket	40.00	8.00	32.00

a. What information is stored in cell B4?

b. What formula will calculate the value in cell C2 from the information in cell B2?

c. What formula will calculate the value in cell D4 from the values in cells B4 and C4?

d. Suppose the regular price of the jacket listed in row 6 was $42.50. What would be stored in cells C6 and D6?

Sample Response

a. the regular price of a pair of sweat pants, $15.00

b. B2 • 0.2

c. B4 − C4

d. C6: 8.50; D6: 34.00

For Exercises 5–8, use the spreadsheet.

English-Metric Conversions

	A	B	C
1	Inches	Centimeters	Millimeters
2	1	2.54	25.4
3	2	5.08	50.8
4	6		
5	10		
6	12		

5. What formula will calculate the value in cell B2 from the information in cell A2?

6. What formula will calculate the value in cell C2 from the information in cell B2?

7. What number belongs in cell B4?

8. Complete rows 4, 5, and 6 of the spreadsheet.

Review PREVIEW

9. The volume of a cube is 64 cubic units. What is the length of an edge of the cube? *(Section 2-9)*

Use a number anywhere along the scale to estimate the probability of each event. *(Section 2-1)*

impossible	unlikely	possible	likely	certain
0%	25%	50%	75%	100%
0	0.25	0.5	0.75	1

10. You will get an A in math this year.

11. There will be snow in your town in January.

Solve each equation. *(Sections 2-7, 2-8)*

12. $5x + 12 = 37$ **13.** $\frac{x}{2} = 9$ **14.** $\frac{x}{3} - 8 = 0$

Mean, Median, and Mode

Find values that are typical of a set of data, identify data values that are not typical of a data set, and use equations to find missing data values.

For certain kinds of data, such as heights or shoe sizes, if you collect data for a great many people and then graph the data, you will get a curve that looks something like the one shown below.

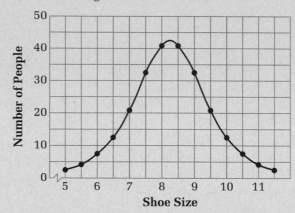

This bell-shaped curve is called a normal curve *and the distribution of data is called a* normal distribution. *In a normal distribution, the mean, median, and mode are all the same number.*

KEY TERMS

EXAMPLE / ILLUSTRATION

KEY TERMS	EXAMPLE / ILLUSTRATION
Mean (p. 136) the sum of the items in a set of data divided by the number of items	Data values: 32, 64, 64, 72, 73, 76, 80, 83, 89, 89, 92 The mean of the data is 74.
Median (p. 136) the middle number in a set of data after the data are put in order (If the number of data items is even, the median is the mean of the two middle numbers.)	The median of the data above (the data is in order) is 76.
Mode (p. 136) the number (or numbers) that occurs most often in a set of data (A data set may have more than one mode.)	There are two modes of the data above, 64 and 89.
Outlier (p. 137) data values that are much larger or smaller than most of the values in a data set (Outliers are *not* typical of the data set.)	There is one outlier in the data above, 32.
Range (p. 137) the difference between the smallest and largest numbers	The range of data above is 60.

UNDERSTANDING THE MAIN IDEAS

Mean, median, and mode

One value from a set of data is often chosen as the most typical value for describing the set. This value may be the mean, which you find by adding all the values and then dividing by the number of values in the set.

However, very large or very small values, called outliers, can make the mean a misleading value for describing the data. The typical value might be the median value, which is the middle value when the values are arranged in order. (If there are two "middle" numbers, the median is the mean of these two numbers.) Or the typical value might be the mode, the value (or values) that occurs most often.

Sample

The weekly salaries of the ten sales clerks at Howard's Book Store are $375, $350, $440, $400, $400, $430, $650, $350, $410, and $210.
  a. Find the mean, median, and mode(s) of the salaries.
  b. What is the salary range?
  c. Are there any outliers?

Sample Response

  a. mean: (375 + 350 + 440 + 400 + 400 + 430 + 650 + 350 + 410 + 210) ÷ 10 = 4015 ÷ 10 = 401.5; $401.50

  median: The ordered list of data is $210, $350, $350, $375, $400, $400, $410, $430, $440, and $650. The two middle numbers are both $400, so the median is $400.

  mode: There are two modes, $350 and $400.

  b. salary range: $650 − $210 = $440

  c. outliers: $210 and $650

For Exercises 1–6, use the following test scores.

45 62 66 66 68 71 71 71 72 74 75 75 76
77 80 80 80 81 83 84 84 86 89 90 95

  1. What is the range of the scores?   **2.** What is the mean of the scores?

  3. What is the median score?   **4.** What are the modes of the scores?

  5. Are there any outliers? If so, what are they?

  6. *Writing* Suppose the grades A, B, C, D, and F are to be assigned to the test scores. How would you group the scores to assign letter grades?

Review **PREVIEW**

  7. You want to show what percent of the people surveyed chose one of five different vegetables as their favorite vegetable. Would you use a *circle graph* or a *line graph* to display the survey results? Explain. *(Section 3-1)*

Write each product as a power. *(Section 1-3)*

  8. 6 • 6 • 6 • 6 • 6   **9.** $y • y • y • y$

Graph each pair of numbers on a number line. Then use the symbol < to write an inequality comparing the two numbers. *(Toolbox Skill 2)*

  10. −4 and −3   **11.** 0 and −5

Use inequalities
to describe number
line graphs.

*Precision in measurement is related to the unit of measure used;
the smaller the unit of measurement, the greater the precision.
The greatest possible error in a measurement is one half the unit
of measure being used. Thus, the actual measure lies within an
interval defined by the possible error.*

Unit of measure: 1 in.
Length of segment: 2 in.

$1\frac{1}{2} \le x \le 2\frac{1}{2}$

Unit of measure: $\frac{1}{4}$ in.

Length of segment: $1\frac{3}{4}$ in.

$1\frac{5}{8} \le x \le 1\frac{7}{8}$

Unit of measure: $\frac{1}{8}$ in.

Length of segment: $1\frac{7}{8}$ in.

$1\frac{13}{16} \le x \le 1\frac{15}{16}$

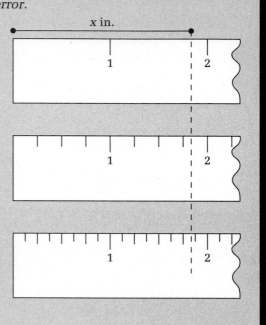

KEY TERMS

EXAMPLE / ILLUSTRATION

KEY TERMS	EXAMPLE / ILLUSTRATION
Inequality (p. 144) a mathematical sentence that contains one of the symbols $<, >, \le,$ or $\ge$	$7 > -2$
Greater than or equal to (p. 144) a relationship between quantities that uses the symbol $\ge$	$x \ge 6.4$
Less than or equal to (p. 144) a relationship between quantities that uses the symbol $\le$	$r \le 10$
Interval (p. 145) a segment on a number line that can be described by a combined inequality	$-1\ 0\ 1\ 2\ 3\ 4\ 5$ $1 < x \le 4$

UNDERSTANDING THE MAIN IDEAS

Graphing inequalities and intervals

The graph of a simple inequality like $x \ge 5$ is the point 5 and all points
to the right of 5 on a number line. The graph of the combined inequality
$-3 \le x < 6$ on a number line consists of the point -3 and all points
between -3 and 6, but *not* the point 6. The combined inequality
$-3 \le x < 6$ is made up of two inequalities, $x \ge -3$ and $x < 6$.

Sample 1

Graph each inequality.

a. $2.5 \leq x$

b. $-3 < x \leq 3$

Sample Response

a.

```
        2.5
  ←+─+─+─●─+─+─+─+─→
    0 1 2 3 4 5 6
```

b.

```
  ←+─○─+─+─+─+─+─●─+─+→
    −4 −3 −2 −1 0 1 2 3 4
```

Sample 2

Graph an interval of the number line to represent the following statement. Then write an inequality to describe the graph.

> The students at Fenmore High School range in age from 14 years old to 19 years old.

Sample Response

```
  ←+─+─+─+─●─+─+─+─●─+─+→
    10   12   14   16   18   20
```

$14 \leq a \leq 19$

Graph each inequality on a number line.

1. $x \geq -1\frac{1}{2}$

2. $0 < x \leq 5$

3. $-2.4 \leq x \leq 1.6$

4. $4 < x < 6$

5. $-3 \leq x < 2$

6. $-6 < x$

Write an inequality to describe each graph.

7.
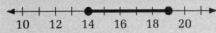
```
        −1½
  ←+─+─●─+─+─+─○─+─+→
   −3 −2 −1 0 1 2 3 4
```

8.
```
  ←+─+─+─○─+─+─○─+─+→
   −3 −2 −1 0 1 2 3 4
```

Review **PREVIEW**

9. Find the mean, the median, and the mode of the data set below. *(Section 3-2)*

Hours worked during a one-week period by employees at Angie's Video Store: 32, 38, 42, 38, 35, 40, 42, 36, 39, 41, 34, 42

10. Give the square roots and the cube root of 64. *(Section 2-9)*

11. Make a bar graph of the data about honor roll students at King High School. *(Toolbox Skill 22)*

Class	Freshman	Sophomore	Junior	Senior
Number of honor roll students	35	33	38	29

INTEGRATED MATHEMATICS 1 **Study Guide**

3-4 Histograms and Stem-and-Leaf Plots

FOCUS

Use histograms, frequency tables, and stem-and-leaf plots to display data.

When the data from the frequency table below is entered in a computer graphics program, the graph shown below results.

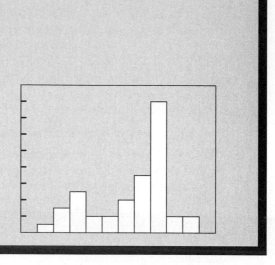

Vehicle Speed (mph)	Number of Cars
50–51	1
52–53	3
54–55	5
56–57	2
58–59	2
60–61	4
62–63	7
64–65	16
66–67	2
68–69	2

KEY TERMS

EXAMPLE / ILLUSTRATION

Histogram (p. 150)

a type of bar graph that shows how many data items occur in each of one or more non-overlapping intervals

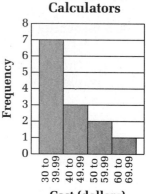

Prices of Scientific Calculators

Frequency (p. 150)

the number of data items in an interval

In the histogram above, the frequency of scientific calculators in the $40 to $49.99 price range is 3.

Frequency table (p. 151)

a table that displays the exact number of data items in an interval

Prices of Scientific Calculators

Prices	Frequency
$30–39.99	7
$40–49.99	3
$50–59.99	2
$60–69.99	1

Stem-and-leaf plot (p. 152)	Prices of Scientific Calculators

Stem-and-leaf plot (p. 152)
a method of displaying data items by separating each item into two parts, a stem and a leaf

Prices of Scientific Calculators

```
3 | 0 0 2 3 5 9
4 | 0 0 7
5 | 0 0
6 | 4
```

UNDERSTANDING THE MAIN IDEAS

Frequency tables and histograms

A histogram is a useful way of displaying data that can be grouped into convenient intervals. The data used to make a histogram is often obtained from a frequency table. In a frequency table, the intervals are defined and the number of pieces of data in each interval is given.

Sample 1

The weights in pounds of 25 players on a high school junior varsity football team are listed below.

142 146 148 150 152 155 158 159 159 160 163 165 166
167 167 168 169 170 173 174 175 177 180 182 191

a. Make a frequency table. Use the intervals 140–149, 150–159, 160–169, 170–179, 180–189, and 190–199.

b. Use your frequency table from part (a) to make a histogram.

Sample Response

a.

Weights of Football Players (in pounds)

Weight	Frequency
140–149	3
150–159	6
160–169	8
170–179	5
180–189	2
190–199	1

b.

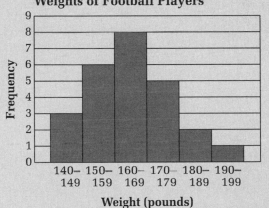

Weights of Football Players

Thirty people were asked to tell how many books they had read in the past year. Here are the results of the survey:

0   2   4   6   6   8 10 12 12 13 14 14 14 14 15 15
15 16 16 18 19 19 20 21 22 24 30 36 48 48

1. Make a frequency table. Use the intervals 0–9, 10–19, 20–29, 30–39, and 40–49.

2. Use your frequency table from Exercise 1 to make a histogram.

INTEGRATED MATHEMATICS 1 Study Guide

Stem-and-leaf plots

A stem-and-leaf plot is a useful way of organizing data into intervals in such a way that each data item is displayed. On a stem-and-leaf plot, each data item is separated into a stem and a leaf. The leaf is the last digit of a data value and the stem is the remaining digit or digits. For example, the stem for the number 32 would be 3 and the leaf would be 2, whereas for the number 185 the stem would be 18 and the leaf would be 5.

Sample 2

Use the stem-and-leaf plot shown at the right.

a. What are the intervals represented by the stems of the data?

b. What is the frequency for each interval?

c. List the individual data items.

d. What information does the stem-and-leaf plot have that the frequency table for Sample 1 does not have?

14	2 6 8
15	0 2 5 8 9 9
16	0 3 5 6 7 7 8 9
17	0 3 4 5 7
18	0 2
19	1

Sample Response

a. The stem gives the first two digits of each interval: 140–149, 150–159, 160–169, 170–179, 180–189, 190–199.

b. The *number* of leaves for a stem is the frequency of each interval. From top to bottom, the frequencies are 3, 6, 8, 5, 2, 1.

c. Combine each leaf with its stem to get the individual data items. The data items in the interval 140–149 are 142, 146, and 148; in the interval 150–159, the data items are 150, 152, 155, 158, 159, and 159; in the interval 160–169, the data items are 160, 163, 165, 166, 167, 167, 168, and 169; in the interval 170–179, the data items are 170, 173, 174, 175, and 177; for the interval 180–189, the data items are 180 and 182; and the only item in the interval 190–199 is 191.

d. The stem-and-leaf plot gives the individual data items, not just the intervals and the frequencies.

For Exercises 3 and 4, use the following test scores.

```
58  60  63  65  65  67  69  70  70  71
74  75  75  75  78  81  81  83  84  84
87  88  90  91  91  93  93  95  96  98
```

3. Make a stem-and-leaf plot of the test scores.

4. Make a histogram from your stem-and-leaf plot.

**Write and graph an inequality to describe the interval referred to in
each statement.** *(Section 3-3)*

5. In Iowa, a person must be 16 years old in order to obtain a
   driver's license.

6. Water is in a liquid state between the temperatures of 0°C and 100°C.

Draw an angle whose measure is the given number of degrees.
(Toolbox Skill 16)

7. 30°　　　　　　　8. 120°　　　　　　　9. 170°

10. Find the median, the range, and the outliers of the salaries listed below.
    (Section 3-2)

$5400	$18,500	$32,000	$12,400	$29,500
$16,200	$25,000	$18,500	$30,000	$27,300
$20,400	$28,800	$55,000	$33,000	$18,500

Box-and-Whisker Plots

Computer graphics are affecting the way in which data is displayed. Many examples of computer graphics can be found in newspapers and magazines. The diagrams below show the stages in changing a two-dimensional circle graph to a three-dimensional pie chart that emphasizes one part of the data.

Recycling Data

☐	Aluminum
⊠	Glass
■	Plastic
▨	Paper
▦	Styrofoam

After you apply the format file, your circle graph looks like this.

Recycling Data

Drag a slice of the graph to make it stand out from the rest of the graph.

Recycling Data

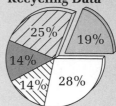

This is the finished pie graph with depth added.

KEY TERMS

EXAMPLE / ILLUSTRATION

Box-and-whisker plot (p. 158) a graph that shows the median, the quartiles, the extremes, and the range of a set of data	The box-and-whisker plot for the data 43, 49, 51, 52, 55, 56, 59, 61, 64, 67, and 70 is shown below. 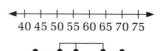
Lower quartile (p. 158) the median of the data in the lower half of a data set	The lower quartile of the data above is 51. It is represented as the left end of the box in the plot.
Upper quartile (p. 158) the median of the data in the upper half of a data set	The upper quartile of the data above is 64. It is represented as the right end of the box in the plot.
Extremes (p. 158) the lowest and highest data values in a data set (The lowest data value is the *lower extreme* and the highest data value is the *upper extreme*.)	The lower and upper extremes of the data above are 43 and 70, respectively. These extremes are shown as the endpoints of the whiskers in the plot.

Sample 1

Eighteen basketball players practiced free throw shots on two separate days. The number of shots made out of 50 free throws by each player are shown below.

Day 1

12	32	42	50	39	38
27	34	42	35	48	36
13	15	23	16	25	43

Day 2

42	17	18	42	28	37
19	14	14	41	21	29
21	17	19	26	31	34

a. Make box-and-whisker plots for the two sets of data.

b. Compare the results for the two days of practice.

Sample Response

a. **Step 1** Write the data items in order for each data set.

Day 1: 12 13 15 16 23 25 27 32 34 35 36 38 39 42
42 43 48 50

Day 2: 14 14 17 17 18 19 19 21 21 26 28 29 31 34
37 41 42 42

Step 2 Find the median, the extremes, and the quartiles of each data set.

Day 1: median: There are two middle numbers, 34 and 35, so the median is $(34 + 35) \div 2 = 34.5$; extremes: 12 and 50; lower quartile: the middle number of the lower half of the data is 23; upper quartile: the middle number of the upper half of the data is 42.

Day 2: median: There are two middle numbers, 21 and 26, so the median is $(21 + 26) \div 2 = 23.5$; extremes: 14 and 42; lower quartile: the middle number of the lower half of the data is 18; upper quartile: the middle number of the upper half of the data is 34.

Step 3 Graph the five values for each data set found in Step 2 below a number line.

Step 4 Draw a box from the lower quartile to the upper quartile. Draw a vertical line in the box through the median.

Step 5 Draw whiskers (line segments) from the ends of the box to the extremes.

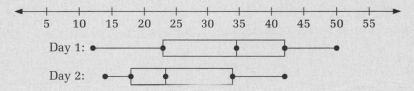

b. The Day 2 results show a much lower performance than the Day 1 results. The upper quartile for the second day was less than the median for the first day, and the median for the second day was only slightly better than the lower quartile for the first day. While the lower extreme was a little higher for the second day, the upper extreme for the second day was much less than that for the first day.

The daily high temperatures for each day of two one-week periods in Chicago in July are given below. Use these temperatures for Exercises 1 and 2.

Week 1: 95   96   93   98   98   101   99
Week 2: 95   85   83   78   79   82   80

1. Make box-and-whisker plots for the two sets of data.

2. Compare the weather in Chicago during each of these two weeks.

3. *Open-ended* Collect two sets of data about a situation. Make box-and-whisker plots and compare the data sets.

 *Review* **PREVIEW**

For Exercises 4–6, use the histogram showing the prices of notebook computers. *(Section 3-4)*

Prices of Notebook Computers

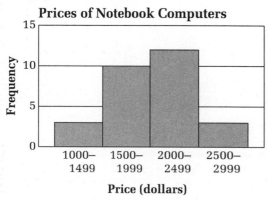

4. How many computer models cost $2000 or more?

5. Which price range has the greatest frequency? What does this mean in terms of the data?

6. What else do you need to know to make a stem-and-leaf plot for the data set?

For Exercises 7 and 8, simplify. *(Section 2-6)*

7. $6x - 2y - 5x + 3y$ 8. $-8a^2 + 6a^2$

9. A birdwatcher records the number of migrating warblers seen in a park each day over a two-week period. Is this data discrete or continuous? Should the birdwatcher use a bar graph or a line graph to display the data? *(Sections 2-1, 3-1)*

Choosing a Data Display

FOCUS

Tell why a data display is a good choice for a data set, choose a good data display for a data set.

For many years, scientists have used two-dimensional graphs of the locations of the epicenters of earthquakes. The one at the left below shows such a graph for earthquake epicenters in the Fiji Islands. Now, a computer graphic like the one at the right below can give a three-dimensional view which adds depth so that scientists can see how the epicenters are stacked on top of each other beneath the crust of the Earth. The viewing angle can be changed to provide even more information.

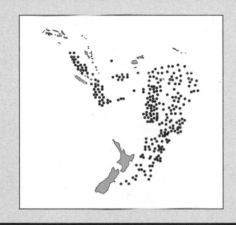

UNDERSTANDING THE MAIN IDEAS

Deciding on a graph

Different kinds of graphs are appropriate for different kinds of data. Here are some general guidelines to follow.

- A *bar graph* is a good choice for displaying data that cannot be put in numerical order, such as types of pets or countries, or data that is in discrete categories, such as consecutive years or days.

- A *circle graph* is a good choice for showing relationships among parts of a whole, such as portions of a budget or fractions of the total student body.

- A *box-and-whisker plot* is a good choice for showing different data sets that relate to similar situations, such as sets of test scores or samples taken on different occasions.

- A *histogram* is a good choice for showing data that can be grouped in intervals, such as salary or price ranges.

- A *line graph* is a good choice for showing continuous data that changes over time, such as temperature changes or stock market trends.

- A *stem-and-leaf plot* is a good choice for displaying small sets of data that can be grouped in intervals, such as test scores for a small group of students or salaries for employees of a small business.

Remember that these are only guidelines; more than one type of graph might be appropriate for the same data set.

Use the information in the table below.

a. Make a graph showing the areas of the continents.

b. Make a graph showing the percentage of the total area occupied by continent.

Continent	Area (million square miles)	Percent of total area
Africa	11.7	20.8%
Asia	17.1	30.4%
Antarctica	5.1	9.1%
Australia	2.9	5.2%
Europe	3.1	5.5%
North America	9.4	16.7%
South America	6.9	12.3%

Sample Response

a. Since the categories are discrete, a bar graph is a good choice for displaying the area data.

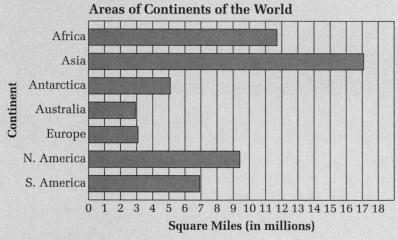

Areas of Continents of the World

b. Since the percents are parts of 100%, a circle graph is a good choice for displaying the percentages.

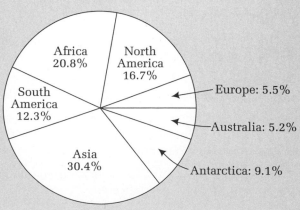

For Exercises 1–3, tell what type of graph you think is a good choice for displaying each data set. Explain your choice.

1. the population growth of the United States during the years 1890–1990

2. the amount of time each day you spend on different activities, such as going to school, sleeping, playing sports, and so on

3. the size of each of the grades at your school

4. The table below shows the areas of the oceans of the world in millions of square miles. Graph the data using (**a**) a bar graph and (**b**) a circle graph.

Ocean	Antarctic	Arctic	Atlantic	Indian	Pacific
Area (million square miles)	7.6	4.8	31.5	28.4	63.8

Review **PREVIEW**

5. Make a box-and-whisker plot of the data in the table. *(Section 3-5)*

Basketball Players' Heights (in inches)			
Chuck	81	Doc	79
Red	72	Clyde	80
Pete	76	Patrick	85
Scottie	83	Ervin	82
Shawn	81	Lon	82
Mike	74	B.J.	71

6. Each grid square on the map at the right represents 100 ft². Estimate the area of the lake. *(Section 2-4)*

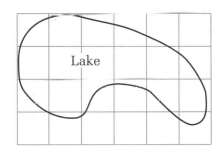

Lake

For Exercises 7 and 8, use the bar graph below. *(Section 3-1)*

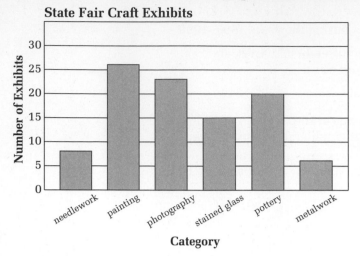

7. Which category had the most exhibitors? How many more exhibitors were there in this category than in the photography category?

8. Tell whether this statement is *True* or *False*: "Almost one third of the exhibitors were painters."

3-7 Analyzing Misleading Graphs

FOCUS

Recognize when graphs do not give an accurate picture of a data set.

For many years, Mercator projection maps were widely used. In a Mercator projection, the surface of the Earth is shown as a rectangle, with the meridians as parallel straight lines spaced at equal intervals. The lines of latitude are parallel lines intersecting the meridians at right angles, but spaced further apart as their distance from the equator increases. Areas on such maps become increasingly distorted, with land masses becoming elongated, toward the poles.

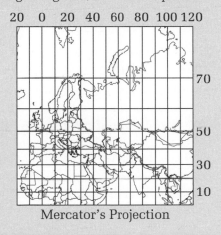

Mercator's Projection

UNDERSTANDING THE MAIN IDEAS

Analyzing graphs

There are a number of ways in which graphs can be distorted, either intentionally or unintentionally.

- They can be distorted by starting either the vertical or the horizontal scale at some point other than zero.

- They can be distorted by using intervals on the scales that are not evenly spaced.

- They can be distorted by using inappropriate area or volume models.

- They can be distorted by using percentages when actual quantities would be more appropriate, or vice versa.

Sample

Use the graph shown below.

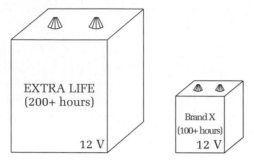

EXTRA LIFE
(200+ hours)

12 V

Brand X
(100+ hours)

12 V

EXTRA LIFE batteries last twice
as long as ordinary batteries!

a. How do the number of hours of use claimed for the Extra Life battery
compare with the number of hours claimed for the Brand X battery?

b. The length, width, and height of the "bar" for the Extra Life battery are
each twice as great as the corresponding measure of the "bar" for the
Brand X battery. How do the volumes of the two "bars" representing the
batteries compare?

c. Why does the graph give a misleading impression of the comparative life
span of the two brands of batteries?

Sample Response

a. The number of hours for the Extra Life battery is twice the number of
hours given for the Brand X battery.

b. Let l = the length of the Brand X "bar," let w = the width, and let
h = the height. Then the length, width, and height of the Extra Life
"bar" would be $2l$, $2w$, and $2h$, respectively. So the volume of the "bar"
for the Brand X battery is lwh and the volume of the "bar" for the Extra
Life battery is $(2l)(2w)(2h) = 8lwh$. Therefore, the volume of the "bar"
for the Extra Life battery is 8 times the volume of the "bar" for the Brand
X battery.

c. The graph is misleading because it gives the impression that the Extra
Life battery will last 8 times as long, not twice as long, as the Brand X
battery.

For Exercises 1–3, use the graphs below.

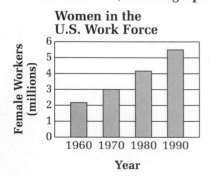

Women in the
U.S. Work Force

Women in the
U.S. Work Force

1. **a.** In the graph at the left, which bar is twice as long as the bar for 1960?
   b. In the graph at the right, which bar is twice as long as the bar for 1960?
   c. In which year was the number of women employed about twice as great as the number employed in 1960?

2. Which graph gives an accurate representation of the data? Why is the other graph misleading?

3. *Writing* Explain why proponents of governmental funding of day-care centers might choose the graph on the right to support their position for increased funding.

4. *Open-ended* Find an example, or make up an example of your own, of a graph that misleads in order to support a specific point of view.

Review  **PREVIEW**

What type of graph is a good choice for displaying each data set? Why?
(Section 3-6)

5. the heights of high jumps in a regional track and field meet

6. a person's daily caloric intake for a month

7. the ages of students enrolling in high school

Write each number in scientific notation. *(Section 2-3)*

8. 945,000   9. 6,400,000   10. 0.025   11. 0.00033

Plot each point on a coordinate plane. *(Toolbox Skill 21)*

12. (3, −2)   13. (−3, 2)   14. (0, −1)   15. (−1, 0)

Unit 3 Review

Complete these exercises for a review of Unit 3. If you have difficulty with a particular problem, review the indicated section.

For Exercises 1–3, use the matrix and the stacked bar graph below. *(Section 3-1)*

\multicolumn{3}{c}{Estimated Number of Recreational Boats in the United States}
Year	**Motorized**	**Non-motorized**
1983	7,100,000	3,400,000
1987	7,900,000	4,100,000
1991	8,600,000	4,700,000

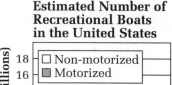
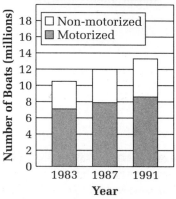

Estimated Number of Recreational Boats in the United States

1. What are the dimensions of the matrix?

2. What does the number in the second row, first column of the matrix represent?

3. What information is shown in the stacked bar graph that is not given in the matrix?

For Exercises 4–6, use the following final exam scores. *(Section 3-2)*

75 83 89 92 91 67 97 95 83 81 82 94 98 95 79
82 65 88 84 90 72 70 80 85 98 77 80 80 93 90

4. Find the median.   **5.** Find the mode.   **6.** Find the mean.

Graph each inequality. *(Section 3-3)*

7. $0 < x < 3$ **8.** $x \geq -1.5$ **9.** $-2 \leq x \leq 0$

For Exercises 10 and 11, use the following data set. *(Section 3-4)*

Thirty people were surveyed to find out how many times they ate pizza during the month of October. Here are the results:

  3   7 12 16 27   8 14 17 22   2   9   5 18   0 10
 24 15 13   6   1 28   7   0 10 16   5 24   4   9 14

10. Make a stem-and-leaf plot of the data.

11. Make a histogram of the data using the intervals 0–9, 10–19, and 20–29.

For Exercises 12 and 13, use the following data sets. *(Section 3-5)*

Books read by students during the first semester
15 20 32 24 18 23 16 24
35 15 20 30 25 19 27

Books read by students during the second semester
17 18 35 20 16 14 10 28
32 14 25 30 27 21 16

12. Make box-and-whisker plots for the number of books read by students during each semester.

13. *Writing* Write at least two statements comparing the data for the two semesters.

14. Name six different ways that data can be displayed. *(Section 3-6)*

15. What kind of graph would you use to show the population growth of a country over a long period of time? Explain your choice. *(Section 3-6)*

16. *Open-ended* Describe three ways in which graphs can be misleading. *(Section 3-7)*

Spiral Review
Units 1–3

Solve.

1. $6x + 3 = 21$ **2.** $4y - 7 = 29$ **3.** $35 = 6p - 1$

Draw all the lines of symmetry for each figure.

4. 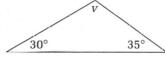   **5.**    **6.**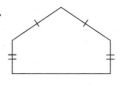

Write and solve an equation to find each unknown angle measure.

7. 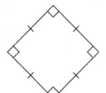   **8.**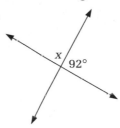

Simplify.

9. $-12.5 + 8.2$ **10.** $-6 - 7.5$ **11.** $(-4)(-1.3)$

Evaluate each expression for $x = 3$, $y = -2$, and $z = -4$.

12. $xy - xz$ **13.** $z(x - y)$ **14.** $xy + yz$

Name the congruent triangles.

15. 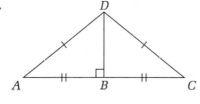   **16.**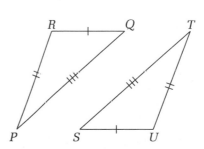

For Exercises 17–19, use the quiz scores below.

25   18   17   21   22   20   20   19   25   24   23   15   20   19   24

17. Find the mean, median, mode(s), and range of the scores.

18. Make a stem-and-leaf plot of the scores.

19. Make a box-and-whisker plot of the scores.

Graph each inequality on a number line.

20. $-3 \leq x < 2$ **21.** $x < 3\frac{1}{4}$ **22.** $-4.5 \leq x \leq -0.7$

INTEGRATED MATHEMATICS 1 Study Guide

4-1 Coordinates for Locations

FOCUS

Use coordinate systems to solve problems about locations in different settings.

"The doctor opened the seals with great care, and there fell out the map of an island, with latitude and longitude, soundings, names of hills, and bays, and inlets, and safe anchorage upon its shores. It was about nine miles long and five across, shaped, you might say, like a fat dragon standing up, and had two land-locked harbors, and a hill in the center part marked 'The Spyglass.'"

from <u>Treasure Island</u> by Robert Louis Stevenson

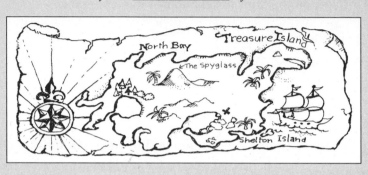

KEY TERMS	**EXAMPLE / ILLUSTRATION**
Coordinate plane (p. 184) a plane determined by a horizontal and a vertical number line (or axis), where ordered pairs indicate points on the plane	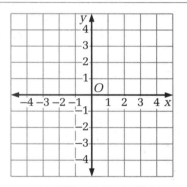
Ordered pair (p. 184) a pair of numbers used to describe the location of a point on a coordinate plane, where the first number corresponds to the horizontal axis and the second number corresponds to the vertical axis	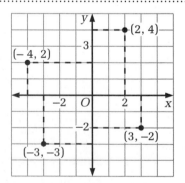
Origin (p. 184) the point on a coordinate plane where the horizontal and vertical axes intersect (The ordered pair for this point is (0, 0).)	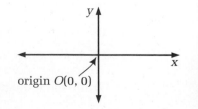 origin O(0, 0)

Quadrant (p. 184)
one of the four regions that are created by the axes of a coordinate plane (The quadrants are numbered beginning in the upper right-hand corner and moving in a counterclockwise direction.)

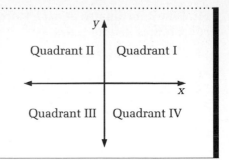

UNDERSTANDING THE MAIN IDEAS

Maps as coordinate systems

Maps often have coordinate systems. Their coordinates describe a square region, not a point. Usually map coordinates are a letter and a number.

> **Sample 1**
>
>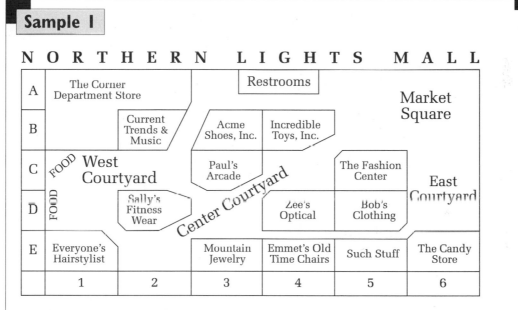
>
> Use the map of the Northern Lights Mall.
> **a.** What store is located in square C3?
> **b.** What are the coordinates of Sally's Fitness Wear?
>
> **Sample Response**
>
> **a.** Move across row C to column 3 to find Paul's Arcade.
>
> **b.** Locate Sally's Fitness Wear on the map. Look to the left to find the letter D and to the bottom of the map to find the number 2. The coordinates are D2.

Use the map of the Northern Lights Mall above for Exercises 1–8.

What store is located in each square?

1. C5   2. D4

3. B2   4. E6

Find the coordinates of each store. If there is more than one pair of coordinates, list all pairs.

5. Acme Shoes, Inc.

6. Bob's Clothing

7. Everyone's Hairstylist

8. Market Square

The globe as a coordinate system

Coordinates are used to locate places on Earth. The grid lines on a globe are lines of latitude and longitude. Places are identified by latitude first, then longitude. The vertical axis of the system is a line from the North Pole to the South Pole which passes through Greenwich, England. This line is called the **prime meridian** and is labeled 0° of longitude; longitude is measured in degrees east or west from the prime meridian. The **equator** is the horizontal axis and is labeled 0° of latitude; latitude is measured in degrees north or south from the equator.

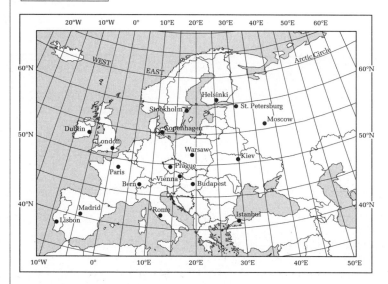

Use the map of Europe.

a. Estimate the latitude and longitude of London, England.

b. What city is located near 60 N, 25 E?

Sample Response

a. Locate London on the map. London has an approximate latitude of 52° north and an approximate longitude of 2° west. These numbers can be found by following the nearest latitude line to the left and the nearest longitude line up. You can write these coordinates as 52 N, 2 W. Notice that the equator is not on this map. The latitudes of any locations below the equator would have been labeled with an "S" for south.

b. Look to the left and find the latitude of 60° north. Follow that line until it intersects with the longitude of 25° east. Notice it is to the right of the prime meridian. The city at this location is Helsinki, Finland.

Use the map of Europe in Sample 2 for Exercises 9–16.

Estimate the latitude and longitude of each city.

9. Rome, Italy   **10.** Madrid, Spain   **11.** Kiev, Ukraine

In Exercises 12–14, what city is near each location?

12. 59 N, 18 E   **13.** 38 N, 8 W   **14.** 47 N, 20 E

15. About how many degrees east of Dublin, Ireland is Warsaw, Poland?

16. About how many degrees south of Moscow, Russia is Istanbul, Turkey?

Review **PREVIEW**

The display below shows the number of children in families of two parents and one parent in the United States for the years 1960–1990.

Children in Families of Two Parents and One Parent, 1960–1990

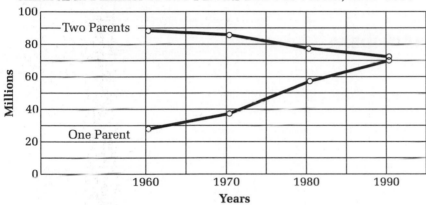

17. a. Interpret the information shown in the display. *(Section 3-6)*
   b. Do you think this is the best way to display the information? Explain why or why not.

18. Quadrilateral *ABCD* has two pairs of parallel sides and at least one right angle. *(Section 1-7)*
   a. Make an accurate sketch of quadrilateral *ABCD*.
   b. Write the special name for quadrilateral *ABCD*.

4-2 Introduction to Coordinate Geometry

Learn about coordinate geometry, identify polygons on a coordinate plane, and find the areas of polygons drawn on a coordinate plane.

Albrecht Dürer (1471–1528), geometer, writer, and artist, described various methods, based on geometric principles, of changing the proportions of human figures. These methods had the effect of producing caricatures by geometry.

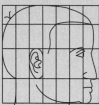 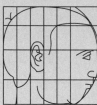 

UNDERSTANDING THE MAIN IDEAS

Describing shapes

A shape can be drawn on a coordinate plane using ordered pairs as its vertices (corners). From this drawing, the type of shape can be determined as well as various characteristics of that shape, such as congruency of sides.

Sample 1

For the set of points $A(-3, -2)$, $B(4, -2)$, $C(4, 5)$, $D(-3, 5)$, follow these steps.

- Plot the points on a coordinate plane. Connect the points in order and connect the last point to the first.

- Write the specific name of the polygon you formed.

- Explain how you know what it is.

Sample Response

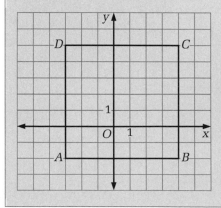

The polygon is a *square* because $AB = BC = CD = AD$ and $\angle A$, $\angle B$, $\angle C$, and $\angle D$ are right angles formed by horizontal and vertical segments.

Use the steps given in Sample 1 for Exercises 1–4.

1. $X(1, 6)$, $Y(1, -4)$, $Z(11, -4)$ 2. $H(0, 5)$, $I(-7, 0)$, $J(0, -5)$, $K(7, 0)$

3. $M(-3, -5)$, $N(2, 8)$, $P(6, -1)$ 4. $Q(-3, 7)$, $R(-7, 3)$, $S(7, 3)$, $T(3, 7)$

Finding areas

Sample 2

Find the area of right triangle XYZ.

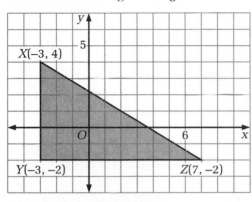

Sample Response

Problem Solving Strategy: Use a diagram

Insert helping lines to build a rectangle.

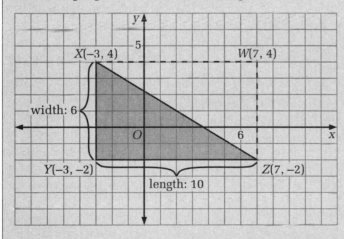

← Label point W.

Area of ◺ = $\frac{1}{2}$ • area of ▱

$= \frac{1}{2}lw$

$= \frac{1}{2}(10)(6)$ ← Substitute 10 for l and 6 for w.

$= 30$

The area of triangle XYZ is 30 square units.

Sample 3

Find the area of trapezoid *RSTU*.

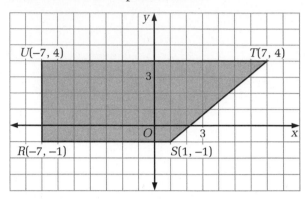

Sample Response

Problem Solving Strategy: Solve a simpler problem

To find the area of the trapezoid, you can solve the simple problems of finding the areas of a rectangle and a right triangle.

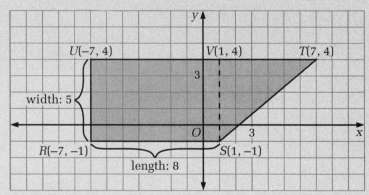

Step 1 First label point *V* to form rectangle *RSVU* and find its area.
Insert a helping line to build the rectangle and triangle.

$A = lw$
  $= 8(5)$
  $= 40$

Step 2 Next, find the area of triangle *STV*.

$A = \frac{1}{2}(5)(6)$ ⟵ Recall the method used in Sample 2.
  $= 15$

Step 3 Now add the areas of rectangle *RSVU* and triangle *STV*.

$40 + 15 = 55$

The area of trapezoid *RSTU* is 55 square units.

Find the area of each polygon. Describe the method you used.

5.

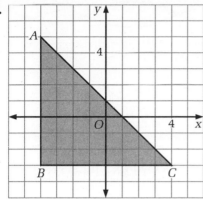

6.

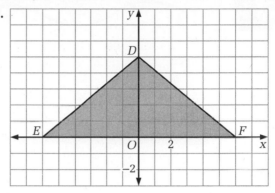

7.

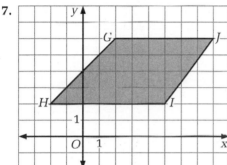

8.

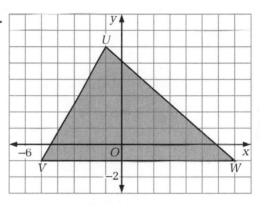

9.

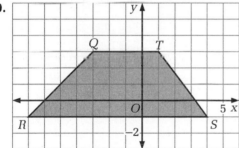

10.

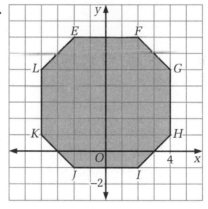

Review **PREVIEW**

For Exercises 11–14, simplify each expression. *(Sections 1-4, 1-5)*

11. $20 - 4(7) + (-2)(-6)$

12. $(-4 - 21) \div 5 + (-9)$

13. $2(7 - 3x) - 3(3 - 4x)$

14. $2x(4y - 1) + 4(1 - 3x)$

15. a. The coordinates of point R are $(-6, -2)$. Graph point R. *(Section 4-1)*

   b. What are the coordinates of a point that is 12 units to the right of R? Label this point S on your graph.

   c. What are the coordinates of a point that is 6 units to the right and 6 units up from R? Label this point T on your graph.

   d. Draw $\triangle RST$. What type of triangle is it?

INTEGRATED MATHEMATICS 1 Study Guide

4-3 Translations

FOCUS

Translate figures on a coordinate plane, recognize translational symmetry.

Kathy Homstad of the United States takes her luge down a straightaway at 60 miles per hour. At this part in the race, she is not turning, only her position is changing. The luge is sliding on the ice. This is an example of a **translation**.

KEY TERMS	EXAMPLE / ILLUSTRATION
Translation (p. 197) the movement of an object without changing its size or shape and without rotating or flipping it	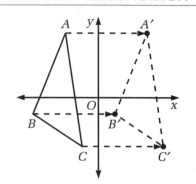
Translational symmetry (p. 199) a symmetry that occurs when an object or pattern is translated, creating copies of the object or pattern at various locations	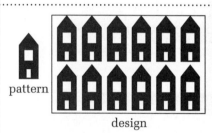 pattern design

UNDERSTANDING THE MAIN IDEAS

Working with translations

Sample 1

Translate △*ABC* 5 units right and 4 units up. What are the coordinates of each vertex after the translation?

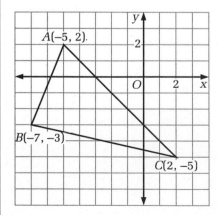

Translate each vertex 5 units right and 4 units up. Then draw the triangle.

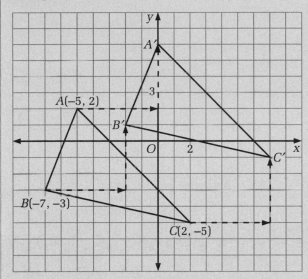

The translation above is written this way: $\triangle ABC \rightarrow \triangle A'B'C'$. The arrow means "goes to." The translation of vertices can be represented in this fashion: $A(-5, 2) \rightarrow A'(0, 6)$; $B(-7, -3) \rightarrow B'(-2, 1)$; $C(2, -5) \rightarrow C'(7, -1)$.

The coordinates of the vertices after the translation are $A'(0, 6)$, $B'(-2, 1)$, and $C'(7, -1)$.

For Exercises 1 and 2, translate $\triangle DEF$ as directed. Find the coordinates of each vertex after each translation.

1. 2 units right and 1 unit up

2. 4 units left and 5 units down

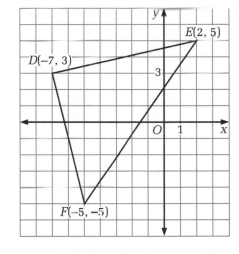

Tell whether the picture shows a translation. If so, describe how the vertices moved.

3.

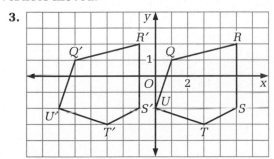

4.

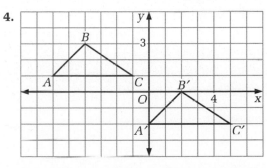

Describing translations using (x, y) coordinates

Another way to describe a translation is to show the change in the
coordinates (x, y) of any point.

Sample 2

Describe the following translation by showing the change in the
coordinates (x, y) of any point of a figure:

3 units right and 4 units down.

Sample Response

The words *right* and *up* are represented by addition and the words *left*
and *down* are represented by subtraction. Since the movements "right"
and "left" happen in the direction of the x-axis, the x-coordinate is
changed by these movements. Similarly, the y-coordinate is changed by
the movements "up" and "down."

Therefore, the given translation indicates an addition to the x-coordinate
and subtraction from the y-coordinate. The translation can be written:
$(x, y) \rightarrow (x + 3, y - 4)$.

**Describe each translation by showing the change in the coordinates
(x, y) of any point.**

   5. 6 units left and 4 units up   **6.** 2 units right and 7 units down

Sample 3

Write the coordinates of P' after the translation $(x, y) \rightarrow (x - 5, y + 4)$
of the point $P(2, 3)$.

Sample Response

In the translation, substitute 2 for x and 3 for y and then solve.
$(x - 5, y + 4) \rightarrow (2 - 5, 3 + 4) = (-3, 7)$

Write the coordinates of P' after each translation of $P(-3, 5)$.

   7. $(x, y) \rightarrow (x + 5, y - 4)$ **8.** $(x, y) \rightarrow (x - 2, y)$

   9. $(x, y) \rightarrow (x - 10, y + 15)$ **10.** $(x, y) \rightarrow (x, y + 6)$

Review **PREVIEW**

11. a. Plot the points $A(-1, -1)$, $B(4, 4)$, $C(0, 8)$, and $D(-4, 4)$. Connect them in
order and connect D to A. *(Section 4-2)*

   b. Write the specific name of the polygon you formed. Explain how you
know what it is.

Solve each equation. *(Sections 2-7, 2-8)*

12. $x + 12 = 19$ **13.** $a - 5 = -15$

4-4 Rotations

FOCUS

Rotations of figures
on a coordinate
plane, rotate
figures on polar
graph paper,
recognize
rotational
symmetry.

The pirouette is an example of a rotation which occurs in ballet. Notice the center of rotation.

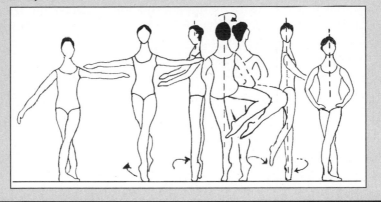

KEY TERMS

EXAMPLE / ILLUSTRATION

Rotation (p. 202)
a turn around a point called the center of rotation
(The direction of a rotation may be clockwise or
counterclockwise.)

direction of rotation

center of rotation

Transformation (p. 202)
a change made to an object or its position (Translating and
rotating are two ways to transform an object.)

TRANSLATION

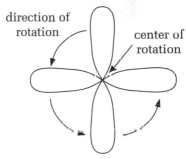

slide

ROTATION

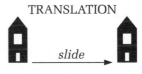

turn

Rotational symmetry (p. 205)
the symmetry that occurs when an object looks the same
after a rotation *of less* than 360° (All objects look the same
after they have been rotated 360°—this does not indicate
rotational symmetry.)

An equilateral triangle has 120°
and 240° rotational symmetry.

original

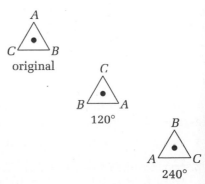

120°

240°

Describing rotation

Sample 1

The graphs below show two different rotations of rectangle *ABCD* around the origin. Describe the direction and amount of each rotation.

a.
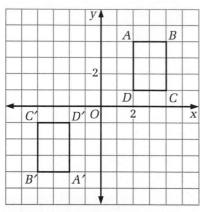

b.
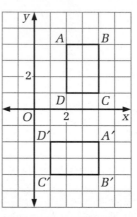

Sample Response

For each graph, draw a line from the center of rotation (in this case the origin) to a point on the original figure. Then draw a line from the center of rotation to the corresponding point on the rotated figure. Measure the angle formed. To completely describe a rotation, you need to state the amount of turn (as a fraction of a full turn or in degrees), the direction (clockwise or counterclockwise), and the center of rotation.

a.
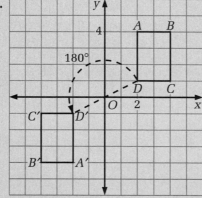

$180°$ or $\frac{1}{2}$ turn around the origin
(Direction does not matter.)

b.
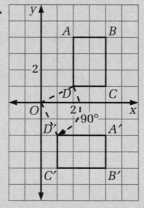

$90°$ or $\frac{1}{4}$ turn clockwise
around the origin

The rotation in part (b) could be described as $270°$ counterclockwise. As a rule, rotations are described by the smaller of the two possible angles.

Graph the given figure and its image on a coordinate plane. Then describe the direction and amount of the rotation of each graph.

1. $\triangle ABC$: $A(3, -2)$, $B(1, -6)$, $C(8, -8)$; $\triangle A'B'C'$: $A'(2, 3)$, $B'(6, 1)$, $C'(8, 8)$

2. trapezoid *DEFG*: $D(-9, -2)$, $E(-2, -2)$, $F(-3, -6)$, $G(-6, -6)$;
   trapezoid *D'E'F'G'*: $D'(-2, 9)$, $E'(-2, 2)$, $F'(-6, 3)$, $G'(-6, 6)$

Drawing rotations

It is easier to draw rotations on a special type of graph paper called polar
graph paper.

Sample 2

Rotate △*QRS* 80° clockwise around
the origin.

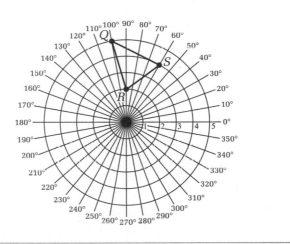

Sample Response

Move each vertex along its circle in a
clockwise direction. The amount of
turn is 80° which is 8 × 10°, so
move the vertices eight lines. Draw
the rotated triangle by connecting
the rotated vertices.

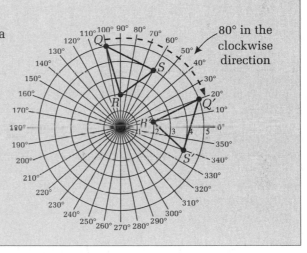

Copy each figure on polar graph paper. Draw each indicated rotation of
the figure around the origin.

3. 150° counterclockwise

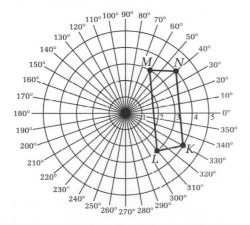

4. 90° clockwise

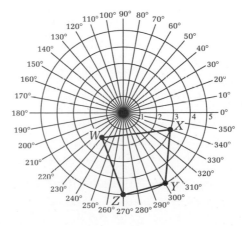

INTEGRATED MATHEMATICS 1 **Study Guide**

Sample 3

Tell whether or not each figure has rotational symmetry. If it does, describe the symmetry.

a. X

b.

Sample Response

a. Yes. This letter has 180° rotational symmetry.

| 90° | 180° | 270° | 360° |
| X → X | → X | → X | → X |

b. Yes. This design has 120° and 240° rotational symmetry.

| 60° | 120° | 180° | 240° | 300° | 360° |

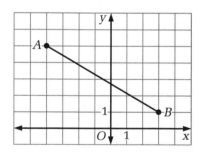

Tell whether each figure has rotational symmetry. If it does, describe the symmetry.

5.

6.

7.

Review **PREVIEW**

8. Translate $\overline{AB}$ 5 units to the right and 4 units down. Draw $\overline{A'B'}$. What are the coordinates of each point after the translation? *(Section 4-3)*

9. Make a graph to show the data. *(Section 3-6)*

National League Baseball Team ERA (July 10, 1993)

Atlanta	Chicago	Cincinnati	Colorado	Florida	Houston	Los Angeles
3.19	4.14	4.15	5.83	3.84	3.83	3.55

Montreal	New York	Philadelphia	Pittsburgh	San Diego	San Francisco	St. Louis
3.87	4.43	3.83	4.82	4.18	3.38	3.67

Scatter Plots

FOCUS

Make and interpret
a scatter plot of
data, use scatter
plots to make
predictions.

*The graphing calculators available
on the market today allow the user
to input a set of ordered pairs and
then have the calculator draw a
scatter plot of the data points.
These calculators can also be used
to determine a fitted line for the
data which can then be added to
the scatter plot.*

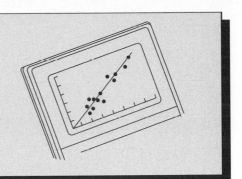

KEY TERMS

EXAMPLE / ILLUSTRATION

Scatter plot (p. 212)
   a graph that shows the relationship between two data sets

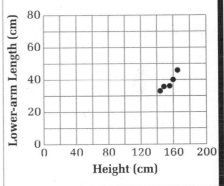

Fitted line (p. 212)
   a straight line drawn on a scatter plot that passes close to
   most of the data points (This line helps to make
   predictions—the stronger the correlation, the more
   accurate the predictions will be.)

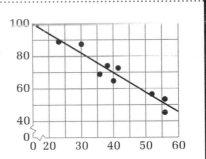

UNDERSTANDING THE MAIN IDEAS

Using a scatter plot of data to make predictions

Sample 1

This table shows the average height and weight for boys from the ages of
1 to 10 years of age.

Age	1	2	3	4	5	6	7	8	9	10
Height (in.)	17	23	36	39	42	45	47	50	52	54
Weight (lb)	21	26	31	34	39	46	51	57	63	69

What average weight could be predicted for a boy that is 60 inches tall?

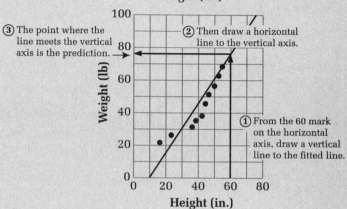
1. The table below shows the heights and weights of girls from 1 to 10 years of age. What average weight could be predicted for a girl 60 in. tall?

Age	1	2	3	4	5	6	7	8	9	10
Height (in.)	17	21	36	39	41	44	47	50	52	54
Weight (lb)	20	25	30	33	38	45	49	56	62	69

Sample 2

State whether each scatter plot shows a *positive correlation*, a *negative correlation*, or *no correlation*.

a.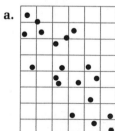

b.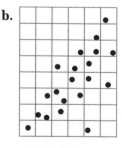

c.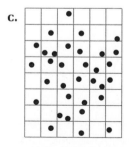

a. Notice that as the points move left to right, they also move from the top to the bottom. Therefore, this scatter plot shows a *negative correlation*.

b. As these points move from left to right, the points also move from bottom to top. This scatter plot shows a *positive correlation*.

c. As the points on this scatter plot move from left to right there is no indication of the points moving up or down. This scatter plot shows *no correlation*.

State whether the following scatter plots show a *positive correlation*, a *negative correlation*, or *no correlation*.

2.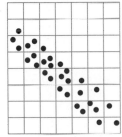

3.

Sample 3

Make a scatter plot for the elevation and the total 1990 precipitation. State whether the scatter plot shows a *positive correlation*, a *negative correlation*, or *no correlation*.

City	Latitude (°N)	Elevation (ft)	Total 1990 Precipitation (in.)	Total 1990 sleet/snow (in.)
Anchorage, AK	61	114	19.0	95.9
Buffalo, NY	42	705	50.9	67.2
Seattle, WA	47	400	44.8	13.6
Omaha, NE	41	997	26.3	27.2
Grand Rapids, MI	43	784	42.6	60.0
Jackson, MS	32	291	54.0	0.0
Fresno, CA	36	328	8.7	0.0
Minneapolis, MN	45	834	33.1	33.9
St. Louis, MO	38	535	45.1	28.7
Tampa, FL	28	19	34.4	0.0

Sample Response

To make a scatter plot for the elevation and the total 1990 precipitation, ordered pairs must be plotted. The ordered pairs for this sample will be in the form (elevation, total precipitation).

Elevation (ft)	Total 1990 Precipitation (in.)	Ordered Pair
114	19.0	(114, 19.0)
705	50.9	(705, 50.9)
400	44.8	(400, 44.8)
997	26.3	(997, 26.3)
784	42.6	(784, 42.6)
291	54.0	(291, 54.0)
328	8.7	(328, 8.7)
834	33.1	(834, 33.1)
535	45.1	(535, 45.1)
19	34.4	(19, 34.4)

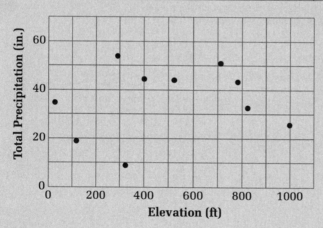

The random arrangement of dots in this scatter plot indicate that there is *no correlation* between elevation and total precipitation.

Make a scatter plot for each relationship using the information given in the table in Sample 3. State whether each scatter plot shows a *positive correlation*, a *negative correlation*, or *no correlation*.

4. the latitude and the total precipitation   **5.** the latitude and the total snow/sleet

Review **PREVIEW**

For Exercises 6–8, graph each inequality on a number line. *(Section 3-3)*

6. $a \geq 7$ **7.** $x \leq -3$ **8.** $-4 \leq k \leq 5$

9. Scott earns $4.25/h as a custodian in a school. Tell how much he earns for each number of hours he works. *(Section 1-2)*

a. 6 hours   **b.** 4 hours   **c.** y hours

Graphs and Functions

Understand what a function is, identify control variables and dependent variables, draw graphs of functions, and recognize functions.

Small-market economics rely on supply and demand. This graph of a demand curve illustrates that the price of wheat depends on the quantity available. As the amount of wheat needed to satisfy the demand increases, the price of the wheat decreases.

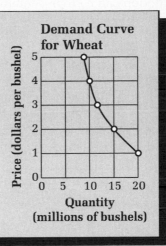

Demand Curve for Wheat

KEY TERMS

EXAMPLE / ILLUSTRATION

Dependent variable (p. 218)
  a variable whose value is determined by one or more other variables

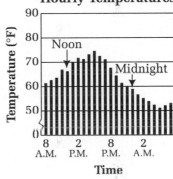

Hourly Temperatures

By examining this bar graph of the hourly temperatures starting from 8 A.M. one day to 7 A.M. the following day, it can be seen that the temperature depends on the time of day. The temperature is the *dependent variable* and the time of day is the *control variable*. Notice also that the time of day is on the horizontal axis and the temperature is on the vertical axis. In general, the control variable and the dependent variable are placed on those respective axes.

Control variable (p. 218)
  a variable which determines the value of another variable (The control variable is sometimes called the *independent variable*.)

Function (p. 220)
  a relationship in which there is only one value of the dependent variable for each value of the control variable

In the graph above, each hour has only one temperature. This is an example of a function.

Functions

A function can be represented many ways: in words, in symbols, with a
table of values, or with a graph.

Sample 1

At a week-long "going out of business" sale, the price of each item is one
third the previous day's price. (Of course, if a customer waits until
tomorrow, what they want may be gone.) Draw a graph of the price of an
$486 item during the sale. Tell whether the graph represents a function.

Sample Response

First make a table of values.

Day of Sale	Price (dollars)
1	486
2	$\frac{1}{3}(486) = 162$
3	$\frac{1}{3}(162) = 54$
4	$\frac{1}{3}(54) = 18$
5	$\frac{1}{3}(18) = 6$
6	$\frac{1}{3}(6) = 2$
7	$\frac{1}{3}(2) = 0.67$

⟵ The original price is $486.

⟵ Multiply the previous day's price by $\frac{1}{3}$.

Then draw a graph. In general,
the dependent variable is put
on the vertical axis and the control
variable on the horizontal axis.
The price depends on the day of
the sale. So the price is the
dependent variable and the day
of the sale is the control variable.

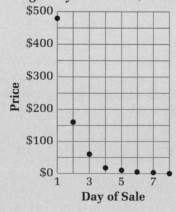

**Daily Sale Price of an Item
Originally Priced at $486**

For each day of the sale, the item has only one price. So the graph
represents a function.

Identify the dependent variable and the control variable in each situation.

1. Bob rides his bike at an average speed of 12 mph. When he rides for different lengths of time throughout the week, he travels different distances.

2. Karla walks or runs for 1 hour each day. She travels different distances each day according to her speed.

Draw a graph for each situation. Tell whether the graph represents a function. Explain.

3. The after-prom committee has a magazine sale every year. This year, they raised $500. They decide to try to raise 1.5 times the amount they raised the previous year for the next four years.

4. Alice earned these scores on her first five tests: 86, 75, 90, 75, and 95.

Vertical-line test for functions

A graph can be used to visualize a function. For each value of the control variable, there should be only one value of the dependent variable. This means that no two points on the graph of a function lie directly above one another. The vertical-line test involves imagining a vertical line drawn through a graph. If the vertical line passes through more than one point on the graph, then the graph does *not* represent a function.

Sample 2

Tell whether the graph represents a function. Explain your answer.

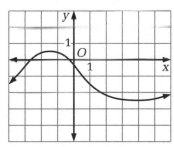

Sample Response

Imagine drawing numerous vertical lines through the graph.

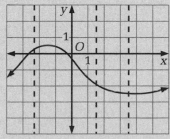

Since no two points of the graph lie on the same vertical line, the graph represents a function.

Tell whether each graph represents a function. Explain your answer.

5.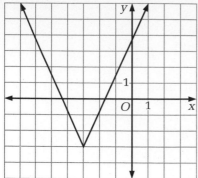

6.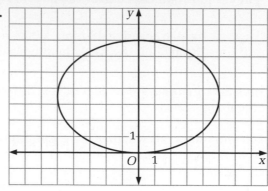

Sample 3

Describe the following situation using the phrase "is a function of."
What is the dependent variable? the control variable?

> Sam owns a house cleaning business. He charges different prices
> for cleaning houses of different sizes.

Sample Response

The cost depends on the size of the house. The cost is a function of the
house size. The cost is the dependent variable. The house size is the
control variable.

**Describe each situation using the phrase "is a function of." What is the
dependent variable? the control variable?**

7. Mark plays golf every day. The more he plays, the lower his score.

8. Martha earns money for each craft item she assembles. The more she
   assembles, the more money she earns.

Review **PREVIEW**

9. Draw a scatter plot that shows a strong negative correlation. *(Section 4-5)*

Give the reciprocal of each number. *(Toolbox Skill 9)*

10. 6

11. $\dfrac{3}{4}$

12. $-\dfrac{5}{16}$

Evaluate each expression when $x = -5$, $x = 0$, and $x = 2$. *(Sections 1-4, 2-2)*

13. $-3x^2$

14. $|x| - 3$

15. $\dfrac{1}{x + 1}$

Functions and Equations

Fireworks create spectacular parabolas.

KEY TERMS

Parabola (p. 230)

a U-shaped graph that can be generated from the equation $y = x^2$ (However, $y = x^2$ is not the only equation that generates a parabola.)

Hyperbola (p. 230)

two U-shaped graphs that mirror each other and share the same line of symmetry (This graph can be generated with the equation $y = \frac{1}{x}$. However, $y = \frac{1}{x}$ is not the only equation that generates a hyperbola.)

EXAMPLE / ILLUSTRATION

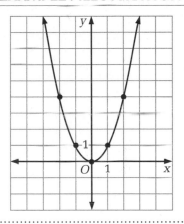

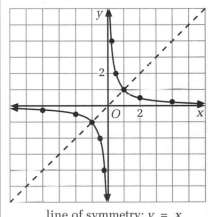

line of symmetry: $y = x$

INTEGRATED MATHEMATICS 1 Study Guide **103**

Writing equations

For a function, x often represents the control variable and y represents the dependent variable.

Sample 1

Write an equation to represent the function given in the table.

x	y
−3	−1
−2	0
−1	1
0	2
1	3
2	4
3	5

Sample Response

Problem Solving Strategy: Identify a pattern

Think about how the y-values relate to the x-values in the table and look for a pattern. Write a rule for the pattern: each y-value is two more than its x-value. Test your rule using the values in the table.

$$-3 + 2 = -1 \qquad -2 + 2 = 0 \qquad -1 + 2 = 1 \qquad 0 + 2 = 2$$
$$1 + 2 = 3 \qquad 2 + 2 = 4 \qquad 3 + 2 = 5$$

Write the rule as an equation: $y = x + 2$.

Write an equation to represent each function.

1.

x	y
−3	3
−2	4
−1	5
0	6
1	7
2	8
3	9

2.

x	y
−3	−12
−2	−8
−1	−4
0	0
1	4
2	8
3	12

3.

x	y
−3	−11
−2	−10
−1	−9
0	−8
1	−7
2	−6
3	−5

Write an equation to represent this function.

> The cost of daycare at the local YMCA depends on the number of
> children receiving care. The fee for the first child in a family is $2.25
> per hour and the fee for each additional child is $1.50 per hour.

Sample Response

The *number of additional children after the first child* is the control
variable. Represent this number by n.

- The number of additional children is n.

The *total cost per hour* is the dependent variable. Represent this cost
by c.

- The total daycare cost per hour in dollars is c.

Because each additional child costs $1.50 per hour, the cost of n
additional children is $1.50 times n.

- The cost per hour of the additional children is $1.5n$.

The total cost per hour is the sum of the first child's cost and the
additional children's costs. Write an equation to represent the function.

- Then $c = 2.25 + 1.5n$.

**Write an equation to represent each function. Tell what your variables
represent.**

4. The cost of a telephone call depends on the number of minutes that it
   lasts. The first minute costs $.32 and each additional minute costs $.15.

5. A group of students plan to rent a hotel room for $200 during the
   upcoming state basketball tournaments. The amount each student pays
   depends on the number of students renting the room.

6. Jacob is 6 years older than Mitch.

Graphing equations

Sample 3

Graph the equation $y = -3x$.

Sample Response

Make a table of values; these values should be written as ordered pairs
(x, y). Choose both positive and negative values for x. Some easy values
to evaluate are -1, 0, and 1. Use other values to show the shape of the
graph better.

Sample Response continues on the next page.

$y = -3x$		
x	y	(x, y)
-1	$-3(-1) = 3$	$(-1, 3)$
0	$-3(0) = 0$	$(0, 0)$
1	$-3(1) = -3$	$(1, -3)$
2	$-3(2) = -6$	$(2, -6)$
3	$-3(3) = -9$	$(3, -9)$

Graph the ordered pairs and connect them.

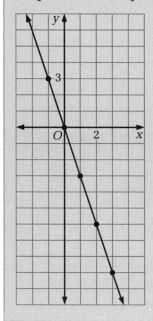

Graph each equation.

7. $y = x - 3$

8. $y = 2|x|$

Write each function as an equation. Then graph the function.

9. A worker earns \$6.15 per hour. The worker's gross pay depends on the number of hours worked.

10. A car traveled for 3 hours. The number of miles traveled depends on the average speed at which the car traveled.

11. The width of a rectangle is three more than two times the length.

Review

12. Draw a graph that does not represent a function. *(Section 4-6)*

Solve each equation. Check each solution. *(Section 2-7)*

13. $2n + 7 = -3$

14. $5x \div 4 = -15$

Unit Check-Up	Complete these exercises for a review of Unit 4. If you have difficulty with a particular problem, review the indicated section.

Use the map of Europe shown in Sample 2 of Section 4-1 for Exercises 1–6.

Estimate the latitude and longitude of each city. *(Section 4-1)*

   1. Copenhagen, Denmark   **2.** Vienna, Austria   **3.** Warsaw, Poland

For Exercises 4–6, what city is near each location? *(Section 4-1)*

   4. 47 N, 8 E   **5.** 59 N, 30 E   **6.** 49 N, 2 E

   7. a. Plot the points $J(-1, 5)$, $K(3, 5)$, $L(3, -2)$, and $M(-1, 1)$ on a coordinate plane. Connect the points in order and connect M to J. *(Section 4-2)*
       b. Write the specific name of the polygon you formed.
       c. Find the area of polygon $JKLM$.

   8. Translate $\triangle ABC$ shown at the right 3 units left and 5 units down. What are the coordinates of each vertex after the translation? *(Section 4-3)*

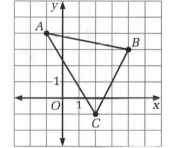

For Exercises 9 and 10, write the coordinates of P' after each translation of $P(-1, 6)$. *(Section 4-3)*

   9. $(x, y) \rightarrow (x - 5, y - 4)$

   10. $(x, y) \rightarrow (x + 3, y - 1)$

   11. ***Open-ended*** Create a design using a right triangle, a rectangle, and a parallelogram. Use your design to make a pattern with translational symmetry. *(Section 4-3)*

   12. Copy the figure at the right on polar graph paper. Draw the figure after a 220° clockwise rotation around the origin. *(Section 4-4)*

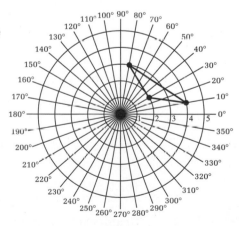

   13. The table below shows the number of push-ups and chin-ups done in one minute by each of six people. Draw a scatter plot of the data and a fitted line. How many chin-ups could be predicted for a person who did 41 push-ups? *(Section 4-5)*

Push-ups	21	28	30	34	34	38
Chin-ups	6	8	9	10	11	12

   14. ***Writing*** Think of a situation that involves two quantities, in which one quantity depends on the other. Describe the situation as a function. Identify the dependent variable and the control variable. Draw a graph of the function. *(Section 4-6)*

Tell whether each graph represents a function. *(Section 4-6)*

15.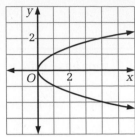

16.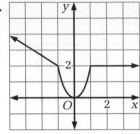

Graph each equation. *(Section 4-7)*

17. $y = -2x + 3$

18. $y = -2|x|$

---

1. Write a variable expression for the amount "16 less than a number n."

Calculate according to the order of operations.

2. $3^3 + 45 \div 5 - 6$

3. $[(8 + 7) \cdot 2 + 6] \div 9$

Simplify.

4. $5y^2 + 4y + 11 + 3y + 8$

5. $3x^2 + x - 2x - x^2 + 4$

Evaluate each expression when $a = 3$ and $b = -5$.

6. $a + b^2$

7. $2b + 6a$

8. $|a + b|$

Solve.

9. $y + 18 = 64$

10. $3x + 4x = 63$

11. $\dfrac{k}{6} + 33 = 26$

For Exercises 12–14, use the data given in the chart at the right.

12. Make a stem-and-leaf plot of the data.

13. Make a box-and-whisker plot of the data.

14. Find the mean, median, mode(s), and range of the data.

15. Draw a scatter plot that shows a strong negative correlation.

16. Graph the function $y = 3x^2$.

Homeroom Class Sizes on the First Day of School				
25	27	32	30	29
31	33	19	36	22
26	21	26	19	20
32	22	24	25	29
33	35	30	33	26

Graph each inequality on a number line.

17. $x \geq -2$

18. $-4 < x \leq 3$

19. $-2 < x < 5$

For Exercises 20–22, use the graph at the right.

20. Find the area of $\triangle LMN$.

21. Translate $\triangle LMN$ 2 units left and 3 units up. What are the coordinates of each vertex after the translation?

22. Rotate $\triangle LMN$ 90° counterclockwise around the origin.

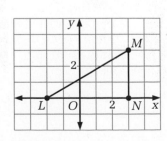

Modeling Problem Situations

FOCUS

Use a table, graph,
or equation to
model situations
and solve
problems.

Suppose a computer is to be rented for two weeks from one of the two businesses whose rental plans are shown below.

COMPUTER CORNER: $75 rental fee plus $8 per day
RENT-A-COMPUTER: $50 rental fee plus $10 per day

You could model the situation with tables, equations, or a graph to determine which plan would be cheaper.

Tables:

Computer Corner

Day	Cost
1	75 + 8
2	75 + 16
⋮	⋮

Rent-A-Computer

Day	Cost
1	50 + 10
2	50 + 20
⋮	⋮

Graph:

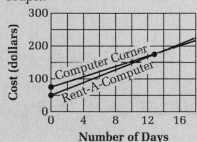

Equations:

Let y = cost and x = number of days.
Computer Corner: $y = 75 + 8x$
Rent-A-Computer: $y = 50 + 10x$

KEY TERMS

EXAMPLE / ILLUSTRATION

Mathematical model (p. 241)
a table, graph, function, equation, or inequality that describes a situation

The graph below is a model for the following problem.
The Celsius temperature that corresponds to 32°F is 0°C. The Celsius temperature that corresponds to 50°F is 10°C. What is the Celsius temperature that corresponds to 86°F?

Converting from °F to °C

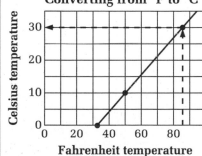

Modeling (p. 241)
making and using a mathematical model

The formula $F = 1.8C + 32$, where F = the Fahrenheit temperature and C = the Celsius temperature, models the problem above by using an equation. Replace F by 86 to get the equation $86 = 1.8C + 32$. Then solve the equation for C.

UNDERSTANDING THE MAIN IDEAS

Using tables, graphs, or equations to model situations and solve problems

A given problem situation can be modeled by a variety of mathematical models. Graphs (both hand-drawn and graphics calculator generated), equations, inequalities, tables, and spreadsheets can be utilized as models. After modeling the situation, the model can be used to solve the situation.

Sample 1

You are driving your car at an average speed of 55 miles per hour. After how many hours will you be 330 miles from your starting point?

Sample Response

Method 1: Use a table to model the situation.

Number of hours	Total distance driven
1	55
2	110
3	165
4	220
5	275
6	330

After 6 hours, you will be 330 miles from your starting point.

Method 2: Use a graph to model the situation.

1. Label the horizontal axis with the number of hours. Label the vertical axis with the distance from the starting point.

2. Start with 0 miles and 0 hours. Mark the origin as the starting point.

3. In one hour, the distance from the starting point will be 55 miles. Plot the point (1, 55).

4. Add 55 miles to the distance for each successive hour and plot the points (2, 110) and (3, 165). Draw a line through the points.

5. Estimate 330 on the vertical scale. Find where the horizontal line through 330 meets the line you drew in step 4.

6. Read down to the horizontal axis to find the number of hours.

After 6 hours, you will be 330 miles from your starting point.

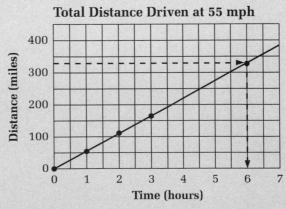

Sample Response continues on the next page.

Method 3: Use an equation to model the situation.

The distance formula, $d = rt$, can be used to write the equation.
In the formula, $d = $ the distance traveled, $r = $ the rate of travel, and
$t = $ the time.

Use the information from the problem to write the equation.

   $d = rt$

$330 = 55t$

Use algebra to solve the equation.

$330 = 55t$

$\dfrac{330}{55} = \dfrac{55t}{55}$ ⟵ Divide both sides by 55.

   $6 = t$

You will be 330 miles from your starting point after 6 hours.

Model each situation with a table, graph, or equation. Do not use the same method for all the exercises. Then solve the problem.

1. A snail travels about 5 feet every 2 minutes. At this rate, how far will the snail travel in 30 minutes?

2. A plumber charges $32.50 for a service call, plus $18.50 per hour while on the job. What would the plumber's charge be for a 3-hour call?

3. Al spent $35.80 for 2 boxes of floppy disks and 3 reams of printer paper. The paper cost $5.00 per ream. How much did each box of disks cost?

Writing situations modeled by given equations

One equation can be the model for a variety of situations.

Sample 2

Describe two situations that could be modeled by the equation
$50 - 2x = 9.5$.

Sample Response

Situation 1: Lila gave the clerk $50 to pay for two books that were the same price. She received $9.50 in change. How much did each book cost?

Caution: You must ⟵ include the fact that both books are the *same* price.

Situation 2: Luis had a 50-ft length of cable. After he cut off two pieces of equal length, he had 9.5 ft of cable left. How long was each of the pieces he cut off?

Describe a situation that could be modeled by each equation.

4. $16 + 2s = 36$

5. $92 = 4p + 4$

Graph each equation. *(Section 4-6)*

6. $y = 1 - |x|$

7. $y = x^2 + 0.5$

Write the opposite of each number. *(Section 2-3)*

8. -1.5

9. 0.01

10. $\frac{2}{3}$

11. 100

Simplify. *(Sections 1-5, 2-3)*

12. $4(x + 2)$

13. $6(k - 4) + 3k$

14. $-5 + 6(8x - 3)$

Opposites and the Distributive Property

FOCUS

Simplify expressions and solve equations involving opposites, the distributive property, and combining like terms.

> *On a multiple-choice test, a student receives 2 points for each correct answer, –2 points for each incorrect answer, and –1 point for each unanswered question. If a student answered 38 items correctly and all the other items incorrectly for a total of 52 points, how many items did the person answer incorrectly? If all the incorrect answers were guesses, how much better would this student's score have been if these items had been left unanswered?*
>
> *The first question can be modeled by the equation $2(38) + (-2)(x) = 52$, where $x =$ the number of incorrect answers. After solving the equation for x, the second question can be answered; the student's score would have been x points higher.*

UNDERSTANDING THE MAIN IDEAS

Simplifying expressions

Mathematical expressions involving numbers, variables, and operations can be simplified by applying the distributive property, by using the opposite operation, and by combining like terms. Recall that the distributive property tells you that a product like $20(8 + 3)$ is equal to the sum $(20 \cdot 8) + (20 \cdot 3)$. You use the opposite of an operation when you use the idea that subtracting a number is the same as adding its opposite. Recall that like terms are constant terms, such as -7 and 5, or terms that contain the same variable raised to the same power, such as $4x$ and $-x$.

Sample 1

Simplify $6n - 3(n + 2)$.

Sample Response

Subtracting is the same as adding the opposite.
$6n - 3(n + 2) = 6n + (-3)(n + 2)$

Now use the distributive property to simplify $(-3)(n + 2)$.
$6n + (-3)(n + 2) = 6n + (-3n - 6)$

Next group like terms.
$6n + (-3n - 6) = (6n + (-3n)) - 6$

Combine like terms.
$(6n + (-3n)) - 6 = 3n - 6$

So, $6n - 3(n + 2) = 3n - 6$.

Simplify each expression.

1. $7(y + 2) - 3y$ **2.** $18 - (5p - 2)$ **3.** $8m - 3(m + 4)$

INTEGRATED MATHEMATICS 1 Study Guide **113**

Solving multi-step equations

You can apply what you know about simplifying expressions to solving
equations. When you solve an equation, the goal is to get the variable
alone on one side of the equation, with its value on the other side.

Sample 2

The perimeter of the rectangle shown at the
right is 50 cm. Find the length of each side.

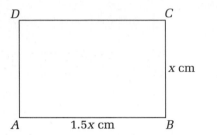

Sample Response

The perimeter of a rectangle is found by using the formula
$P = 2l + 2w$.

Substitute 50 for P, $1.5x$ for l, and x for w.

$50 = 2(1.5x) + 2(x)$
$50 = 3x + 2x$
$50 = 5x$ ⟵ Combine like terms.
$\frac{50}{5} = \frac{5x}{5}$ ⟵ Divide both sides by 5.
$10 = x$

The length of the rectangle is $1.5 \cdot 10 = 15$ cm, and the width is 10 cm.

Sample 3

Solve the equation $3n - 7n - 10 = 24$.

Sample Response

Remember that you want terms with variables alone on one side of the
equation.

$3n - 7n - 10 = 24$
$3n - 7n - 10 + 10 = 24 + 10$ ⟵ Add 10 to both sides.
$3n - 7n = 34$
$-4n = 34$ ⟵ Combine like terms $3n$ and $-7n$.
$\frac{-4n}{-4} = \frac{34}{-4}$ ⟵ Divide both sides by -4.
$n = -8.5$

The solution is -8.5.

For Exercises 4–6, solve.

   4. $5(y - 3) + y = 24$ **5.** $3s - 2(5 - s) = 8$ **6.** $-24 = -x + 18$

   7. *Writing* What property of opposites tells you that there is a distributive property for multiplication and subtraction?

Review **PREVIEW**

   8. Model and solve this situation. *(Section 5-1)*

     Renting a floor sander costs $50 plus $10.50 per hour of use. How much will it cost the Sarahanda family to rent a floor sander for 8 hours?

   9. Use a number anywhere along the scale below to estimate the probability that snow will fall in Bismarck, ND, in January. *(Section 4-4)*

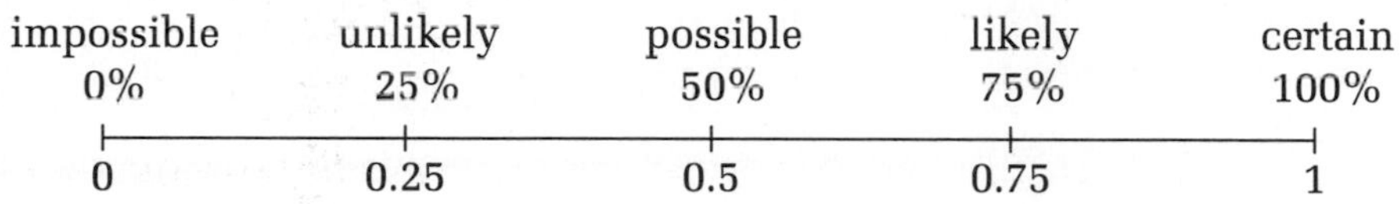

impossible	unlikely	possible	likely	certain
0%	25%	50%	75%	100%
0	0.25	0.5	0.75	1

Solve. *(Section 2-8)*

10. $2n + (-8n) = -60$ **11.** $46 + 6 + (-3y) = 19$

12. $9x - 6x + 10 = -8$ **13.** $18 + 3d - 6d = -15$

Variables on Both Sides

Model situations and solve equations that have a variable on both sides of the equals sign.

The House of Exercise health club placed the advertisement at the right in the local newspaper. New members have two plans to choose from, so they must compare the plans in order to choose the plan better suited to their needs. An equation can be used to help them determine the number of visits under Plan I required in order to be of the same value as Plan II.

HOUSE OF EXERCISE

Membership Plans

Plan I: $250 yearly membership fee plus $10 per visit

Plan II: $25 per visit

KEY TERMS

EXAMPLE / ILLUSTRATION

Variable terms (p. 256)
  terms that contain variables

In the equation $2r = 5r - 90$, the terms $2r$ and $5r$ are variable terms.

UNDERSTANDING THE MAIN IDEAS

Variables on both sides of the equation

Very often the equation you write to model a situation has the variable on both sides of the equals sign. One step in solving the equation is to move all the variable terms to one side of the equals sign. You can move variable terms just as you move numbers, by adding or subtracting the same term from both sides.

Sample 1

Solve $5x = 4 + 3x$.

Sample Response

The algebraic steps used to solve the equation are shown on the left, while the corresponding model (using tiles) of each step is shown on the right.

Let ▭ represent x and ▢ represent 1.

$$5x = 4 + 3x$$

Sample Response continues on the next page.

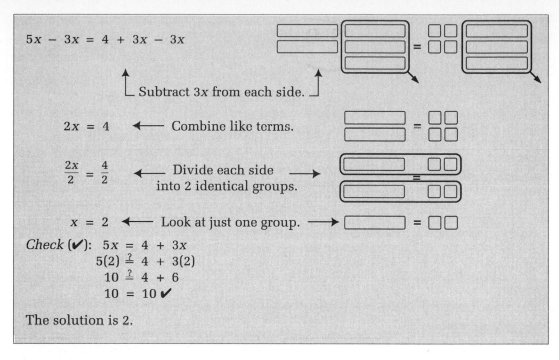

$$5x - 3x = 4 + 3x - 3x$$

↑ Subtract 3x from each side. ↑

$$2x = 4 \quad \longleftarrow \text{Combine like terms.}$$

$$\frac{2x}{2} = \frac{4}{2} \quad \longleftarrow \begin{array}{l} \text{Divide each side} \\ \text{into 2 identical groups.} \end{array} \longrightarrow$$

$$x = 2 \quad \longleftarrow \text{Look at just one group.} \longrightarrow$$

Check (✔): $5x = 4 + 3x$

$$5(2) \stackrel{?}{=} 4 + 3(2)$$
$$10 \stackrel{?}{=} 4 + 6$$
$$10 = 10 ✔$$

The solution is 2.

Let ⬓ represent *x* and ⬜ represent 1. Model and solve
each equation.

1. $4x + 7 = 6x + 1$ **2.** $3x + 4 = 4x + 1$ **3.** $5x + 4 = 2x + 10$

Sample 2

The same amount of
fencing is needed to
enclose these two
flower beds. What is
the value of *x*?

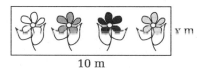

10 m

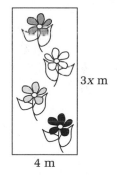

3x m

4 m

Sample Response

Use the perimeter formula $P = 2l + 2w$ to help you write an equation.
Since the perimeters are equal, you can write the following equation.

$$2(10) + 2(x) = 2(4) + 2(3x)$$
$$20 + 2x = 8 + 6x$$
$$20 + 2x - 8 = 8 + 6x - 8 \quad \longleftarrow \text{Subtract 8 from both sides.}$$
$$12 + 2x = 6x \quad \longleftarrow \text{Combine like terms.}$$
$$12 + 2x - 2x = 6x - 2x \quad \longleftarrow \text{Subtract 2x from both sides.}$$
$$12 = 4x$$
$$\frac{12}{4} = \frac{4x}{4} \quad \longleftarrow \text{Divide both sides by 4.}$$
$$3 = x$$

Sample Response continues on the next page.

INTEGRATED MATHEMATICS 1 Study Guide **117**

4. The perimeters of the two triangles at the right are equal. What is the value of x?

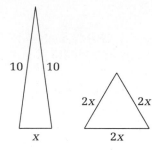

Solve.

5. $3(6 + 2k) = 3k$

6. $1 - n = 2n - 11$

7. $-2a = 4a + 42$

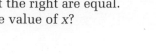
Review **PREVIEW**

Solve. *(Section 5-2)*

8. $-16 + 3y = 5$ **9.** $2(3x - 4) = 10$ **10.** $7 - (4t + 3) = 16$

For Exercises 11–13, write using exponents. *(Section 1-3)*

11. $4 • 4 • 4$ **12.** six squared   **13.** ten to the third power

14. Choose the statement represented by the graph below. *(Section 3-3)*

$$-5 \ -4 \ -3 \ -2 \ -1 \ \ 0 \ \ 1 \ \ 2 \ \ 3 \ \ 4 \ \ 5$$

a. $x \leq -2$ **b.** $x \geq -2$ **c.** $x < 2$ **d.** $x > -2$

15. A quart of orange juice contains at least 30 oz of juice and at most 33 oz of juice. Write an inequality to represent the situation. *(Section 3-3)*

Inequalities with One Variable

FOCUS

Understand how adding, subtracting, multiplying, and dividing affect an inequality and model situations with inequalities.

After five dives, the leader in a regional diving competition has a composite score of 9.2. The second-place diver has scores of 9.1, 9.0, 8.9, and 9.3. What score must the second-place diver make on her fifth dive in order to take the lead? This situation can be modeled by an inequality. Solving the inequality will give you the answer.

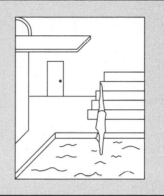

KEY TERMS

Equivalent inequalities (p. 263)
    inequalities that have the same solution

EXAMPLE / ILLUSTRATION

Because the inequalities $12 \geq -2n$ and $-6 \leq n$ have the same solution, they are equivalent inequalities.

UNDERSTANDING THE MAIN IDEAS

Solving inequalities

You use the same steps to solve inequalities that you use to solve equations. The goal is to get the variable alone on one side of the inequality. The one important difference is that when you multiply or divide an inequality by a negative number, you reverse the inequality. The resulting inequality is equivalent to the original inequality.

Sample 1

Solve and graph the inequality $-4x - 2 \geq 6$.

Sample Response

$$-4x - 2 \geq 6$$
$$-4x - 2 + 2 \geq 6 + 2 \quad \longleftarrow \text{ Add 2 to both sides.}$$
$$-4x \geq 8$$
$$\frac{-4x}{-4} \leq \frac{8}{-4} \quad \longleftarrow \text{ Divide by } -4 \text{ and reverse the inequality.}$$
$$x \leq -2 \quad \longleftarrow \text{ This inequality is equivalent to the original one.}$$

The solution is all numbers less than or equal to -2. The graph is shown at the right.

$$\xleftarrow{\ \ } \ \underset{-4}{+} \ \underset{-3}{+} \ \underset{-2}{\bullet} \ \underset{-1}{+} \ \underset{0}{+} \ \underset{1}{+} \ \underset{2}{+} \ \underset{3}{+} \ \underset{4}{+} \xrightarrow{\ \ }$$

Sample Response continues on the next page.

Check (✔): Choose a value of x that is less than or equal to –2, say –4. Substitute –4 for x in the original inequality to see if a true statement results.

$$-4x - 2 \geq 6$$
$$-4(-4) - 2 \overset{?}{\geq} 6$$
$$16 - 2 \overset{?}{\geq} 6$$
$$14 \geq 6 \text{ ✔}$$

Solve each inequality and write the letter of its graph.

1. $-3x > 3$

2. $x + 5 \leq 8$

3. $2(x + 3) \geq 10$

4. $-(x - 3) < 7$

A.
$$-4\ -3\ -2\ -1\ \ 0\ \ 1\ \ 2\ \ 3\ \ 4$$

B.
$$-4\ -3\ -2\ -1\ \ 0\ \ 1\ \ 2\ \ 3\ \ 4$$

C.
$$-4\ -3\ -2\ -1\ \ 0\ \ 1\ \ 2\ \ 3\ \ 4$$

D.
$$-4\ -3\ -2\ -1\ \ 0\ \ 1\ \ 2\ \ 3\ \ 4$$

Solve and graph each inequality.

5. $-6q \leq 12$

6. $4(n - 6) \leq 2$

7. $10 > -2(x - 5)$

Modeling situations with inequalities

Often, real-world situations can be modeled by inequalities. Solving the inequality gives the solution to the situation.

Sample 2

To get an A in her math course, Kim needs to attain an average score of 90 or above on three tests. She scored 85 and 91 on the first two tests. What is the lowest score she can make and still get an A?

Sample Response

Let s = Kim's score on the third test. Then the average of the three scores, 85, 91, and s must be greater than or equal to 90. The situation can be modeled by the inequality

$$\frac{85 + 91 + s}{3} \geq 90.$$

Solve the inequality.

$$\frac{85 + 91 + s}{3} \geq 90$$

$$3\left(\frac{85 + 91 + s}{3}\right) \geq 90 \cdot 3 \quad \longleftarrow \text{ Multiply both sides by 3.}$$

$$85 + 91 + s \geq 270$$
$$176 + s \geq 270$$
$$176 + s - 176 \geq 270 - 176 \quad \longleftarrow \text{ Subtract 176 from both sides.}$$
$$s \geq 94$$

Sample Response continues on the next page.

Check (✔): One solution of $s \geq 94$ is 96. Try 96 in the original inequality

$$\frac{85 + 91 + s}{3} \geq 90$$

$$\frac{85 + 91 + 96}{3} \overset{?}{\geq} 90$$

$$\frac{272}{3} \overset{?}{\geq} 90$$

$$90.7 \geq 90 ✔$$

The least number that is a solution of $s \geq 94$ is 94. So, the lowest score Kim can make in order to get an A is 94.

Write and solve an inequality for each problem.

8. A rectangle is twice as long as it is wide. What can its dimensions be if its perimeter is less than 30 in.?

9. Ms. Willis has a $15-a-day food budget on her vacation. On the first full day of her trip, she spent $3.75 for breakfast and $4.50 for lunch. What is the most she can spend for dinner and stay within her budget?

Review  **PREVIEW**

Solve. *(Sections 2-7, 2-8, 5-3)*

10. $10a - 11 = 89$ **11.** $-3x = -51$ **12.** $7x + 3 - 2x = 73$

13. $2(4y + 1) = 34$ **14.** $2x + 20 = 6x$ **15.** $n - 3 = 4n + 6$

For each formula, tell what each variable represents. *(Sections 2-4, 2-5)*

16. $V = \pi r^2 h$ **17.** $A = 2\pi r^2 + 2\pi rh$ **18.** $A = 6s^2$

Rewriting Equations and Formulas

FOCUS

Learn to rewrite formulas to make them easier to use.

In business, the formula Percentage = Base × Rate, or P = BR, is used to figure profits, discounts, taxes, and so on. Percentage is an amount found by multiplying the base amount by the percent, or rate. If the base and rate are known, then the formula P = BR is used to find the percentage. If the percentage and base are known, then the formula is easier to use after rewriting it in the form $R = \frac{P}{B}$. Similarly, if the percentage and rate are known, then the formula is rewritten as $B = \frac{P}{R}$.

UNDERSTANDING THE MAIN IDEAS

Rewriting formulas

Formulas and equations can be rewritten to make them easier to use for a specific problem. To solve a formula for one of its variables, you use steps similar to those used to solve an equation.

Sample

In the formula $F = \frac{9}{5}C + 32$, $F =$ the Fahrenheit temperature and $C =$ the Celsius temperature. In this form, the Fahrenheit temperature can easily be found if you know the Celsius temperature. Rewrite the formula so that you can easily find the Celsius temperature that corresponds to a given Fahrenheit temperature.

Sample Response

Solve the formula for C.

$$F = \frac{9}{5}C + 32$$

$$F - 32 = \frac{9}{5}C + 32 - 32 \quad \longleftarrow \text{ Subtract 32 from both sides.}$$

$$F - 32 = \frac{9}{5}C \quad \longleftarrow \text{ Combine like terms.}$$

$$5(F - 32) = 5\left(\frac{9}{5}C\right) \quad \longleftarrow \text{ Multiply both sides by 5.}$$

$$5(F - 32) = 9C$$

$$\frac{5(F - 32)}{9} = \frac{9C}{9} \quad \longleftarrow \text{ Divide both sides by 9.}$$

$$\frac{5}{9}(F - 32) = C$$

Solve each equation for the variable indicated.

1. $P = 4s$ for s

2. $C = np$ for p

3. $d = \dfrac{m}{v}$ for v

4. $C = \dfrac{Wtc}{1000}$ for t

5. a. Solve the surface area formula $S = 2lw + 2lh + 2hw$ for h.

   b. Find the height of a rectangular prism with $S = 236$ square units, $l = 8$ units, and $w = 6$ units.

Review **PREVIEW**

For Exercises 6–8, solve and graph each inequality. *(Section 5-4)*

6. $3s \geq -27$

7. $-4x < 64$

8. $2(1.5 - x) > 33$

9. Find the mean of 91%, 78%, 86%, 90%, and 80%. *(Section 3-2)*

Find the reciprocal of each number. *(Toolbox Skill 9)*

10. $-\dfrac{2}{3}$

11. 5

12. $\dfrac{7}{4}$

13. $-\dfrac{12}{10}$

5-6 Using Reciprocals

FOCUS

Use reciprocals to solve equations.

Focusing a camera is modeled by an equation that involves the distance of the object from the lens, the distance of the image from the lens, and the focal length of the lens. The equation uses the reciprocals of the object distance, p, the image distance, q, and the focal length, f: $\frac{1}{p} + \frac{1}{q} = \frac{1}{f}$.

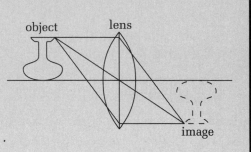

KEY TERMS	EXAMPLE / ILLUSTRATION
Reciprocals (p. 275) numbers that when multiplied together give a product of 1	Since $-\frac{5}{2} \cdot \left(-\frac{2}{5}\right) = 1$, $-\frac{5}{2}$ and $-\frac{2}{5}$ are reciprocals of each other.

UNDERSTANDING THE MAIN IDEAS

Solving equations by using reciprocals

One step you can use when solving an equation where the variable term has a coefficient other than 1 is to multiply both sides by the reciprocal of the coefficient.

Sample 1

Solve $\frac{5}{2}x = 35$.

Sample Response

$$\frac{5}{2}x = 35$$

$$\frac{2}{5} \cdot \frac{5}{2}x = 35 \cdot \frac{2}{5} \quad \longleftarrow \text{ Multiply both sides by } \frac{2}{5}, \text{ the reciprocal of } \frac{5}{2}.$$

$$1x = 14 \quad \longleftarrow \text{ The product of the reciprocals is 1.}$$

$$x = 14$$

Check ($\checkmark$): $\frac{5}{2}x = 35$

$$\frac{5}{2} \cdot 14 \overset{?}{=} 35$$

$$35 = 35 \ \checkmark$$

Solve.

1. $\frac{1}{4}x + 2 = 3$ 2. $7 - \frac{3}{2}y = 22$ 3. $-6m = -20$

4. $-\frac{3}{4}n + 2 = 8$ 5. $\frac{4}{3}d - 4 = -\frac{1}{6}$ 6. $-8r + 11 = -19$

Sample 2

Solve $6x - \frac{3}{2}y = 10$ for y.

Sample Response

$$6x - \frac{3}{2}y = 10$$

$$6x - \frac{3}{2}y - 6x = 10 - 6x \qquad \longleftarrow \text{ Subtract } 6x \text{ from both sides.}$$

$$-\frac{3}{2}y = 10 - 6x \qquad \longleftarrow \text{ Combine like terms on the left side.}$$

$$-\frac{2}{3}\left(-\frac{3}{2}y\right) = -\frac{2}{3}(10 - 6x) \qquad \longleftarrow \text{ Multiply both sides by } -\frac{2}{3}, \text{ the reciprocal of } -\frac{3}{2}.$$

$$y = -\frac{20}{3} + \frac{12}{3}x \qquad \longleftarrow \text{ Use the distributive property.}$$

$$y = 4x - \frac{20}{3} \qquad \longleftarrow \text{ Simplify.}$$

For Exercises 7–10, solve each equation for the indicated variable.

7. $4x - 2y = 18$, for y 8. $3x + 6y = 10$, for x

9. $\frac{3}{4}x - \frac{1}{4}y = 1$, for y 10. $\frac{5}{9}x + \frac{5}{6}y = 2$, for x

11. **_Writing_** The steps for solving the lens equation $\frac{1}{p} + \frac{1}{q} = \frac{1}{f}$ for f are shown below. Explain what has been done in going from one step to the next.

a. $\frac{1}{p} + \frac{1}{q} = \frac{1}{f}$

b. $\frac{f}{p} + \frac{f}{q} = 1$

c. $f + f\frac{p}{q} = p$

d. $fq + fp = pq$

e. $f(q + p) = pq$

f. $f = \frac{pq}{q + p}$

   INTEGRATED MATHEMATICS 1 **Study Guide**

Solve each equation for the variable indicated. *(Section 5-5)*

12. $V = I(R + r)$ for r **13.** $2y - x = 12$ for x **14.** $8x + 5y = 35$ for y

15. Describe the pattern in the table. *(Section 1-1)*

x	−4	−1	0	2	3	8
y	−2	1	2	4	5	10

Evaluate each expression when $r = 4$, $s = 6$, and $t = \frac{2}{5}$. *(Section 2-2)*

16. rs^2 **17.** $\frac{1}{2}st$ **18.** $\frac{2}{3}(r + s)$ **19.** $t(r + 21)$

5-7 Area Formulas

FOCUS

Use the formulas for the area of a parallelogram, a triangle, and a trapezoid to solve problem situations.

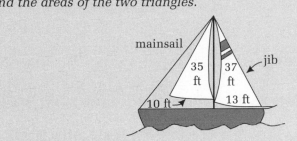

The two triangular sails on the sailboat are made of canvas. To find the amount of canvas needed to make these sails, you need to know how to find the areas of the two triangles.

KEY TERMS

EXAMPLE / ILLUSTRATION

Base (pp. 281, 282)
in a parallelogram or triangle, the length of any side; in a trapezoid, the length of one of the two parallel sides

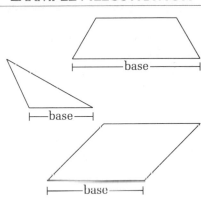

Height (pp. 281, 282)
in a parallelogram or trapezoid, the perpendicular distance to the base from a point on the opposite side; in a triangle, the perpendicular distance to the base from the opposite vertex

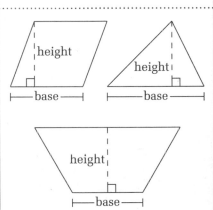

UNDERSTANDING THE MAIN IDEAS

Area of a parallelogram

The area of a parallelogram is found by multiplying its base by its height, that is $A = bh$. The dimensions must be in the same unit and the resulting area is in square units.

Sample I

Find the area of the parallelogram shown at the right.

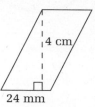

4 cm

24 mm

Sample Response

Method 1: Use the formula $A = bh$. First, change 4 cm to 40 mm.

$A = bh$
$A = 24(40)$ ◄——— Substitute 24 for b and 40 for h.
$A = 960$

The area is 960 mm².

Method 2: Use the formula $A = bh$. First, change 24 mm to 2.4 cm.

$A = bh$
$A = 2.4(4)$ ◄——— Substitute 2.4 for b and 4 for h.
$A = 9.6$

The area is 9.6 cm².

Find the area of each parallelogram.

1.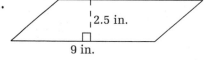

2.5 in.

9 in.

2.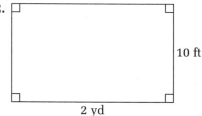

10 ft

2 yd

Sample 2

Find the base of a parallelogram with height 6 ft and area 10 yd².

Sample Response

Solve the formula $A = bh$ for b.

$A = bh$

$\dfrac{A}{h} = \dfrac{bh}{h}$ ◄——— Divide both sides by h.

$\dfrac{A}{h} = b$

Sample Response continues on the next page.

Before substituting for A and h in the formula $\frac{A}{h} = b$, change 6 ft
to 2 yd.

$\frac{10}{2} = b$ ◄──── Substitute 10 for A and 2 for h.

$5 = b$

The base is 5 yd.

3. Find the area of a parallelogram with base 4 m and height 105 cm.

4. Find the height of a parallelogram with area 4 mi^2 and base 2 mi.

5. In Sample 2, if you change the area to 90 ft^2, what is the length of the base in feet?

Area of a triangle

The area of a triangle is found by multiplying $\frac{1}{2}$ by the product of the

base and height, that is $A = \frac{1}{2}bh$.

Sample 3

Find the area of the triangle shown at the right.

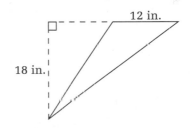

Sample Response

Use the formula $A = \frac{1}{2}bh$.

$A = \frac{1}{2}bh$

$A = \frac{1}{2}(12)(18)$ ◄──── Substitute 12 for b and 18 for h.

$A = 108$

The area is 108 in.^{2}.

Find the area of each triangle.

6.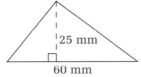
25 mm
60 mm

7. 18 in.
9 in.

8. Find the area of a triangle with base 2.4 km and height 3 km.

9. Find the height of a triangle with base 10 ft and area 16 ft².

Area of a trapezoid

The area of a trapezoid is found by multiplying $\frac{1}{2}$ by the product of the sum of the two bases and the height of the trapezoid, that is

$A = \frac{1}{2}(b_1 + b_2)h.$

Sample 4

Find the area of the trapezoid shown at the right.

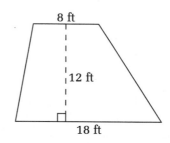

8 ft

12 ft

18 ft

Sample Response

Use the formula $A = \frac{1}{2}(b_1 + b_2)h.$

$A = \frac{1}{2}(b_1 + b_2)h$

$A = \frac{1}{2}(18 + 8)12$ ⟵ Substitute 18 for b_1, 8 for b_2, and 12 for h.

$A = \frac{1}{2}(26)12$

$A = 13(12)$

$A = 156$

The area is 156 ft².

Find the area of each trapezoid.

10.

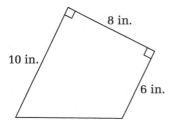

8 in.

10 in.

6 in.

11.

7 m

2 m

5 m

Solving area problems

Area formulas are useful models for many situations. Substituting known values into the appropriate area formula is a useful technique in solving problems involving area.

Sample 5

The Creative Cooking School supplies its students with aprons to wear during classes. The main part of the aprons is trapezoidal in shape. How much fabric will the cooking school need for the main part of 25 aprons?

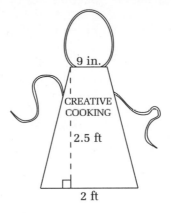

9 in.

CREATIVE COOKING

2.5 ft

2 ft

Sample Response

Use the formula $A = \frac{1}{2}(b_1 + b_2)h$, to find the amount of fabric needed for *one* apron. First, change 9 in. to 0.75 ft.

$A = 0.5(2 + 0.75)2.5$ ◄── Substitute 2 for b_1, 0.75 for b_2, 2.5 for h; use 0.5 for $\frac{1}{2}$.

$A = 0.5(2.75)2.5$

$A = 3.4375$

For one apron, the school will need about 3.5 ft^2 of fabric. To find the amount for 25 aprons, multiply by 25:

$3.5 \cdot 25 = 87.5$.

The school will need about 87.5 ft^2 of fabric for 25 aprons.

Use a formula to solve each problem.

12. The walkway in a shopping mall is paved in stones that repeat the pattern shown at the right. Each stone is 18 in. at the base and has a height of 12 in. What is the area of each paving stone in square inches?

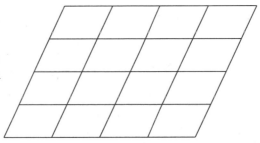

13. Find the amount of canvas needed for the two sails on the boat shown at the right.

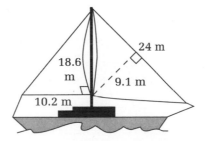

24 m

18.6 m

9.1 m

10.2 m

For Exercises 14–16, solve. *(Section 5-6)*

14. $\frac{5}{2}x = 30$ **15.** $\frac{3}{4}y - 3 = -9$ **16.** $27 = -\frac{2}{3}x + 3$

17. A quadrilateral has vertices at $A(-6, 2)$, $B(-1, 2)$, $C(1, -2)$, and $D(-8, -2)$. If the quadrilateral is translated 5 units to the right, find the coordinates of the new vertices. *(Section 4-3)*

Solve each equation for y. *(Section 5-5)*

18. $3y - x = 2$ **19.** $4x + 4y = 12$ **20.** $20 = \frac{5}{8}y - 5x$

5-8 Systems of Equations in Geometry

Model situations and solve equations with two variables using substitution.

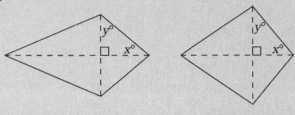

Two kites are shown below. The one on the left will glide faster than the one on the right, but it is more difficult to control. The relationship between the measures of the angles labeled x and y affects the properties of the kites.

KEY TERMS

EXAMPLE / ILLUSTRATION

KEY TERMS	EXAMPLE / ILLUSTRATION
System of equations (p. 291) two or more equations which state relationships that must all be true at the same time	System of two equations in two variables: $y = 3x$ $x + y + 40 = 180$
Solution of a system (p. 291) an ordered pair of values for the variables found in a system of two equations that make both equations true	The solution of the system above is (35, 105).

UNDERSTANDING THE MAIN IDEAS

Solving systems of equations in two variables

One way to solve a system of two equations in two variables is to solve one equation for one of the variables and then to substitute that value for the variable in the other equation. The resulting equation in one variable is then solved to find the value of that variable. This value can then be substituted in either equation to find the value of the other variable.

Sample

In $\triangle ABC$, the measures of $\angle B$ and $\angle C$ are the same, and $\angle A$ is twice the measure of $\angle B$. Find the measure of each angle.

Sample Response

First make a sketch. Since $\angle B$ and $\angle C$ have the same measure, label both measures $x°$.

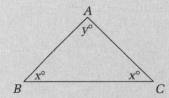

Sample Response continues on the next page.

Write two equations to show the relationships among the angles.
Remember that the sum of the measures of the angles of a triangle
is 180°.

$x + x + y = 180$

$y = 2x$

The equation $y = 2x$ tells you that $2x$ is another name for y.

$x + x + 2x = 180$ ⟵ Substitute $2x$ for y in the equation $x + x + y = 180$.

$\quad\quad 4x = 180$ ⟵ Combine like terms.

$\quad\quad \dfrac{4x}{4} = \dfrac{180}{4}$ ⟵ Divide both sides by 4.

$\quad\quad\quad x = 45$

To find y, substitute 45 for x in either equation.
Choose $y = 2x$.

$y = 2x$
$y = 2(45)$
$y = 90$

Check (✔): Substitute the values of x and y in the other equation.

$\quad x + x + y = 180$

$45 + 45 + 90 \overset{?}{=} 180$ ⟵ Substitute 45 for each x and 90 for y.

$\quad\quad\quad 180 = 180$ ✔

The measures of $\angle B$ and $\angle C$ are 45°, and the measure of $\angle A$ is 90°.

For Exercises 1–3, solve each system of equations.

1. $5m = n$
$\quad 2m + 3n = 51$

2. $7x + 3y = 13$
$\quad\quad y = 2x$

3. $r = s - 4$
$\quad 5r + 2s = 8$

4. Two angles are supplementary. The measure of one angle is 20° less than
the measure of the other. What is the measure of each angle?

5. Find the values of x, y, and z in the diagram below.

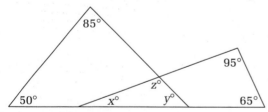

Review PREVIEW

6. Compare the heights of a triangle and a parallelogram if both have
$A = 36$ square units and $b = 9$ units. *(Section 5-7)*

Solve and graph each inequality. *(Section 5-4)*

7. $4c \le 18$

8. $-10 > -2p$

9. $x - 6 \ge -4$

Write each fraction or decimal as a percent. *(Toolbox Skill 11)*

10. $\dfrac{4}{25}$

11. 3.2

12. 0.18

13. $\dfrac{5}{8}$

Unit 5 Review

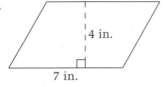

| Unit Check-Up | Complete these exercises for a review of Unit 5. If you have difficulty with a particular problem, review the indicated section. |

1. Use a graph to model the following situation. Then read the answer from the graph.

   The population of Chicago, Illinois, was about 2,800,000 in 1990. If the population decreases each year by about 20,000, when will the population be less than 2,500,000? *(Section 5-1)*

2. ***Writing*** Describe a situation that could be modeled by the equation $530 = 500 + 500r$. *(Section 5-1)*

3. Simplify $9x - 3(5 - 2x)$. *(Section 5-2)*

4. Solve $2(m - 6) = 0$. *(Section 5-2)*

5. Solve $9x = 4(2x + 3)$. *(Section 5-3)*

6. Write and solve an equation for this problem.

   The trip from Wilton to Bradford takes t hours at a speed of 40 mi/h. The trip can be made in 3 fewer hours if the speed is 55 mi/h. How many hours does the trip take at 40 mi/h? *(Section 5-3)*

7. Solve and graph the inequality $-4(x + 2) \geq 8$. *(Section 5-4)*

8. ***Open-ended*** Describe a situation that can be modeled by an inequality. Then solve the inequality. *(Section 5-4)*

9. Solve $I = prt$ for r. *(Section 5-5)*

10. Solve $y = mx + b$ for b. *(Section 5-5)*

11. Solve $16 + \frac{1}{2}y = 17$. *(Section 5-6)*

12. Solve $V = \frac{1}{3}\pi r^2 h$ for h. *(Section 5-6)*

In Exercises 13 and 14, find the area of each figure. *(Section 5-7)*

13.

4 in.

7 in.

14.

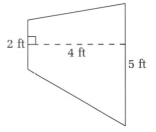

2 ft

4 ft

5 ft

In Exercises 15 and 16, solve using a system of equations.

15. The perimeter of a triangle is 32 m. Two sides are the same length and the third side is twice as long as the other two sides. Find the lengths of the sides of the triangle. *(Section 5-8)*

16. In a triangle, the measure of the largest angle is twice the measure of the smallest angle. The measure of the third angle is 15° less than the measure of the largest angle. Find the measures of the angles of the triangle. *(Section 5-8)*

Find the mean of each set of numbers.

1. 24, 18.2, 21.1, 27, 15.5, 22.3, 31.4, 13.3

2. 36,500; 21,800; 12,900; 30,000; 19,750; 28,600

3. 97, 93, 90, 88, 96

Name the congruent polygons. Then list the pairs of corresponding sides.

4.

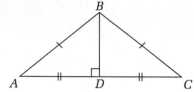

5.

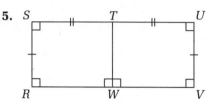

6. Translate △KLM 3 units left and 2 units up. What are the coordinates of each vertex after the translation?

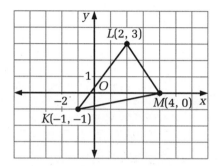

7. Rotate quadrilateral *ABCD* 90° clockwise about the origin. What are the coordinates of each vertex after the rotation?

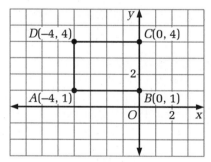

Solve.

8. $5x + 7 = 42$

9. $2y - 9 = -11$

10. $6a - 3a = 48$

11. $0.5s + 6 = 9$

12. $-2t - 1.5 = 8.5$

13. $7 = 5n - 12n$

14. $3x + 7 = 5x - 3$

15. $-3(r - 6) = 21$

16. $m - 4(5 - m) = 50$

17. $-6x \leq -36$

18. $8(d - 4) < 24$

19. $6 - 2c > 32$

In Exercises 20–22, solve each system of equations.

20. $y = 5x$
    $3x + y = -96$

21. $4a - 3b = 54$
    $b = -2a$

22. $n = 3p - 4$
    $2p - 3n = -2$

23. The measure of one acute angle of a right triangle is five times the measure of the other acute angle. Find the measure of both acute angles.

6-1 Ratios and Rates

A recipe for salad dressing calls for one part vinegar mixed with three parts oil. The ratio of vinegar to oil is 1 to 3, or 1 : 3. If you use one cup of vinegar, then the recipe calls for 3 cups of oil. If you use one cup of oil, then you need only $\frac{1}{3}$ cup of vinegar. To make one cup of dressing, you use $\frac{1}{4}$ cup vinegar and $\frac{3}{4}$ cup oil. No matter how much dressing you make, you use three times the amount of oil as vinegar.

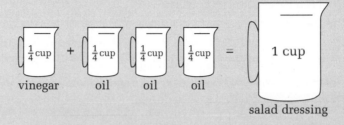

KEY TERMS	EXAMPLE / ILLUSTRATION
Ratio (p. 301) a quotient of two numbers or two quantities	In this design, the ratio of circles to line segments is 2 : 1. Another way to write this is $\dfrac{\text{circles}}{\text{segments}} = \dfrac{2}{1}$.
Percent (p. 302) a special ratio in which the second number is 100	A basketball player made 18 free throws in 20 attempts. Since $\dfrac{18}{20} = \dfrac{90}{100}$, she made 90% of her free throws.
Rate (p. 302) a ratio of two different types of measurements	*Miles per hour*, *cost per pupil*, *beats per measure*, and *revolutions per minute* are all rates.
Unit rate (p. 302) a rate for one unit of a given quantity	Two inches of rain fell in four hours. The unit rate is $\dfrac{2}{4} = \dfrac{1}{2} = 0.5$ inches per hour.

Writing and using ratios

The ratio comparing quantity m to quantity n can be written
$\frac{m}{n}$, $m : n$, or m to n. Ratios should be given in simplest form.

Sample 1

The Department of Fish and Game plans to stock a pond with 200 bass and 150 trout.

a. What is the ratio of trout to bass?

b. To the nearest tenth, what percentage of the stocked fish are bass?

c. Next year the department plans to add 700 trout and bass in the same ratio. How many of the fish will be trout and how many will be bass?

Sample Response

a. Write a fraction with the number of trout on top and the number of bass on the bottom.

$$\frac{\text{trout}}{\text{bass}} = \frac{150}{200} \longleftarrow$$

Caution: The first quantity goes on top.

$\left(\text{The ratio of "bass to trout" would be } \frac{200}{150}. \right)$

Now simplify.

$$\frac{150}{200} = \frac{3}{4}$$

The ratio of trout to bass is $\frac{3}{4}$, $3 : 4$, or 3 to 4.

b. Of the 350 total fish, 200 are bass.

$$\frac{200}{350} = \frac{4}{7}$$
$$\approx 0.5714$$
$$\approx 57.1\%$$

Of the stocked fish, about 57.1% were bass.

c. The ratio $\frac{\text{trout}}{\text{bass}} = \frac{3}{4}$ means that for every 7 fish, 3 are trout and 4 are bass. So for every $7x$ fish, $3x$ are trout and $4x$ are bass.

$$\text{trout } + \text{ bass } = 700$$
$$3x + 4x = 700$$
$$7x = 700$$
$$x = 100 \longleftarrow$$

Caution: $x = 100$ is not the answer to the question.

The number of trout: $3x = 3(100) = 300$
The number of bass: $4x = 4(100) = 400$

Of next year's 700 fish, 300 will be trout and 400 will be bass.

1. A rectangle is 12 in. wide and 18 in. long. Write the ratio of length to width in simplest form.

2. The sales tax on a $90 dress was $4.50. What is the percentage rate of the sales tax?

3. A gear with 100 teeth drives a smaller gear, called the pinion, with 20 teeth. What is the *gear ratio* (the ratio of teeth)?

Sample 2

The 2-qt size of laundry detergent costs $2.99, while the 50-oz size costs $4.99. Which is the better buy?

Sample Response

Find the unit price for each size of detergent. The one with the lower unit price is the better buy.

Both unit prices must be written in the same units, so, first change quarts to ounces.

For the smaller size, the unit price is

$$\frac{\$2.99}{2 \text{ qt}} = \frac{\$2.99}{32 \text{ oz}} \quad \longleftarrow \quad 1 \text{ qt} = 16 \text{ oz, so } 2 \text{ qt} = 2(16) = 32 \text{ oz.}$$

$$\approx \$0.0934/\text{oz.}$$

For the larger size, the unit price is

$$\frac{\$4.99}{50 \text{ oz}} = \$0.0998/\text{oz.}$$

The 2-qt size is the better buy.

For Exercises 4–6, find the unit rate.

4. A 999-mi car trip takes 18 h.

5. A school of 513 students has 27 teachers.

6. Your new car goes 462 mi on 15 gal of gas.

7. A new sedan goes 440 mi on 16 gal of gas. A new station wagon goes 409 mi on 14 gal of gas. Which car uses gas more efficiently?

Review **PREVIEW**

For Exercises 8–10, solve each system of equations. *(Section 5-8)*

8. $x = 2y$
   $3x + y = 14$

9. $t = 9s - 7$
   $10s + 11t = 32$

10. $m = n + 3$
    $20 = 5m - 4n$

11. **Open-ended** What does a weather forecaster mean by "there is a 70% chance of rain?" *(Section 2-1)*

6-2 Investigating Probability

FOCUS

Describe how likely it is that something will happen.

Manufacturers must test their products to determine if they meet quality standards. For example, a sneaker manufacturer might take a sample of 100 pairs and inspect them closely to see if they meet all the company's standards. The manufacturer then uses the results of this inspection to estimate the probability that <u>any</u> pair of sneakers meets the standards.

KEY TERMS

EXAMPLE / ILLUSTRATION

KEY TERMS	EXAMPLE / ILLUSTRATION
Outcome (p. 308) a possible result of an experiment	A three-way race for Senator involving a Republican, a Democrat, and an Independent is an experiment with three possible outcomes: the Republican wins, the Democrat wins, or the Independent wins.
Event (p. 308) a particular outcome or combination of outcomes of an experiment	In the election described above, the event "the Independent loses" can happen in one of two ways (outcomes): the Republican wins, or the Democrat wins.
Probability (p. 308) a number from 0 to 1 (where 0 indicates impossibility and 1 indicates certainty) that describes how likely it is that an event will occur	Weather forecasts are given in probabilities (or chances). A "70% chance of rain" means that the probability of rain is 0.70.
Experimental probability (p. 308) probability that is based on the results of an experiment, an activity in which data is observed and recorded	Researchers find that a medicine they are testing improved the condition of 270 out of 300 patients. Using experimental probability, they conclude that the probability the medicine will help a patient who takes it is $\frac{270}{300} = 0.9$, or 90%.
Theoretical probability (p. 309) probability found without having to do an experiment, based on the assumption that all outcomes of an experiment are equally likely to occur	You buy 2 tickets for a charitable lottery. Eighty-five tickets in all are sold. Since each ticket is equally likely to be drawn, you can use theoretical probability to reason that your chances of winning are $\frac{2}{85}$, or about 0.024.

Complementary events (p. 310)	
two events, the event E and the event "E does not happen" (The sum of the probabilities of complementary events is 1.)	In a lottery, the events "you win" and "you lose" are complementary.

UNDERSTANDING THE MAIN IDEAS

Experimental probability

The experimental probability of an event E can be calculated using the formula

$$P(E) = \frac{\text{number of times event } E \text{ occurs}}{\text{number of times the experiment is done}}.$$

The more times the experiment is conducted, the more reliable is the computed value of $P(E)$.

Sample 1

A vending machine dispenses five different types of fruit drinks. The owner of the machine has kept records on the last 2000 sales from the machine.

Fruit punch	746
Citrus punch	524
Apple juice	98
Orange juice	282
Cranberry juice	350

What is the probability that a randomly-chosen purchase from the machine will be a punch?

Sample Response

Of the five types of juice, two are punches: fruit punch and citrus punch.

$P(\text{purchasing a punch}) = \dfrac{\text{number of times a punch was purchased}}{\text{number of times a purchase was made}}$

$\qquad = \dfrac{746 + 524}{2000}$ ← Add the number of fruit punches and citrus punches.

$\qquad = \dfrac{1270}{2000}$

$\qquad = 0.635$

The probability that a punch is bought is 0.635, or $63\frac{1}{2}\%$.

For Exercises 1 and 2, use the information provided in Sample 1.

1. Find the probability that a randomly-selected customer buys
   a. apple juice.
   b. apple juice or cranberry juice.
   c. seltzer water.

2. Of the next 50 drinks sold, how many are likely to be orange juice?

Theoretical probability

When all the possible outcomes of an experiment are equally likely, the following ratio is used to determine the theoretical probability of an event E.

$$P(E) = \frac{\text{the number of outcomes that are in event } E}{\text{the number of possible outcomes}}$$

If you know the probability of an event E, then the probability that event E does *not* happen is $1 - P(E)$.

Sample 2

The letters of the alphabet are printed on cards (one letter per card) and placed in a box. You close your eyes and choose one card. What is the probability that the card you chose is

a. the first letter of your first name?

b. a vowel?

c. *not* a vowel?

Sample Response

Each card is equally likely to be chosen, so theoretical probability can be used.

a. Of the 26 cards, only one has your initial on it.

$P(\text{choosing your first initial}) = \dfrac{1}{26}$

b. There are five vowels (A, E, I, O, U), so the event "choosing a vowel" can happen in 5 ways.

$P(\text{choosing a vowel}) = \dfrac{5}{26}$

c. "Choosing a vowel" and "not choosing a vowel" are complementary events.

$$\begin{aligned} P(\text{not choosing a vowel}) &= 1 - P(\text{choosing a vowel}) \\ &= 1 - \frac{5}{26} \\ &= \frac{21}{26} \end{aligned}$$

3. In Sample 2, what is the probability that Maria Carvalho chooses one of her two initials? that Alan Adams chooses one of his initials?

4. What is the probability that the last digit of your teacher's phone number is "1?"

5. Which of these pairs of events are complementary?
   a. passing Math, failing Math
   b. getting a traffic ticket, driving safely
   c. reading, watching television

For Exercises 6–9, use the spinner at the right. Find each probability.

6. $P(\text{odd number})$ **7.** $P(\text{number less than 3})$

8. $P(3)$ **9.** $P(\text{not 4})$

10. Using the spinner at the right, describe two complementary events.

Write each ratio as a fraction in simplest form. *(Section 6-1)*

11. $10 : 55$ **12.** 82 to 100   **13.** $18 : 48$

Find the square root and cube root of each number. Round decimal answers to the nearest hundredth. *(Section 2-9)*

14. 36   **15.** 125   **16.** 91

Solve each equation. *(Section 5-6)*

17. $13x = 39$ **18.** $\dfrac{x}{1.7} = 4$ **19.** $\dfrac{x}{-6} = \dfrac{8}{3}$

Solving Proportions

The state of Massachusetts has a 5% "flat rate" sales tax. A customer pays a $5 sales tax on a $100 purchase and a $2 sales tax on a $40 purchase. These tax charges are in proportion since $\frac{5}{100} = \frac{2}{40}$.

KEY TERMS

EXAMPLE / ILLUSTRATION

Proportion (p. 314) a statement that two ratios are equal	$\frac{10}{2} = \frac{80}{16}, \frac{x}{7} = \frac{5}{15}$, and $\frac{3}{y} = \frac{5}{1}$ are all proportions.
Terms of a proportion (p. 314) the numerators and denominators of the ratios (fractions) in a proportion	The *terms* of $\frac{5}{a} = \frac{b}{4}$ are 5, a, b, and 4. (*Note:* Every proportion has four terms.)
Cross products (p. 315) the products formed by multiplying the numerator of one fraction in a proportion by the denominator of the other fraction (For any proportion, the two cross products are equal.)	The cross products of the proportion $\frac{4}{9} = \frac{12}{x}$ are $4 \cdot x = 9 \cdot 12$.

UNDERSTANDING THE MAIN IDEAS

Solving proportions

If a proportion has a variable, you can solve for the value of the variable either by using the techniques for solving equations with fractions in them, or by using the fact that *the cross products of a proportion are equal.*

> **Sample 1**
>
> Solve the proportion $\frac{2x}{9} = \frac{7}{3}$ in two ways.

Method 1: To get x alone on one side, multiply both sides of the equation by $\frac{9}{2}$; remember that $\frac{9}{2}$ and $\frac{2}{9}$ are *reciprocals* and $\frac{9}{2} \cdot \frac{2}{9} = 1$.

$$\frac{9}{2} \cdot \frac{2x}{9} = \frac{9}{2} \cdot \frac{7}{3}$$

$$x = \frac{63}{6}$$

$$x = 10.5$$

Method 2: Use cross products.

$$\frac{2x}{9} = \frac{7}{3}$$

$$3 \cdot 2x = 9 \cdot 7 \quad \longleftarrow \quad \text{cross products}$$

$$6x = 63$$

$$\frac{6x}{6} = \frac{63}{6}$$

$$x = 10.5$$

1. *Writing* How are the two methods in Sample 1 the same? different?

For Exercises 2–4, solve each proportion.

2. $\dfrac{19}{4} = \dfrac{x}{8}$ 　　　　3. $\dfrac{4}{15} = \dfrac{5}{y}$ 　　　　4. $\dfrac{3000}{x} = \dfrac{150}{3}$

5. Write at least four proportions with the terms x, 3, 5, and 20 and solution $x = 12$.

Using proportions to solve problems

In situations with a steady rate, like driving at 45 miles per hour or paying $1.09 per gallon of gas, you can use proportions to solve for an unknown.

Sample 2

A work crew lays 0.5 mi of new road in 1 week. At this rate, how long will it take to lay 3 mi of new road?

Sample Response

Since the rates for laying 0.5 mi and 3 mi are the same, a proportion can be used.

Let t = the number of weeks it takes to lay 3 mi of road.

$$\frac{0.5}{1} = \frac{3}{t} \quad \longleftarrow \quad \frac{\text{miles}}{\text{weeks}} = \frac{\text{miles}}{\text{weeks}}$$

$0.5 \cdot t = 3 \cdot 1 \quad \longleftarrow$ When the variable is on the bottom of one of the fractions, use cross products to solve.

$0.5t = 3 \quad \longleftarrow$ Multiply both sides by 2, the reciprocal of 0.5.

$$t = 6$$

It will take 6 weeks to lay 3 mi of new road.

6. Three grams of oxygen unite with 24 grams of hydrogen to form water. How many grams of oxygen unite with 1 kg of hydrogen?

7. Property taxes in a town are based on a flat rate per square foot of land. If a person owning 6500 ft^2 of property pays $1450 in property taxes, what does a person owning 5400 ft^2 pay?

8. The scale on a map indicates that 1 in. on the map represents 10 mi. What distance on the map represents 25 mi?

Review  **PREVIEW**

The graph at the right shows the number of orders for men's sweatpants received by a catalog company. Use the graph for Exercises 9–11. *(Section 6-2)*

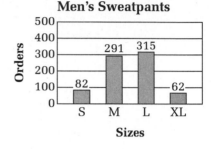

Men's Sweatpants

9. What is the probability that a randomly-selected order for sweatpants will be for size extra large (XL)?

10. What is the probability that a randomly selected order for sweatpants will be for size medium (M) or large (L)?

11. Of the next 300 orders that are received, estimate the number that will be for size large (L).

Identify the control variable and dependent variable for each function. *(Section 4-6)*

12. The closer a light source is to an object, the brighter the object is illuminated.

13. The lower the price of baseball tickets, the more people will attend games.

Find each number. *(Toolbox Skill 14)*

14. 3% of 900   15. 32% of 9   16. 30% of 180,000

Sampling and Making Predictions

Medical researchers use sampling frequently. For example, an epidemiologist *is a scientist who studies the spread and control of diseases. If epidemiologists need to know the percentage of the population who carry a virus, they have to study a sample of the population because they cannot administer a blood test to everyone. They use the branch of mathematics called* statistics *to properly select the sample and to draw accurate conclusions about the prevalence of the virus in the whole population.*

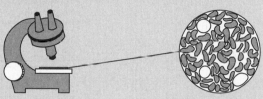

KEY TERMS

EXAMPLE / ILLUSTRATION

KEY TERMS	EXAMPLE / ILLUSTRATION
Population (p. 321) a whole group of people, animals, or objects	A radio ratings service wants to know the listening habits of people in their city. They telephone 100 people to ask them how they use the radio. The *population* is all the people in the city; this is the group they want to know about.
Sample (p. 321) a part of a group	The *sample* in the example above is the 100 people the service actually interviews.
Margin of error (p. 323) an estimate of the interval that is most likely to contain the exact result for the population	Suppose 42% of the people in the radio survey say they listen to the radio in the late afternoon. The ratings service may conclude that 42% of the city's population listens in the late afternoon, but they should give a *margin of error*, such as "plus or minus 5%." This means between 37% and 47% of the population listen to the radio in the late afternoon.

UNDERSTANDING THE MAIN IDEAS

Sampling

Samples can be used to make predictions or draw conclusions about the population.

Sample 1

A biologist needs to estimate the frog population in a large pond. She captures 75 frogs, tags them, and releases them back into the pond. One week later she captures 50 frogs and observes that 7 are tagged. About how many frogs are in the pond?

Sample Response

Use a proportion. Let x = the total population of frogs.

$$\frac{75}{x} = \frac{7}{50} \quad \longleftarrow \quad \frac{\text{total no. of tagged frogs in pond}}{\text{total no. of frogs in pond}} = \frac{\text{no. of tagged frogs in sample}}{\text{no. of frogs in sample}}$$

$$75(50) = 7x \quad \longleftarrow \text{Use cross products.}$$

$$\frac{3750}{7} = \frac{7x}{7}$$

$$536 \approx x$$

There are about 536 frogs in the pond.

For Exercises 1–3, use the information given in Sample 1.

1. In the study described above, what is the population? the sample?

2. After another week passes, the biologist captures 60 frogs and notes that 8 are tagged. Estimate the frog population based on this new sample.

3. Combine the sample in Exercise 2 with that in Sample 1, for one large sample of 110 frogs. What estimate does this sample give for the size of the frog population in the pond?

Margin of error

All results based on samples are estimates and contain some error. A margin of error describes how large the error is likely to be.

Sample 2

Using a capture-recapture method like that in Sample 1, a biologist estimates that a pond has a frog population of 1256, with a margin of error of ±5%. Give the interval that most likely includes the exact number of frogs in the pond.

Sample Response

Find 5% of the estimate.

$$0.05(1256) = 62.8$$

Now add and subtract the result from the estimate to get the upper and lower limits of the interval.

$$1256 + 62.8 = 1318.8 \approx 1319 \quad \longleftarrow \text{ upper limit}$$
$$1256 - 62.8 = 1193.2 \approx 1193 \quad \longleftarrow \text{ lower limit}$$

There are most likely somewhere between 1193 and 1319 frogs in the pond.

4. Change the margin of error in Sample 2 to ±10%. What is the resulting interval for the size of the frog population?

5. A pretzel manufacturer samples 100 bags of pretzels and finds that 3 are underweight. If the company manufactures 20,000 bags each week, approximately how many bags are underweight each week?

6. The company determines that the sample in Exercise 5 has a margin of error of ±3%. What interval most likely contains the actual number of underweight bags of pretzels manufactured each week?

 *Review* **PREVIEW**

For Exercises 7–9, solve each proportion. *(Section 6-3)*

7. $\dfrac{15}{80} = \dfrac{x}{32}$
           8. $\dfrac{2}{90} = \dfrac{6}{y}$
           9. $\dfrac{18}{z} = \dfrac{3}{4}$

10. List the pairs of corresponding sides; $\triangle ABC \cong \triangle XYZ$. *(Section 1-6)*

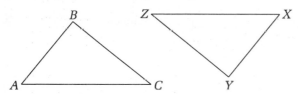

Find the perimeter of each triangle. *(Toolbox Skill 17)*

11.

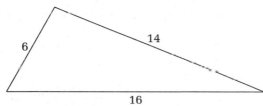

12.

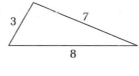

INTEGRATED MATHEMATICS 1 Study Guide

Similar Polygons

FOCUS

Apply proportions to problems using similar figures and scale drawings.

In the figure shown at the right, the midpoints of the sides of the large equilateral triangle have been joined to form four triangles that are similar to the original triangle.

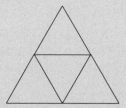

Two repetitions of this process are shown below. (Notice that the process is _not_ repeated on the inverted triangle, but only on the "outer" three triangles.) All the triangles are similar.

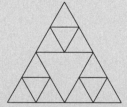 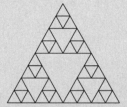

Continuing the process indefinitely results in a geometric figure called a fractal. _One of the main characteristics of a fractal is self-similarity. Fractals have useful applications in fields such as cartography, where they are used in making accurate maps of irregular coastlines._

KEY TERMS **EXAMPLE / ILLUSTRATION**

Similar figures (p. 329)
    two figures with the same shape (They may be the same size or different sizes.)

These designs are similar.

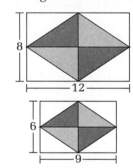

The designs have the same shape (corresponding angles are the same), and the length of the sides are in the ratio 4 : 3.

Scale drawing (p. 330)
    a drawing which represents an actual object (Objects in a scale drawing have the same shape as in real life.)

A road map is a scale drawing of the roads in an area.

Scale (p. 330)
    the ratio of the size of the drawing to the actual size of the object which it represents

The _scale_, such as "1 in. = 50 mi", can be found on any road map. It tells you how distances on the map correspond to distances on the actual roads.

UNDERSTANDING THE MAIN IDEAS

Similar polygons

Similar polygons have corresponding angles congruent and
corresponding sides in proportion. Two triangles are similar if they have
two pairs of corresponding angles congruent.

Sample 1

Trapezoid *LMNP* ~ trapezoid *QRST*.

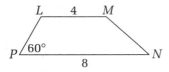 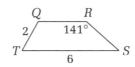

Use the figure to find each measure.

a. *LP*　　　　　　**b.** *QR*　　　　　　**c.** ∠*M*

Sample Response

a. Use a proportion involving *LP* and *QT*, the length of the side
corresponding to $\overline{LP}$. Look at the trapezoids for corresponding sides
whose lengths are known: *NP* and *ST*.

$$\frac{LP}{QT} = \frac{NP}{ST} \longleftarrow$$　Set up the ratios to correspond. Here the lengths
from the larger trapezoid are on the top and those
from the smaller trapezoid are on the bottom.

Let $x = LP$.

$$\frac{x}{2} = \frac{8}{6} \longleftarrow$$　Substitute the known lengths.

$$6 \cdot x = 2 \cdot 8$$

$$\frac{6x}{6} = \frac{16}{6}$$

$$x = 2\frac{2}{3}$$

So, $LP = 2\frac{2}{3}$.

b. Use a proportion. Let $y = QR$. $\overline{LM}$ corresponds to $\overline{QR}$.

$$\frac{QR}{LM} = \frac{ST}{NP}$$

$$\frac{y}{4} = \frac{6}{8}$$

$$8 \cdot y = 4 \cdot 6$$

$$\frac{8y}{8} = \frac{24}{8}$$

$$y = 3$$

So, $QR = 3$.

c. ∠*M* corresponds to ∠*R*, which measures 141°. Since *corresponding*
angles are congruent, ∠*M* = 141°.

　　INTEGRATED MATHEMATICS 1 **Study Guide**

For Exercises 1–6, triangle *DEF* ~ triangle *XYZ*.

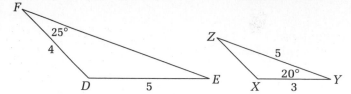

Find each measure.

1. *FE*   **2.** ∠*Z*   **3.** *XZ*   **4.** ∠*D*

Tell why each statement is false.

5. triangle *EFD* ~ triangle *YXZ*   **6.** $\frac{EF}{YZ} = \frac{XZ}{DF}$

Sample 2

Use the map below. The scale is 1 in. = 200 yd.

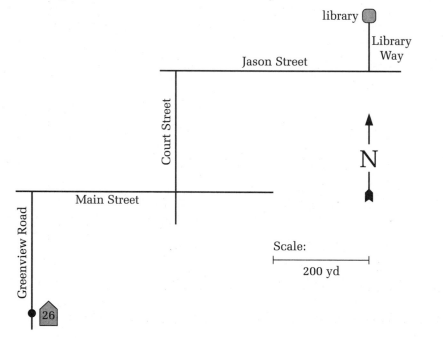

How far is it (along the streets) from 26 Greenview Road to the library?

Sample Response

Use a ruler to measure the distance on the map and use the scale to find the actual distance.

26 Greenview north to Main	$1\frac{1}{4}$ in.
Greenview and Main east to Main and Court	$1\frac{1}{2}$ in.
Main and Court north to Jason and Court	$1\frac{1}{4}$ in.

Sample Response continues on the next page.

Jason and Court east to Jason and Library Way	2 in.
Jason and Library Way north to the library entrance	$\frac{1}{2}$ in.
Total	$6\frac{1}{2}$ in.

Use the scale 1 in. = 200 yd to find the walking distance to the library.
Let x = the unknown distance.

$$\frac{1 \text{ in.}}{200 \text{ yd}} = \frac{\text{inches on map}}{\text{actual distance in yards}}$$

$$\frac{1}{200} = \frac{6.5}{x}$$

$$x = 6.5(200)$$

$$x = 1300$$

The library is 1300 yd away.

7. A scale drawing of a snowflake has the scale 50 : 1. If the drawing is 17 cm in diameter, what is the diameter of the snowflake?

8. Make a scale drawing of a rectangular swimming pool with dimensions 225 ft by 60 ft. Give the scale of your drawing.

9. A slide projector enlarges the image on the slide to a similar image on the screen. On the slide, a person is $\frac{5}{8}$ in. tall. The image on the screen is 2 ft 1 in. high. What is the scale of the enlargement?

For Exercises 10 and 11, use the figure at the right. To measure the distance between points A and B, a scout puts stakes in the ground at points C, D, and E, so that A, C, and D are on the same line and the angles at B and E are right angles. The scout then measures these distances: $BC = 500$ ft, $CE = 9$ ft, $CD = 59$ ft, and $DE = 56$ ft.

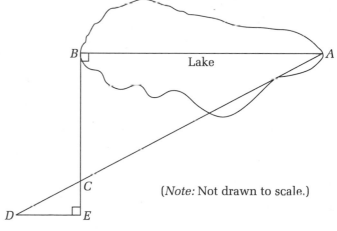

(*Note:* Not drawn to scale.)

10. How does the scout know that the two triangles are similar?

11. What is the distance across the lake from point A to point B?

Review **PREVIEW**

12. A recipe for spaghetti sauce calls for 1 cup of chopped onion and 15 tomatoes. How much onion should be used with 20 tomatoes?

13. Find the mean, median, and mode(s) of these test scores. *(Section 3-2)*

84	98	90	75	88	67	78	92	90	99
76	85	93	88	85	80	94	93	87	88

14. Plot the points $A(-1, 3)$, $B(3, 2)$, $C(2, -2)$, and $D(-2, -1)$ on a coordinate plane. Connect the points in order and connect D to A. Write the specific name of the polygon you formed. *(Section 4-2)*

6-6 Dilations

Inflating the balloon causes the picture to be enlarged while keeping the same shape. This transformation is a dilation.

KEY TERMS

EXAMPLE / ILLUSTRATION

Image (p. 337)

the result of a transformation

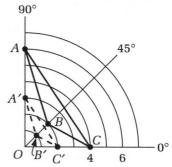

In the figure, the smaller triangle, $\triangle A'B'C'$, is the *image* of the larger triangle, $\triangle ABC$.

Dilation (p. 337)

a transformation in which the original figure and its image are similar (When the image is larger than the original, the dilation is called an *enlargement*. When the image is smaller, the dilation is called a *reduction*.)

The transformation above is a *dilation*. $\triangle A'B'C' \sim \triangle ABC$. Since the image is smaller than the original, the dilation is a *reduction*.

Scale factor (p. 337)

in a dilation, the ratio of any length on the image to the corresponding length on the original

The scale factor of the dilation above is $\frac{1}{2}$ since each side of the image is half as long as the corresponding side in the original.

Center of dilation (p. 338)

the point which does not move under a dilation

The center of dilation of the transformation above is the origin O. Notice that

$OA' = \frac{1}{2}OA$, $OB' = \frac{1}{2}OB$, and

$OC' = \frac{1}{2}OC$.

UNDERSTANDING THE MAIN IDEAS

In a dilation, each image point lies on the ray from the center of dilation through the original point. In an enlargement, the image points are farther from the center than the originals. In a reduction, the image points are closer to the center.

Sample

Copy quadrilateral *ABCD* on graph paper and find its image under the dilation with center *O*(0, 0) and scale factor 3.

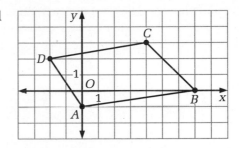

Sample Response

After copying quadrilateral *ABCD*, use a ruler to draw rays from the center through each vertex. On each ray, place the image point of the vertex so that it is three times as far from the center as the original point.

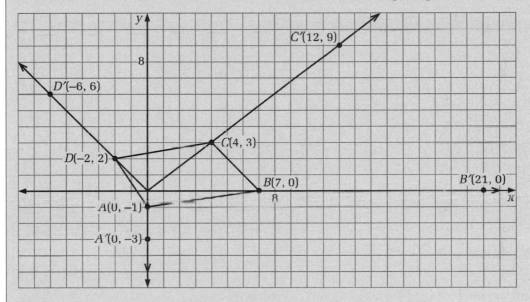

Finally, connect the image points to form the image quadrilateral.

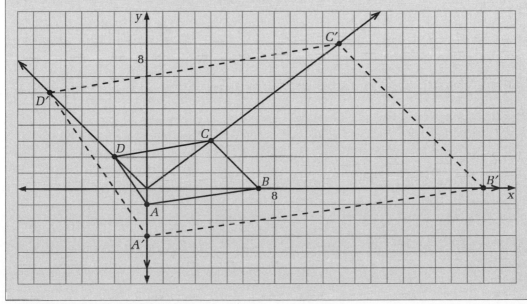

1. Use a protractor to measure all the angles in quadrilaterals *ABCD* and *A′B′C′D′* in the Sample. Are the corresponding angles congruent?

2. Copy quadrilateral *ABCD* on another sheet of graph paper. Draw the dilation of *ABCD* with center at (0, −2) and scale factor 3.

3. Are the images in the Sample and in Exercise 2 similar? Are they congruent?

4. On graph paper, draw △*JKL* with vertices *J*(0, 6), *K*(4, 6) and *L*(6, 0). Draw the dilation of △*JKL* with center (−2, 0) and scale factor $\frac{1}{3}$.

5. Draw △*JKL* from Exercise 4 again. Draw the dilation of △*JKL* with center *K* and scale factor $\frac{1}{2}$.

6. Are the images in Exercises 4 and 5 similar? Are they congruent?

In each figure, △*A′B′C′* is the image of △*ABC*. Give the coordinates of the center and the scale factor.

7.
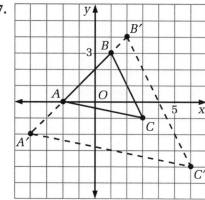

8.
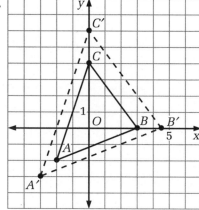

 Review **PREVIEW**

9. Find all the missing side and angle measures. In the figure, △*RST* ~ △*XYZ*. *(Section 6-5)*

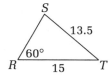

Solve. *(Section 5-3)*

10. $5x + 6 = x - 10$

11. $2n + 13 = 5n - 23$

12. $2a - 11 = -3a + 4$

13. $4w + 11 = -2w - 13$

Write each ratio in simplest form. *(Section 6-1)*

14. $\frac{12}{60}$

15. 18 to 72

16. 26 : 91

6-7 Sine and Cosine Ratios

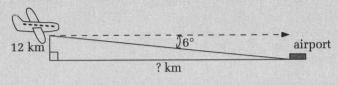

FOCUS

Learn to use two special right triangle ratios, *sine* and *cosine*, to solve problem situations.

Trigonometric ratios are used in engineering, surveying, and navigation. For example, a pilot who wants to approach an airport at a 6° angle of descent can use trigonometry to determine when to start the descent.

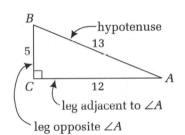

12 km

6°

airport

? km

KEY TERMS

EXAMPLE / ILLUSTRATION

Sine (p. 344)
the ratio of the length of the leg opposite an acute angle of a right triangle to the length of the hypotenuse (abbreviated *sin*)

B — hypotenuse

13

5

C 12 A

leg adjacent to $\angle A$

leg opposite $\angle A$

Cosine (p. 344)
the ratio of the length of the leg adjacent to an acute angle of a right triangle to the length of the hypotenuse (abbreviated *cos*)

In $\triangle ABC$, $\sin A = \frac{5}{13}$ and $\cos A = \frac{12}{13}$.

(There are no sine or cosine ratios associated with $\angle C$, because it is not acute.)

Trigonometric ratios (p. 344)
ratios associated with the acute angles of a right triangle involving the lengths of sides

For $\triangle ABC$ above, $\sin A = \frac{5}{13}$, $\cos A = \frac{12}{13}$, $\sin B = \frac{12}{13}$, and $\cos B = \frac{5}{13}$.

UNDERSTANDING THE MAIN IDEAS

Sine and cosine ratios

The lengths of the legs and the length of the hypotenuse of a right triangle are used to find the sine and cosine of any acute angle.

Sample 1

Write each trigonometric ratio as a fraction and as a decimal rounded to hundredths.

a. $\sin Y$ **b.** $\cos Y$

X 0.8 Y

0.6 1.0

Z

Use a calculator to write each ratio as a decimal rounded to hundredths. (Be sure your calculator is in degree mode.)

1. sin 36°   **2.** cos 15°   **3.** sin 15°   **4.** cos 75°

For Exercises 5–10, use the figures at the right.

5. Why is $\triangle LMN \sim \triangle PQR$?

6. Use proportions to find MN and PQ to the nearest tenth.

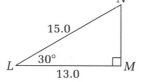
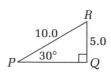

7. Use ratios to find sin L and sin P.

8. Use ratios to find cos L and cos P.

9. Why are the answers in Exercise 7 and the answers in Exercise 8 the same?

10. Use a calculator to find sin 30° and cos 30°. Compare the results with your answers to Exercises 7 and 8.

Using trigonometric ratios to solve problems

You can use the sine and cosine ratios, which are found using calculators or tables, to solve problems involving right triangles.

Sample 2

An anchor is attached to a rowboat by a 20-yd rope. You drop the anchor and let the boat drift until the rope is taut. At that time, the rope makes a 28° angle with the surface of the water. To the nearest tenth of a yard, how deep is the lake at the point you dropped the anchor?

Sample Response

Make a sketch. Label the known lengths and angles. Let d = the depth of the water.

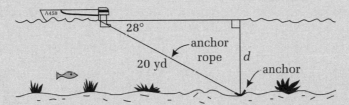

Notice that the known angle, 28°, the known length, 20 yd, and the unknown depth, d, are all parts of a right triangle. Write an equation involving a trigonometric ratio.

$\sin 28° = \dfrac{d}{20}$ ← Use sine because d is *opposite* the 28° angle.

Solve for d.

$20 \cdot \sin 28° = 20 \cdot \dfrac{d}{20}$

$20(0.4695) \approx d$ ⟵ Use the $\boxed{\text{SIN}}$ key on your calculator.

$9.39 \approx d$

The lake is about 9.4 yd deep where the anchor was dropped.

11. In Sample 2, how far has the boat drifted from the point where you dropped the anchor?

Write an equation you could use to find x. Then find x to the nearest tenth.

12.

13.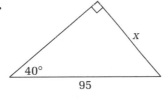

14. The diagonal of a rectangle makes a 37° angle with the base of the rectangle. The diagonal is 24 in. long. To the nearest tenth, what are the dimensions of the rectangle?

Review **PREVIEW**

15. Draw a dilation of △JKL (shown at the right) with center M and a scale factor of 2. *(Section 6-6)*

16. Describe one way that a graph can be misleading. *(Section 3-7)*

17. A box contains 8 blue marbles, 10 red marbles, and 6 green marbles. The marbles are all the same size. If a marble is picked at random, what is the probability that it is red? *(Section 6-2)*

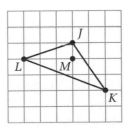

INTEGRATED MATHEMATICS 1 Study Guide **159**

| Unit Check-Up | Complete these exercises for a review of Unit 6. If you have difficulty with a particular problem, review the indicated section. |

1. What is the unit price of shampoo costing $3.89 for 15 oz? *(Section 6-1)*

Use the figure at the right. *(Section 6-1)*

2. What is the ratio of squares to rectangles that are not squares in this design?

3. What percent of the design is black?

Estimate each probability for the order of the next customer in Donnie's Diner. The table shows the orders of the last 200 customers. *(Section 6-2)*

Main Dish	Number of Orders
Meatloaf	42
Chicken	58
Roast Beef	34
Pasta	55
Chef's Salad	11

4. P(meatloaf)

5. P(chicken or roast beef)

6. P(not pasta)

Find each probability for a roll of a fair die. *(Section 6-2)*

7. P(odd number)

8. $P(2)$

For Exercises 9 and 10, solve each proportion for x. *(Section 6-3)*

9. $\dfrac{6}{3.5} = \dfrac{x}{14}$

10. $\dfrac{0.02}{7} = \dfrac{0.05}{x}$

11. In 1991, about 16% of all the automobiles manufactured in the world were made in the United States. About 5.4 million cars were made in the U.S. that year. How many cars were manufactured worldwide? *(Section 6-3)*

12. Forest Rangers captured 50 foxes, tagged them, and released them back into the same region. Later, another 40 foxes were captured. Of these foxes, 13 had tags. Estimate the size of the fox population in the area. *(Section 6-4)*

13. A public opinion poll shows that 43% of a sample of voters has a favorable impression of a candidate. If there are 20,000 qualified voters and the poll has a margin of error of 5%, give a range for the number of voters with a favorable opinion of the candidate. *(Section 6-4)*

For Exercises 14 and 15, refer to the figure at the right. *(Section 6-5)*

14. Why is $\triangle ABC$ similar to $\triangle EDC$?

15. Find DC and CE.

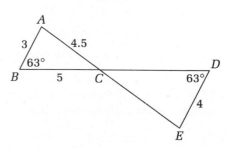

16. A scale model of a mountain was built using the scale of 1 in. : 100 ft. At the peak, the model is 2 ft high. How high is the actual mountain? *(Section 6-5)*

Draw a dilation of each polygon using the given center of dilation and scale factor. *(Section 6-6)*

17. center $P(1, 0)$; scale factor 2

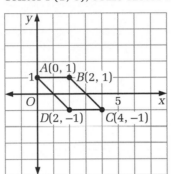

18. center $P(0, 0)$; scale factor $\frac{1}{3}$

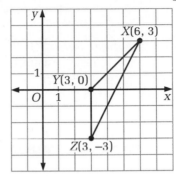

For Exercises 19 and 20, express each trigonometric ratio as a fraction in simplest form. *(Section 6-7)*

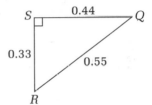

19. $\cos Q$

20. $\sin Q$

21. A board bracing a wall makes an angle of 62° with the ground and reaches 20 ft up the wall. How long is the board? *(Section 6-7)*

Spiral Review
Units 1–6

Tell whether each pattern has *translational symmetry*, *rotational symmetry*, or *neither*.

1.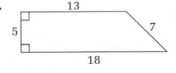

2.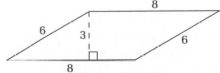

3.

Use the data on jogging times and distances given in the table at the right.

4. Make a scatter plot of the data. Draw a fitted line.

5. Is there a *positive correlation*, *negative correlation*, or *no correlation* between the times and the distances?

6. Predict the distance jogged if the time is 56 min.

Day	Time (min)	Distance (mi)
Monday	40	5
Tuesday	48	6
Wednesday	65	7.5
Thursday	20	3
Friday	36	4
Saturday	50	6
Sunday	25	3.5

Find the perimeter and area of each figure.

7.

8.

7-1 Direct Variation, Slope, and Tangent

FOCUS

Explore three relationships that involve constant ratios.

In San Francisco, there are many steep streets, some with brick walls along them. You can judge the slope of such a street by counting bricks.

(The bricks are $8\frac{1}{8}$ inches long and $2\frac{5}{8}$ inches wide, including the mortar.)

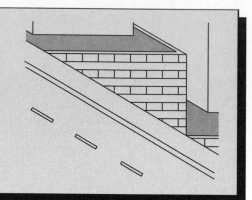

KEY TERMS

EXAMPLE / ILLUSTRATION

Direct variation (p. 360)
the relationship between two variable quantities that have a constant ratio

a	b	c
2	0.6	0.3
3	0.9	0.3
5	1.5	0.3

The quantities a and b are in direct variation because the ratio $\frac{b}{a}$ is always the same.

Variation constant (p. 360)
the constant ratio in a direct variation

The variation constant in the example above is 0.3.

Slope of a line (p. 361)
the ratio of rise to run for any two points on the line (The slope is a measure of the steepness of a line.)

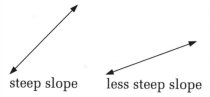

steep slope   less steep slope

Rise (p. 361)
the vertical change between two points

Run (p. 361)
the horizontal change between two points

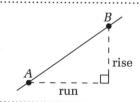

Tangent ratio (p. 361)
a ratio associated with an acute angle of a right triangle that compares the length of the two legs of a right triangle (It is the ratio of the length of the leg opposite the angle to the length of the leg adjacent to the angle:

$$\tan A = \frac{\text{leg opposite } \angle A}{\text{leg adjacent to } \angle A}.)$$

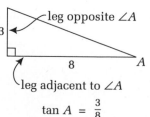

leg opposite $\angle A$

leg adjacent to $\angle A$

$$\tan A = \frac{3}{8}$$

Slope

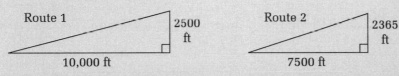

Sample 1

Decide which of two straight highways is steeper: Route 1, which ascends 2500 ft in a horizontal distance of 10,000 ft, or Route 2, which climbs 2365 ft in a horizontal distance of 7500 ft.

Sample Response

Make a sketch.

Route 1
2500 ft
10,000 ft

Route 2
2365 ft
7500 ft

Calculate the slope of each route and compare the slopes.

Slope of Route 1 $= \dfrac{\text{rise}}{\text{run}} = \dfrac{2500}{10{,}000} = 0.25$

Slope of Route 2 $= \dfrac{\text{rise}}{\text{run}} = \dfrac{2365}{7500} \approx 0.32$

Since the slope of Route 2 is greater than the slope of Route 1, Route 2 is steeper. Notice that even though Route 1 climbs higher, it is not as steep as Route 2.

1. Suppose Route 1 continues horizontally for another 5000 ft. How much farther does the roadway rise?

2. The figure at the right shows the front view of a tent that is 4 ft high and 6 ft across. Find the slope of the sides of the tent. (*Hint:* The peak of the tent is centered over the width of the tent.)

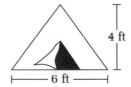

4 ft

6 ft

3. A ramp is to be built from the ground to a loading dock, which is 3 ft high. The slope of the ramp is to be 0.2. How far from the loading dock must the ramp begin?

4. The figure below shows a swimming pool that is 4 ft deep at the shallow end and 12 ft deep at the deep end. What is the slope of the floor of the pool?

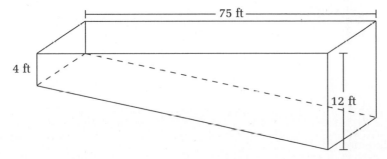

75 ft

4 ft

12 ft

The tangent ratio

Sample 2

a. Find tan A to the nearest hundredth.

b. Use the inverse tangent key of a scientific calculator to find the measure of $\angle A$ to the nearest degree.

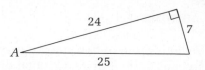

Sample Response

a. $\tan A = \dfrac{\text{leg opposite } \angle A}{\text{leg adjacent to } \angle A} = \dfrac{7}{24} \approx 0.29$

b. Press these keys on your calculator:

$7 \;\boxed{\div}\; 24 \;\boxed{=}\; \boxed{\text{INV}}\; \boxed{\text{TAN}}$ ← *Caution:* Be sure the calculator is in *degree* mode.

The result, 16.2602..., means that $A = 16°$ to the nearest degree.

For Exercises 5–7,

  a. find tan A to the nearest hundredth.

  b. find the measure of $\angle A$ to the nearest degree.

5.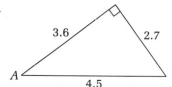

6.

7.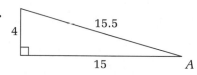

Find the length of $\overline{XY}$ to the nearest tenth.

8.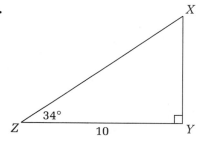

9.

Z, 7, X, 48°, Y

```
        Z
        |\
        | \
       7|  \
        |   \
        |48° \
   X----+-----Y
```

Review **PREVIEW**

10. Use $\triangle QRS$ to find sin Q and cos Q. *(Section 6-7)*

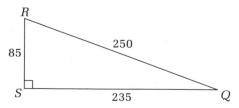

Solve. *(Sections 2-7, 2-8)*

11. $5x = 13$

12. $\dfrac{x}{13} = 5$

13. $5 = 13x$

14. Write an equation to model this statement:

    A child's height at age 2 is about half the height the child will reach as an adult. *(Section 5-1)*

A Direct Variation Model

FOCUS

Model a direct variation situation and use the model to make predictions. Find the slope of a line in a coordinate plane.

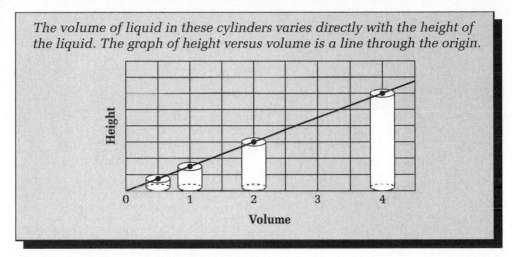

The volume of liquid in these cylinders varies directly with the height of the liquid. The graph of height versus volume is a line through the origin.

UNDERSTANDING THE MAIN IDEAS

Modeling a direct variation

Real-world data almost never fits a line exactly, but when the ratio of two quantities is *approximately* constant, you can use a direct variation graph or equation to model their relationship.

The graph of a direct variation will be a line through the origin with slope equal to the constant ratio. The equation of a direct variation will be of the form $y = kx$, where k is the constant ratio.

Sample 1

Imagine someone has prepared a box full of hundreds of table tennis balls, some of which are painted red. You are not told how many table tennis balls are in the box or how many are red. You perform the following experiment five times.

The table tennis balls are stirred thoroughly and you use a fishing net to scoop some up. Then you count the total number of table tennis balls and also the number that are red.

Suppose that the results shown below are obtained.

Total number of table tennis balls in net	Number of red table tennis balls in net
38	11
46	14
29	9
42	13
31	9

Sample 1 continues on the next page.

a. Show why direct variation is a good model for this situation.
b. Give a direct variation equation which models the situation.
c. Use the model to predict the number of red table tennis balls that will be in the net if there are a total of 33 table tennis balls in the net.
d. Use the model to predict the total number of table tennis balls that should be scooped up in the net in order to collect 12 red table tennis balls.

Sample Response

a. To decide if direct variation is a good model, look at the ratio of red table tennis balls (R) to total number of table tennis balls (T) in each experiment.

T	R	$\dfrac{R}{T}$
38	11	0.289...
46	14	0.304...
29	9	0.310...
42	13	0.309...
31	9	0.290...

The ratios are not exactly equal, but they are all approximately 0.3 (rounded to the nearest tenth). Since the ratios are approximately equal, a direct variation is a good model.

b. Since $\dfrac{R}{T} \approx 0.3$, a possible equation would be $\dfrac{R}{T} = 0.3$, or $R = 0.3T$.

c. Substitute 33 for T in the equation from part (b) and solve for R.
$R = 0.3(33)$
$\quad = 9.9$
$\quad \approx 10$ ◀—— Round to the nearest whole table tennis ball.

A net with a total of 33 table tennis balls will have about 10 red table tennis balls in it.

d. Substitute 12 for R in the equation from part (b) and solve for T.
$12 = 0.3T$
$\dfrac{12}{0.3} = \dfrac{0.3T}{0.3}$
$40 = T$

The model predicts that if 40 table tennis balls are scooped up then the net will have 12 red table tennis balls in it.

For Exercises 1–3, refer to the results given in the table in Sample 1.

1. How many red table tennis balls can you expect to find among 51 table tennis balls scooped up in the net?

2. Predict the total number of table tennis balls in a net if 8 of them are red.

3. What can you conclude about the proportion of red table tennis balls in the box?

Determine whether direct variation is a good model for the data in each table. Explain your reasoning.

4.

Perimeter	Area
16	16
8	4
20	25
12	9

5.

Number of customers	Total sales
15	$41.25
22	$60.10
8	$22.10
18	$49.40
11	$30.35

Graphing direct variation

Sample 2

A wallpaper manufacturing company offers this graph to help customers determine how much wallpaper they need to buy.

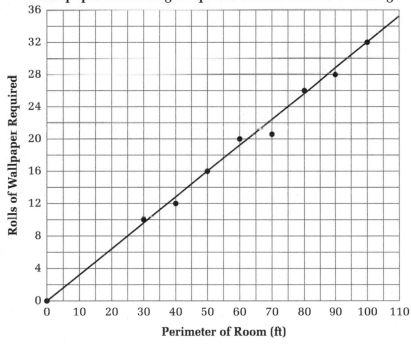

Wallpaper Estimating Graph for Rooms with 10-ft Ceilings

a. The fitted line shown in the figure is a direct variation model. Estimate the variation constant.

b. Use the fitted line to estimate the number of rolls of wallpaper needed to paper a room 15 ft long and 12 ft wide.

INTEGRATED MATHEMATICS 1 ***Study Guide***

a. The variation constant is the slope of the fitted line. To find the slope of the line, find two points *on the line* whose coordinates you know.

The points (50, 16) and (100, 32) are on the fitted line.

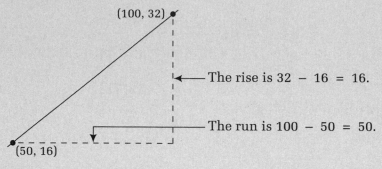

(100, 32)

The rise is 32 − 16 = 16.

The run is 100 − 50 = 50.

(50, 16)

$$\text{slope} = \frac{\text{rise}}{\text{run}} = \frac{16}{50} = 0.32$$

The variation constant is 0.32.

b. To use the graph, you need to know the perimeter of the room.

$$\begin{aligned}\text{perimeter} &= 2 \times \text{length} + 2 \times \text{width}\\ &= (2 \times 15) + (2 \times 12)\\ &= 30 + 24\\ &= 54\end{aligned}$$

Now, locate the point on the fitted line corresponding to a perimeter of 54 ft by drawing a vertical line up from 54 on the horizontal axis. Then draw a horizontal line from this point on the fitted line to the *y*-axis.

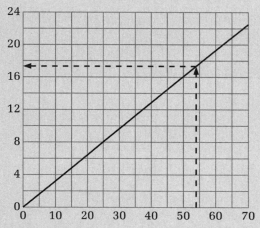

The horizontal line meets the *y*-axis at a point between 17 and 18. In situations like this you should always overestimate, so 18 rolls of wallpaper will be needed.

For Exercises 6–8, use the wallpaper estimating graph given in Sample 2.

6. Estimate the number of rolls of wallpaper needed to paper a room 26 ft long and 20 ft wide.

7. The graph gives estimates for wallpapering rooms with 10-ft ceilings. How would the graph be different if it were for rooms with 8-ft ceilings?

8. According to the graph, what is the approximate area (in square feet) covered by 8 rolls of wallpaper?

The amount of plant fertilizer to be put on a vegetable garden varies directly with the area of the garden. The fertilizer manufacturer recommends putting one gallon of fertilizer on four square feet of garden.

9. Draw a graph with garden area on the horizontal axis and gallons of fertilizer on the vertical axis.

10. Find the variation constant.

11. Use your graph to estimate the gallons of fertilizer needed for a 15 sq ft garden.

Review **PREVIEW**

12. Find the tangent ratio of $\angle A$. *(Section 7-1)*

Graph each equation. *(Section 4-7)*

13. $y = -4x$ 14. $y = \dfrac{2}{5}x$ 15. $y = \dfrac{1}{x}$

Write an expression for the perimeter of each figure. *(Section 2-4)*

16.   17. 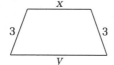   18.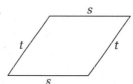

Circumference and Arc Length

In one revolution of a car wheel, the car moves forward a distance equal to the circumference of the wheel. For example, if the radius of the wheel is 14.5 in., then the car moves forward about 91 in. during one revolution. During the revolution, a point P on the rim of the wheel takes a curved path, called a cycloid. The distance traveled by point P for this wheel with 14.5 in. radius is about 116 in.

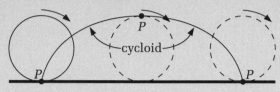

cycloid

KEY TERMS	**EXAMPLE / ILLUSTRATION**
Diameter (p. 375) the distance across a circle at its widest part (All diameters pass through the center of the circle.)	diameter center
Circumference (p. 375) the distance around the circle	circumference
Arc (p. 377) a part of a circle	arc →
Arc length (p. 377) the length of an arc (The arc length is a fraction of the circumference.)	arc length →
Central angle of an arc (p. 377) the angle, with vertex at the center, determined by the endpoints of an arc	arc → central angle center

UNDERSTANDING THE MAIN IDEAS

The ratio pi

In all circles, the ratio of the circumference to the diameter is a constant, represented by the Greek letter pi (π). This ratio cannot be represented exactly as a fraction or decimal. A good decimal approximation for the value of π is 3.14. To find the circumference, C, of a circle, use the formula $C = \pi d$, where d represents the diameter of the circle.

Sample 1

Find the diameter of a circular water tower that is 53 m around.

Sample Response

Use the formula for circumference, $C = \pi d$.

$$C = \pi d$$
$$53 \approx (3.14)d \quad \longleftarrow \quad \text{The "distance around" the tower, 53 m, is the circumference.}$$
$$\frac{53}{3.14} \approx \frac{3.14d}{3.14}$$
$$16.9 \approx d \quad \longleftarrow \quad \text{This answer is given to the nearest tenth.}$$

The diameter of the tower is approximately 16.9 meters.

1. What is the radius of a circle with circumference 11 ft?

2. You want to plant 100 tulip bulbs 6 in. apart in a circle. To the nearest foot, what is the diameter of the plot that the tulips will border?

3. How much fencing will be needed to enclose a circular plot measuring 15 ft in diameter?

Arc length

Arc length is a fraction of the circumference of the circle. To find the length of an arc, you can use this proportion:

$$\frac{\text{arc length}}{\text{circumference}} = \frac{\text{measure of central angle of arc}}{360°}$$

Sample 2

Find the arc length.

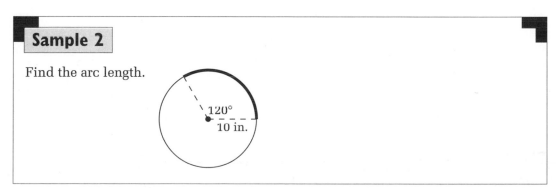

Use a proportion. Let l stand for the arc length.

$$\frac{l}{C} = \frac{\text{measure of central angle}}{360°}$$

Since the radius of the circle is 10 in., the diameter is 20 in. So, the circumference is $C = \pi d \approx 3.14(20)$, or about 62.8 in.

$$\frac{l}{62.8} = \frac{120}{360}$$

$$\frac{l}{62.8} = \frac{1}{3} \quad \longleftarrow \quad \text{Write the ratio in lowest terms.}$$

$$62.8\left(\frac{l}{6.28}\right) = 62.8\left(\frac{1}{3}\right)$$

$$l \approx 20.9$$

The arc length is approximately 20.9 in.

Find each arc length. Give answers to the nearest tenth.

4.

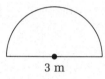

3 m

5.

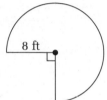

8 ft

6.

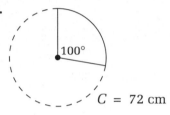

100°

$C = 72$ cm

7. The clock on the city hall has a minute hand one meter long. A bug sits on the tip of the minute hand for two minutes. What distance does it ride? Give your answer to the nearest centimeter.

8. Find the distance around the toy racetrack shown. Give your answer to the nearest tenth.

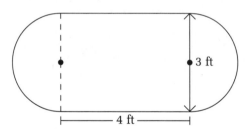

3 ft

4 ft

Review **PREVIEW**

Draw a line through the points and find its slope. *(Section 7-2)*

9. (0, 0) and (3, −2)

10. (4, 2) and (−3, 8)

11. Draw a box-and-whisker plot for the times customers waited in line for service at a bank. *(Section 3-5)*

Customer waiting times (minutes)				
7	4	6	12	8
8	5	2	5	7
9	10	6	15	3

Evaluate each expression for the given value of the variable. *(Section 2-2)*

12. $-6x$ when $x = -2$

13. $0.125x$ when $x = 160$

Direct Variation with $y = kx$

Recognize general characteristics of direct variation equations and graphs. Understand negative slope.

Many formulas in science are examples of direct variations. For instance, the weight of an object on another planet varies directly with its weight on Earth; that is, weight on another planet = k(weight on Earth). The value of k is different for each planet, as shown in these tables.

Planet	k
Mercury	0.385
Venus	0.905
Mars	0.385
Jupiter	2.545

Planet	k
Saturn	0.935
Uranus	0.795
Neptune	1.195
Pluto	0.055

KEY TERMS

General form for direct variation (p. 383)
the equation $y = kx$ (The graph of $y = kx$, for all values of k, will always pass through the origin.)

EXAMPLE / ILLUSTRATION

These are graphs of direct variation equations:

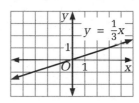

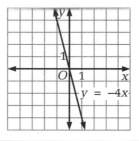

UNDERSTANDING THE MAIN IDEAS

When one variable quantity varies directly with another variable quantity, you can model the situation with an equation of the form $y = kx$. (Another form of this equation is $\frac{y}{x} = k$.) In the equation, recall that y is the dependent variable and x is the control variable.

Sample 1

Use the information in the tables on this page.

a. How much would a 120-pound person weigh on Jupiter?

b. What is the ratio of the weight of a spaceship on Venus to its weight on Earth?

INTEGRATED MATHEMATICS 1 **Study Guide**

a. From the previous page you know that the weight of an object on Jupiter varies directly with the weight of the object on Earth. Use the general form for direct variation to write an equation.

[weight on Jupiter]   [varies directly with]   [weight on Earth]
$$y \qquad = \qquad k \qquad \times \qquad x$$

$y = kx$
$y = 2.545x$ ◄—— From the table, the value of k for Jupiter is 2.545.
$y = 2.545(120)$
$y = 305.4$

A 120-pound person would weigh 305.4 pounds on Jupiter.

b. Use the form $\frac{y}{x} = k$. This means that

$$\frac{\text{weight of an object on Venus}}{\text{weight of the object on Earth}} = k.$$

The table gives the value of k for Venus as 0.905. The ratio is 0.905.

1. An object weighs 3000 lb on Jupiter. What would it weigh on Earth?

2. Write the general equation that gives the weight on Saturn of an object on Earth. Use the equation to find the weight on Saturn of a 120-pound person.

3. On which planet would you weigh the most? the least?

For Exercises 4–5, write the direct variation equation that models each situation. Identify the control variable and dependent variable, and give the value of k.

4. The perimeter of a regular pentagon varies directly with the length of a side.

5. During the summer reading program, the children's librarian gave each child one sticker for every three books the child read.

Direct variation graphs

The graph of a direct variation equation $y = kx$ is a line passing through the origin. The variation constant k is the slope of the line. Recall that if the slope is *negative*, the line falls from left to right. If the slope is *positive*, the line rises from left to right.

Sample 2

Write an equation for the direct variation graph shown at the right.

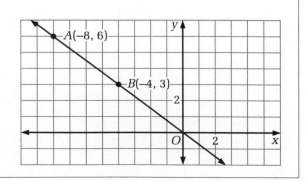

The graph is a line passing through the origin, so the equation takes the form $y = kx$. Since the line falls from left to right, expect k to be negative.

To find the value of k, use two points on the line whose coordinates you know. Sketch a right triangle to calculate rise and run.

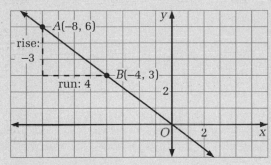

← *Caution:* When calculating rise and run, be sure to start at one point and travel to the other. Here the rise is *negative*, since the path indicates movement down.

$$\text{slope} = \frac{\text{rise}}{\text{run}} = -\frac{3}{4}$$

The value of k equals the slope of the line, so $k = -\frac{3}{4}$. The equation of the function is $y = -\frac{3}{4}x$.

Write an equation of the form $y = kx$ to describe each line.

6.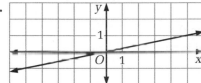

7.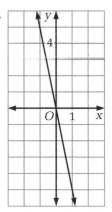

Graph each equation.

8. $y = -1.25x$

9. $y = \frac{2}{3}x$

Review **PREVIEW**

Find the circumference of each circle. *(Section 7-3)*

10. radius = 3 m

11. diameter = 24 cm

Simplify. *(Section 5-2)*

12. $-5(2x + y)$

13. $-2(6x - 4)$

14. $-3(-r - 5s)$

Multiply. *(Toolbox Skill 10)*

15. $\frac{3}{5} \times \frac{5}{4} \times \frac{10}{9}$

16. $\frac{14}{33} \times \frac{55}{21} \times \frac{15}{7}$

17. $\frac{5}{6} \times \frac{1}{10} \times \frac{2}{7} \times \frac{21}{4}$

Using Dimensional Analysis

Use dimensional analysis to work with the units in rates and conversion factors.

Ancient units of length were based on the human body measurements. Around 3000 B.C., the Egyptians used the cubit, *a unit of length based on the length of the arm from the elbow to fingertips. The cubit was subdivided into* 28 digits, *the width of one finger. Four digits made a* palm, *while five digits made a* hand.

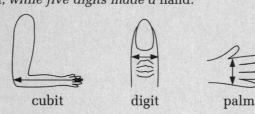

cubit   digit   palm   hand

KEY TERMS

EXAMPLE / ILLUSTRATION

Dimensional analysis (p. 392) a problem solving strategy in which you cancel units of measurement as if they are numbers	To convert 3 pints to cups: $3 \text{ pints} \times \dfrac{2 \text{ cups}}{1 \text{ pint}} = 6 \text{ cups}$ Thus, 3 pints = 6 cups.
Conversion factor (p. 393) a ratio of two equal (or approximately equal) quantities that are measured in different units	The conversion factor $\dfrac{2 \text{ cups}}{1 \text{ pint}}$ was used above.

UNDERSTANDING THE MAIN IDEAS

Conversion factors

You can cancel units of measurement as if they are numbers. To convert from one unit of measurement to another, multiply by one or more conversion factors.

Sample 1

You wish to estimate the distance around your schoolyard. You begin by pacing around the perimeter of the schoolyard, counting a total of 423 paces. You then measure the length of your stride and find that 9 paces cover 25 feet. Assuming that all your paces are about the same length, what is the distance in feet around the schoolyard?

1. Convert 1175 ft first to yards and then to miles. Round your answers to the nearest tenth of a unit.

For Exercises 2–5, each expression shows the units of a conversion problem. Use dimensional analysis to find the unit(s) of the answer.

2. $\dfrac{\text{revolutions}}{\text{s}} \times \dfrac{\text{s}}{\text{min}} = \underline{\quad?\quad}$

3. $\dfrac{\text{dollars}}{\text{week}} \times \dfrac{\text{weeks}}{\text{month}} = \underline{\quad?\quad}$

4. $\dfrac{\text{cents}}{\text{yd}} \times \dfrac{\text{dollars}}{\text{cents}} \times \dfrac{\text{yd}}{\text{ft}} = \underline{\quad?\quad}$

5. $\dfrac{\text{mi}}{\text{h}} \times \dfrac{\text{ft}}{\text{mi}} \times \dfrac{\text{h}}{\text{min}} \times \dfrac{\text{min}}{\text{s}} = \underline{\quad?\quad}$

6. Are you "worth your weight in gold?" Suppose gold is selling at $350 per troy ounce. A troy ounce equals 1.097 ordinary ounces, and there are 16 ordinary ounces in a pound. Calculate your "worth" in gold.

Converting the units of a rate

You can use dimensional analysis to convert rates to different units. This often requires more than one conversion factor.

Sample 2

A tank is emptying at the rate of 2 liters per second. How fast is it emptying in gallons per minute?

Sample Response

The problem gives a rate, 2 liters per second (or 2 L/s). You need to convert liters to gallons and seconds to minutes. The necessary conversions are:

$$1 \text{ qt} = 0.95 \text{ L} \qquad 60 \text{ s} = 1 \text{ min} \qquad 4 \text{ qt} = 1 \text{ gal}$$

Sample Response continues on the next page.

While the conversion from seconds (s), to minutes (min), can be done in one step, the conversion from liters (L), to gallons (gal), will be in two steps, first from L to qt and then from qt to gal.

$$2\text{ L/s} \times \frac{?}{?} \times \frac{?}{?} \times \frac{?}{?} = \underline{\quad ?\quad}\text{ gal/min}$$

Arrange the units first.

$$\frac{2\text{ L}}{1\text{ s}} \times \boxed{\frac{?\text{ s}}{?\text{ min}}} \times \boxed{\frac{?\text{ qt}}{?\text{ L}}} \times \boxed{\frac{?\text{ gal}}{?\text{ qt}}} = \frac{?\text{ gal}}{?\text{ min}}$$

— Cancels qt and leaves gal on the top.

— Cancels L and leaves qt on the top.

— Cancels s and leaves min on the bottom.

Now complete the conversion factors.

$$\frac{2\text{ L}}{1\text{ s}} \times \boxed{\frac{60\text{ s}}{1\text{ min}}} \times \boxed{\frac{1\text{ qt}}{0.95\text{ L}}} \times \boxed{\frac{1\text{ gal}}{4\text{ qt}}} = \frac{?\text{ gal}}{?\text{ min}}$$

Finally, cancel the units and do the calculations.

$$\frac{2\text{ L̸}}{1\text{ s̸}} \times \frac{60\text{ s̸}}{1\text{ min}} \times \frac{1\text{ qt̸}}{0.95\text{ L̸}} \times \frac{1\text{ gal}}{4\text{ qt̸}} = \frac{120\text{ gal}}{3.8\text{ min}} \approx 31.5789\text{ gal/min}$$

The tank is emptying at about 31.6 gal/min.

7. The minute hand of a clock revolves 360 degrees in one hour. Convert this measure to degrees per minute.

8. Convert 60 miles per hour to feet per second.

9. Convert 55 miles per hour to kilometers per hour.

Review **PREVIEW**

Graph. *(Section 7-4)*

10. $y = -\frac{3}{5}x$

11. $y = -x$

Solve each proportion. *(Section 6-3)*

12. $\dfrac{x}{300} = \dfrac{50}{60}$

13. $\dfrac{12}{240} = \dfrac{15}{x}$

14. $\dfrac{450}{x} = \dfrac{90}{64}$

Find each value for x. *(Sections 2-5, 2-7)*

15.

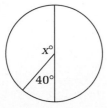

16.

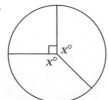

17.

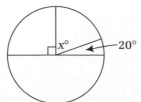

Areas of Circles and Sectors

Use the formulas for the area of a circle and find the area of a sector.

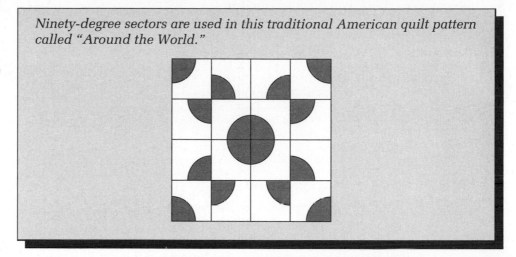

Ninety-degree sectors are used in this traditional American quilt pattern called "Around the World."

KEY TERMS

Sector (p. 402)
   the region of a circle formed by a central angle and its arc

EXAMPLE / ILLUSTRATION

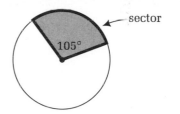

UNDERSTANDING THE MAIN IDEAS

Areas of circles

For all circles, the ratio of the area of the circle to the *square* of the radius of the circle is π. To find the area of a circle, use the formula $A = \pi r^2$.

Sample 1

Find the area of the circle shown at the right. Give your answer to the nearest tenth.

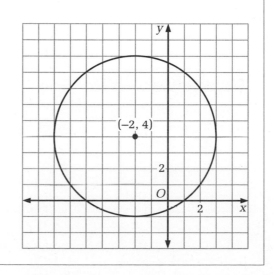

To use the formula $A = \pi r^2$ to find the area of the circle, you need to know the length of the radius of the circle. You can determine this information from the graph. Since the circle passes through $(-7, 4)$, the radius of the circle is $-2 - (-7) = 5$.

Substitute $r = 5$ and $\pi \approx 3.14$ into the formula $A = \pi r^2$:

$A \approx (3.14)(5^2)$
$A \approx 3.14(25)$
$A \approx 78.5$

The area of the circle is approximately 78.5 square units.

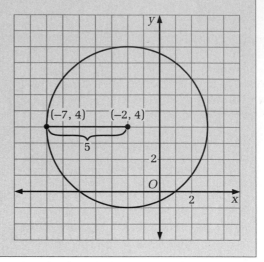

For Exercises 1–3, find the unknown measurement for each circle. Give your answers to the nearest tenth.

1. radius = 6 in.
   area = ___?___

2. area = 201 km^2
   radius = ___?___

3. area = 18.1 m^2
   diameter = ___?___

4. Graph the circle with center at $(3, -2)$ and area 16π square units.

Area of a sector

To find the area of a sector, use this proportion:

$$\frac{\text{area of a sector}}{\text{area of the circle}} = \frac{\text{measure of the central angle}}{360°}.$$

Notice that the "Around the World" quilt pattern on the first page of this study lesson is made with 15 rotations and translations of the square shown at the right.

If the sides of the square measure 5 in. and the radius of the shaded sector is 4 in., find the area of the light-colored cloth used in this square.

Break the problem into parts: (1) Find the area of the square. (2) Find the area of the dark-colored sector. (3) Subtract the area of the sector from that of the square.

(1) Area of square = $5^2 = 25$ in.^{2}

Sample Response continues on the next page.

(2) To find the area of the sector, use the proportion

$$\frac{\text{area of sector}}{\text{area of circle}} = \frac{\text{measure of the central angle}}{360°}.$$

Since the central angle of the sector is one corner of the square, its measure is 90°. Recall that the radius of the sector is 4 in., so the area of the circle is $\pi(4^2) \approx 50.24$ in.^{2}. Letting A = area of the sector:

$$\frac{A}{50.24} = \frac{90}{360}$$

$$\frac{A}{50.24} = \frac{1}{4}$$

$$A = \frac{50.24}{4}$$

$$A = 12.56 \text{ in.}^2$$

(3) Now subtract to find the area of the light-colored cloth:

area of light cloth = area of square − area of sector
$$= 25 - 12.56$$
$$= 12.44$$

The area of the light-colored cloth is approximately 12.44 in.^{2}.

In Exercises 5–7, find the area of each sector to the nearest tenth.

5.

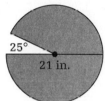

25°
21 in.

6.

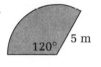

120°
5 m

7.

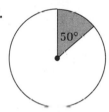

50°

The area of the circle is 121π km^2.

8. Which is larger: a slice of a 12-in. pizza which has been cut into 6 equal pieces, or a slice of a 14-in. pizza which has been cut into 8 equal pieces? Both pizzas have the same thickness.

Review **PREVIEW**

For Exercises 9 and 10, use conversion factors. *(Section 7-5)*

9. Convert 0.06 mi/h to feet per second.

10. Convert 5¢/in. to dollars per yard.

11. The graph at the right shows a rotation around the origin. What is the direction of the rotation and the amount of turn? *(Section 4-4)*

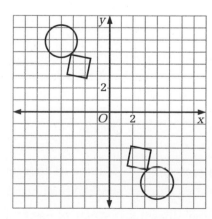

Solve. *(Sections 2-7, 2-8)*

12. $-4 = 0.25x + 6$

13. $\frac{x}{12} - 3 = 42$

14. $5 = -3x - 16$

INTEGRATED MATHEMATICS 1 **Study Guide**

Unit Check-Up	Complete these exercises for a review of Unit 7. If you have difficulty with a particular problem, review the indicated section.

1. Using $\triangle ABC$ at the right, express tan 35° as a ratio of the length of two sides of the triangle. *(Section 7-1)*

2. Use a calculator to find tan 35°. *(Section 7-1)*

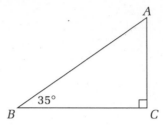

3. If $BC = 100$ m in $\triangle ABC$, find the length of $\overline{AC}$ to the nearest 0.1 m. *(Section 7-1)*

The volumes of four cylinders, all with the same diameter, are given in the table below. Use this information for Exercises 4–6. *(Section 7-1)*

Height h (cm)	4	10	16	20
Volume V (cm³)	24.8	62.0	99.2	124.0

4. Find the ratio $\dfrac{V}{h}$, to the nearest tenth, for each height in the table.

5. Write an equation for V in terms of h.

6. Find the volume of a cylinder 30 cm tall.

For Exercises 7 and 8, decide whether direct variation is a good model for the data in each table. Explain your reasoning. *(Section 7-2)*

7.

Height	Weight
2	16.6
2.5	20.8
3	25
4	33

8.

Diameter	Weight
2	12.6
4	100.8
10	1527
14	4322

9. The sun is approximately 93 million miles from Earth. The orbit of Earth is approximately circular. About how many miles does Earth travel in its yearly orbit of the sun? *(Section 7-3)*

Find each arc length to the nearest tenth. *(Section 7-3)*

10.

11.

The circumference of the circle is 42π m.

Rusty can mow 300 yd² of lawn in 20 min. *(Section 7-4)*

12. Model this situation with a direct variation equation in general form.

13. How long does it take Rusty to mow 1500 yd²?

Write an equation of the form $y = kx$ to describe each line. *(Section 7-4)*

14.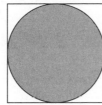

15.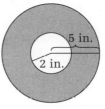

16. Convert 7446 days to years. *(Section 7-4)*

17. A point on the equator of Earth travels about 25,000 miles per day as the Earth rotates on its axis. Convert 25,000 miles per day to feet per second. *(Section 7-4)*

Find the area, to the nearest tenth, of each shaded region. *(Section 7-6)*

18.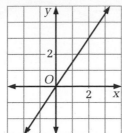

19.

20.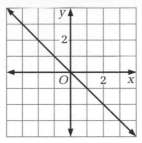

The area of the square is 36 m².

For Exercises 1 and 2, solve each system of equations.

1. $a + 4b = 100$
   $a = b - 10$

2. $x = 2y + 4$
   $3x + y = 5$

3. Two angles are supplementary. The measure of one angle is 10° less than the measure of the other angle. Find the measure of each angle.

For Exercises 4 and 5, solve the inequalities and graph.

4. $19x - 18 > 2 - x$

5. $-6x \leq -45$

6. *Open-ended* Give an example of a number that is a solution to *both* inequalities in Exercises 4 and 5.

Describe each situation using the phrase "is a function of." What is the dependent variable? the control variable?

7. The turkey gets warmer the longer it stays in the oven.

8. The faster the wind blows, the lower the wind chill factor.

Tell whether each graph represents a function. Explain your answer.

9.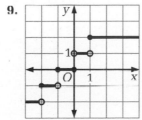

10.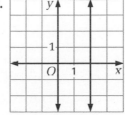

Linear Growth and Decay

FOCUS

Recognize how the rate and initial value in a real-life situation appear in an equation and a graph representing the situation.

"*And how many hours a day did you do lessons?*" said Alice, in a hurry to change the subject.

"*Ten hours the first day,*" said the Mock Turtle, "*nine the next, and so on.*"

"*What a curious plan!*" replied Alice.

"*That's the reason they're called lessons,*" the Gryphon replied, "*because they lesson from day to day.*"

This was quite a new idea to Alice, and she thought it over a little before she made her next remark. "*Then the eleventh day must have been a holiday?*"

"*Of course it was,*" said the Mock Turtle.

"*And how did you manage on the twelfth?*" Alice went on eagerly.

"*That's enough about lessons,*" the Gryphon interrupted in a very decided tone, "*tell her something about the games now.*"

from Alice in Wonderland *by Lewis Caroll*

KEY TERMS

Slope (p. 418)
the ratio of rise to run of a line (For a line modeling linear growth or decay, the slope is the rate of growth or decay.)

EXAMPLE / ILLUSTRATION

Marching Band Membership Drive

The slope is $\frac{70 - 40}{5 - 0} = \frac{30}{5} = 6$
(6 members/week).

Vertical intercept (p. 418) the value of the function when the control variable equals zero, or where the graph of a line crosses the vertical axis	The vertical intercept of the line in the graph on the previous page is 40, since the band starts with 40 members.
Slope-intercept form of an equation (p. 418) the form $y = mx + b$, where m is the slope and b is the vertical intercept (Here x is the control variable and y is the dependent variable.)	The equation of the line in the graph on the previous page is $y = 6x + 40$.
Linear growth (p. 420) change caused by repeatedly adding the same value (A graph modeling linear growth is a line slanting upward from left to right, that is, a line with a positive slope.)	The graph on the previous page shows that membership is increasing by 6 people every week. This is linear growth.
Linear decay (p. 420) change caused by repeatedly subtracting the same value (A graph modeling linear decay is a line slanting downward from left to right, that is, a line with a negative slope.)	The Mock Turtle's study plan is an example of linear decay. Each day the time spent on lessons is one hour less than the day before.

UNDERSTANDING THE MAIN IDEAS

Linear growth and decay

A situation in which a quantity increases at a steady rate is an example of *linear growth*. It can be modeled by a line with a positive slope. If a quantity decreases at a steady rate, the situation is an example of *linear decay*. It can be modeled by a line with a negative slope.

Sample

A hiker descends from the top of Mt. Washington at the rate of 800 ft/h. The base of Mt. Washington is about 2000 ft above sea level, while the summit is about 6300 ft above sea level.

a. Model this situation with a table of values and a graph.

b. Write an equation for the hiker's height above sea level as a function of the time.

Sample Response

The hiker is descending at a steady rate, 800 ft/h, so this is an example of linear decay.

a. The hiker's height above sea level depends on how long the hiker has been descending. Let $t = $ the time in hours and let $h = $ the height in feet above sea level. Set up a table using the information given in the problem.

Sample Response continues on the next page.

INTEGRATED MATHEMATICS 1 **Study Guide**

Time t	Height h
0	6300
1	5500
2	4700
3	3900
⋮	⋮

The hiker starts out at the summit, which is 6300 ft above sea level.

At the end of each hour, the hiker is 800 ft lower:
6300 − 800 = 5500;
5500 − 800 = 4700;
4700 − 800 = 3900.

The table could be continued until $h = 2000$ (the base of the mountain), but these four points are enough to draw a graph.

Plot the dependent variable, h, on the vertical axis and the control variable, t, on the horizontal axis. Plot the points (0, 6300), (1, 5500), (2, 4700), and (3, 3900) from the table and draw a line through the points as shown below.

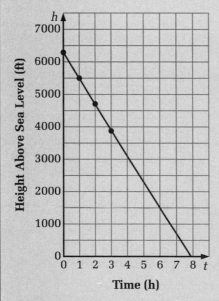

Time (h)

b. Since this is an example of linear decay, the equation will take the form

$$\begin{matrix} \text{dependent} \\ \text{variable} \end{matrix} = \begin{pmatrix} \text{rate of} \\ \text{decay} \end{pmatrix} \begin{pmatrix} \text{control} \\ \text{variable} \end{pmatrix} + \begin{matrix} \text{vertical} \\ \text{intercept} \end{matrix}.$$

The rate is −800 ft/h since the height is decreasing, the control variable is the time, t, and the vertical intercept is the height when $t = 0$, or 6300 ft. Therefore, the equation is $h = -800t + 6300$.

For Exercises 1 and 2, do these things:
  a. Model each situation with a table and a graph.
  b. Find the slope and the vertical intercept of each line. Explain how they are related to the original situation.
  c. Model each situation with an equation.

  1. A teacher's classroom supply budget is $100 plus $3 per pupil.

  2. Gregg starts swimming at a point 2000 ft from shore and swims toward shore at a rate of 250 ft/min.

For Exercises 3 and 4, do these things:

  a. **Find the slope and the vertical intercept of each graph.**

  b. **Write an equation for each line.**

  c. **Tell whether each graph is an example of** *linear growth* **or** *linear decay*.

3.

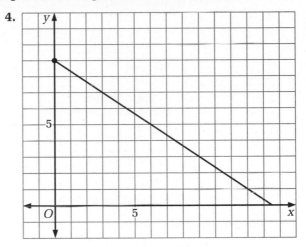

4.

![Review PREVIEW]

5. A window has the shape of a half-circle with diameter 4 ft. What is the area of the window? *(Section 7-6)*

6. What is the slope of a line passing through the origin and the point $(-3, 8)$? *(Section 7-2)*

Evaluate each expression when $x = -2$ and $y = 4$. *(Section 2-2)*

7. $2x - 7$ 8. $-x + 2y$ 9. $4x + 2y$ 10. $\frac{1}{3}x - \frac{2}{3}y$

Solve for y. *(Section 5-5)*

11. $x - y = 12$ 12. $3x - 2y = k$ 13. $210 = 5y + 2x$

Linear Combinations

FOCUS

Use the standard form of an equation for a line to model real-life situations. Find intercepts from the standard form and go from standard form to slope-intercept form.

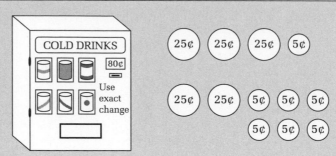

Here are two ways you can pay for an 80¢ cold drink with quarters and nickels. Both ways are solutions of the equation $25q + 5n = 80$, where $q = $ the number of quarters and $n = $ the number of nickels.

KEY TERMS	EXAMPLE / ILLUSTRATION
Solution of an equation with two variables (p. 426) an ordered pair of numbers that make the equation true	The ordered pair $(x, y) = (3, 5)$ is a solution to $5x + 3y = 30$ because $5(3) + 3(5) =$ $15 + 15 = 30$.
Graph of an equation (p. 426) all the points whose coordinates are solutions of the equation	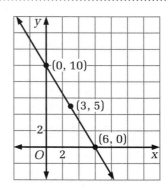
Linear equation (p. 427) the equation for a line	One form of the equation of the line graphed above is $5x + 3y = 30$.
Standard form of a linear equation (p. 427) the form $ax + by = c$, where x and y are the variables and a, b, and c are numbers	The equation above is in standard form.
Horizontal intercept (p. 428) the value of the control variable that makes the value of the dependent variable zero, or where the graph of a line crosses the horizontal axis	The horizontal intercept of the line graphed above is 6. (The line crosses the horizontal axis at the point (6, 0).)

UNDERSTANDING THE MAIN IDEAS

A linear equation, like $2x + 4y = 20$, can be used to model situations where two quantities are being related. The graph of such an equation is a *line*. The intercepts of the graph are found by substituting zero for one of the variables and solving for the other variable.

Sample

The pentagon at the right is formed by an equilateral triangle with sides of length s on top of a rectangle with length s and width w. The perimeter of the pentagon is 50 units.

a. Write an equation that models this situation.

b. Make a table of four possible solutions for s and w.

c. Graph the equation found in part (a).

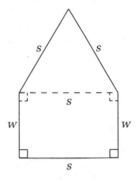

Sample Response

a. An expression for the perimeter of the pentagon is
$s + s + w + s + w = 3s + 2w$, so an equation for this situation is
$3s + 2w = 50$ ($s > 0$ and $w > 0$).

b. A solution of the equation from part (a) is an ordered pair of numbers
(s, w) that make the equation true. To find such an ordered pair, pick a
number for s and determine the value of w that makes the equation true.

First solve the equation for w:

$$3s + 2w = 50$$
$$3s - 3s + 2w = 50 - 3s$$
$$2w = -3s + 50$$
$$\frac{2w}{2} = \frac{-3s + 50}{2}$$
$$w = -\frac{3}{2}s + 25 \quad \longleftarrow \quad \text{This is the slope-intercept form of the equation.}$$

Now choose any reasonable values for s, use the equation above to find
the corresponding value of w, and record the values in a table.

s	$-\frac{3}{2}s + 25$	w
2	$-\frac{3}{2}(2) + 25 = -3 + 25$	22
6	$-\frac{3}{2}(6) + 25 = -9 + 25$	16
10	$-\frac{3}{2}(10) + 25 = -15 + 25$	10
14	$-\frac{3}{2}(14) + 25 = -21 + 25$	4

Other values of s $\left(0 < s < 16\frac{2}{3}\right)$ can also be used.

Sample Response continues on next page.

INTEGRATED MATHEMATICS 1 Study Guide **189**

c. All solutions lie on the graph of the line $3s + 2w = 50$, or $w = -\frac{3}{2}s + 25$. (These two forms of the equation, the standard form and the slope-intercept form, are equivalent and thus have the same graph.)

From part (b) you already know four points on the line. Set up the axes and plot the points, (s, w). The control variable, s, should be plotted on the horizontal axis and the dependent variable, w, should be plotted on the vertical axis.

The original problem asked for the lengths of the sides of a pentagon. The line $w = -\frac{3}{2}s + 25$ passes through many points (for example, $(-2, 28)$) that could not be the lengths of the sides of a pentagon. The solutions of the problem make up the part of the line that lies in Quadrant I, because that is where s and w are both positive.

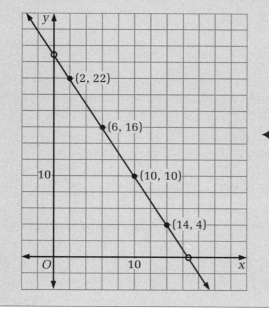

The intercepts are *not* solutions because neither s nor w, the lengths of sides of the pentagon, can be 0.

For Exercises 1–3, refer to the Sample.

1. Sketch each of the four pentagons indicated by the values in the table for part (b).

2. Complete this table:

s	w
4	
12	
15	
	24
	0.5

3. Can $w = 25$? Can $s = 17$? Tell why or why not.

For Exercises 4–6, do these things.

   a. Write an equation modeling each situation.

   b. Give three possible solutions.

4. To make 4 gallons of punch, mix x gallons of fruit juice with y gallons of seltzer water.

5. A basketball team scores 2 points for each field goal and 1 point for each free throw. In one game, the team scored 52 points with g field goals and f free throws.

6. To pay for a used car, Liora put d dollars down and made 12 monthly payments of m dollars each. She paid a total of $3400 for the car.

Find the intercepts of the graph of each equation.

   7. $4x - 6y = 12$ **8.** $-1.5x - 0.9y = 3$ **9.** $\frac{2}{3}x + \frac{1}{5}y = 6$

10–12. Rewrite the equations in Exercises 7–9 in slope-intercept form.

Review **PREVIEW**

13. A membership in Diamond Dave's Health Club costs $85 for registration and $25 per month. *(Section 8-1)*

   a. Model the situation with a graph.

   b. Find the slope and the vertical intercept of the line. Explain how they are related to the original situation.

14. **a.** Graph the points $A(4, -2)$, $B(4, 0)$, $C(4, 1)$, and $D(4, 4)$. *(Section 4-6)*

   b. What pattern do you see in the graph? in the coordinates?

   c. Is the graph a function? Explain why or why not.

15. Repeat Exercise 14 using the points $P(6, -2)$, $Q(3, -2)$, $R(0, -2)$, and $S(-4, -2)$. *(Section 4-6)*

Horizontal and Vertical Lines

FOCUS

Describe slopes of horizontal and vertical lines and write equations for horizontal and vertical lines.

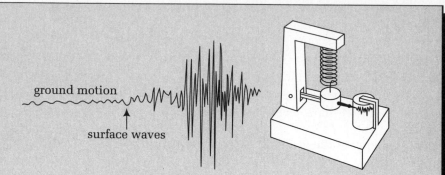

Geologists use seismometers to measure the strength and duration of earthquakes. This instrument records large and small tremors of the ground. The readout is almost horizontal during calm periods, and forms almost vertical peaks during quakes.

UNDERSTANDING THE MAIN IDEAS

Here is a table summarizing the facts about horizontal and vertical lines.

Type of line	Slope	Equation	Function?
horizontal	0	$y = a$	yes
vertical	no slope (undefined)	$x = b$	no

Sample 1

Sketch the line through the points (2, −2) and (6, −2). Then write an equation for the line.

Sample Response

Plot the two points and draw the line passing through them.

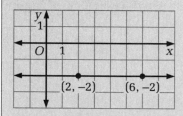

$$\text{slope} = \frac{\text{rise}}{\text{run}} = \frac{-2 - (-2)}{6 - 2} = \frac{-2 + 2}{4} = \frac{0}{4} = 0$$

The slope is zero. The y-coordinate of all the points on this line is −2.

The equation of the line is $y = -2$.

Sample 2

Graph the equation $4x - 24 = 0$ on the coordinate plane.

Sample Response

Most linear equations have two variables in them. When a linear equation has only one variable, you know that the line is either horizontal or vertical, depending on the variable involved.

Solve the equation for x:

$$4x - 24 = 0$$
$$4x - 24 + 24 = 0 + 24$$
$$4x = 24$$
$$\frac{4x}{4} = \frac{24}{4}$$
$$x = 6$$

To graph this line, plot several points (x, y) where the value of x is 6: $(6, 0)$, $(6, 1)$, $(6, 4)$, $(6, 6)$.

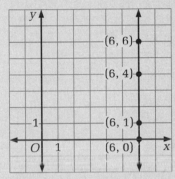

The line is vertical.

$$\text{slope} = \frac{\text{rise}}{\text{run}} = \frac{4 - 1}{6 - 6} = \frac{3}{0}$$

Since division by zero is undefined, the slope is undefined.

For Exercises 1–4, do these things.
  a. Tell whether the line is *horizontal* or *vertical*.
  b. Graph the line.
  c. Find the slope of the line.

1. $y = 0.1$ **2.** $2x = 72$ **3.** $2.6 = \frac{y}{5}$ **4.** $0x - 1.8y = 9.0$

Write an equation for each line.

  5. The line is vertical, and the point $(6, 1)$ is on the line.

  6. The points $(3, -1)$ and $(-10, -1)$ are on the line.

  7. The slope is zero, and the point $\left(1, \frac{1}{5}\right)$ is on the line.

  8. The slope is undefined, and the point $(0, 4)$ is on the line.

INTEGRATED MATHEMATICS 1 **Study Guide**

Find the slope of each line and write an equation for each line.

9.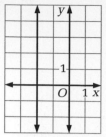

10.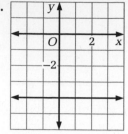

Review **PREVIEW**

Rewrite each equation in slope-intercept form. If it is not possible to do so, explain why not.   *(Section 8-2)*

11. $5x + 9y = 45$ **12.** $0x - 11y = 22$ **13.** $6x - 7y = 14$

For Exercises 14–16, solve.   *(Sections 2-7, 5-2, 5-3)*

14. $-2(x + 4) = 8$ **15.** $3t + 7 = 5 - 2t$ **16.** $9.81 = 3.12 + 3m$

17. Graph the line that contains the points $(-4, 8)$ and $(4, -2)$. Find the slope and the vertical intercept of the graph. Write an equation for the line. *(Section 8-1)*

8-4

Writing Equations for Lines

FOCUS

Use two points or
the slope and one
point to write an
equation for a line.
Use an equation for
a line to solve
problems.

*This is a graph shown in the book <u>A Scientific Approach to Distance
Running</u>, by David L. Costill. The author has used a fitted line to model
the relationship between a runner's maximal heart rate while running at
10 mi/h and performance in a 10-mi race.*

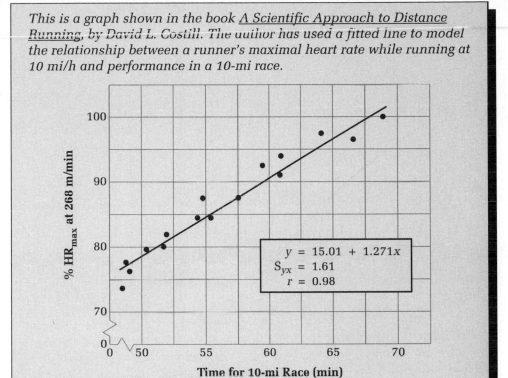

$$y = 15.01 + 1.271x$$
$$S_{yx} = 1.61$$
$$r = 0.98$$

UNDERSTANDING THE MAIN IDEAS

This table summarizes how to find the equation of a line in
slope-intercept form.

If you know . . .	Follow these steps.
The slope and the vertical intercept	Substitute the slope for m and the vertical intercept for b in the equation $y = mx + b$.
The slope and one point on the line	1. Substitute the slope for m and the coordinates of the point for x and y in the equation $y = mx + b$. 2. Solve for b. 3. Substitute the known values for m and b in the equation $y = mx + b$.
Two points on the line	1. Use the coordinates of the two points to find the slope m. 2. Use the slope and the coordinates of one of the two known points to write the equation, following the steps in the second situation above.

Note: If the slope is 0 or undefined, refer to the procedures in Section 8-3.

Sample

Find the equation of the line containing the points (6, 2) and (1, 4).

INTEGRATED MATHEMATICS 1 Study Guide **195**

Sample Response

First, find the slope of the line:

$$m = \frac{\text{change in } y}{\text{change in } x}$$

$$= \frac{2 - 4}{6 - 1} \quad \longleftarrow \quad \textit{Caution: Be sure the subtractions are in the same order.}$$
$$\text{Start with the same point each time.}$$

$$= -\frac{2}{5}$$

Second, use the slope and the coordinates of one of the two points to find the value of b:

$$y = mx + b$$

$$4 = -\frac{2}{5}(1) + b \quad \longleftarrow \quad \text{The point } (1, 4) \text{ is used here.}$$

$$4 = -\frac{2}{5} + b$$

$$4 + \frac{2}{5} = -\frac{2}{5} + b + \frac{2}{5}$$

$$\frac{22}{5} = b$$

Finally, substitute m and b into the slope-intercept form of an equation:

$$y = -\frac{2}{5}x + \frac{22}{5}$$

Check (✔): It is a good idea to check your equation by substituting the other known point in the equation. The coordinates of this point should make the equation true.

$$y = mx + b$$

$$2 \stackrel{?}{=} -\frac{2}{5}(6) + \frac{22}{5} \quad \longleftarrow \quad x = 6, y = 2$$

$$2 \stackrel{?}{=} -\frac{12}{5} + \frac{22}{5}$$

$$2 \stackrel{?}{=} \frac{10}{5}$$

$$2 = 2 \ ✔$$

The equation of the line is $y = -\frac{2}{5}x + \frac{22}{5}$.

For Exercises 1–4, write an equation for each line.

1. The points $(3, -10)$ and $(-2, 6)$ are on the line.

2. The vertical intercept is 8 and the horizontal intercept is -3.

3. The vertical intercept is -2 and the line has the same slope as the line $y = \frac{7}{10}x + 8$.

4. The slope is $\frac{1}{3}$ and the point $(7, 9)$ is on the line.

For Exercises 5 and 6, write an equation for the graphed line.

5.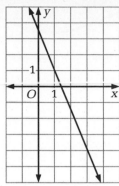

6.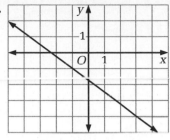

7. Carla has a job cataloging books in the library's new computer. One day after working for 3 h at a steady pace, her supervisor told her she had 475 books left to catalog. After 5 h, she had 285 books left.

   a. What is the control variable? the dependent variable?

   b. Represent the given information as two points on a graph.

   c. Write an equation for the line through the two points.

   d. What do the slope and vertical intercept of the graph mean in terms of the original situation?

   e. Use your graph to predict how long it will take her to catalog all the books.

8. An 11-mi bike path connects the towns of Arlington and Bedford. At every mile there is a "milestone" telling the distance from Arlington. Tomás gets on the path somewhere between Arlington and Bedford, and rides toward Bedford at a steady rate. After riding two minutes, he passes the "Mile 3" marker. It takes him a total of 42 minutes to reach the end of the path.

   a. What is the control variable? the dependent variable?

   b. Represent the given information as two points on a graph.

   c. Write an equation for the line through the two points.

   d. What do the slope and vertical intercept of the graph mean in terms of the original situation?

Review **PREVIEW**

Write an equation for each line.   *(Section 8-3)*

9. The slope is 0, and the point (5, 9) is on the line.

10. The points (12, 8) and (12, −2) are on the line.

Solve each system of equations.   *(Section 5-8)*

11. $y = 4x$
    $2x - y = 10$

12. $y = x - 8$
    $3x - 2y = 14$

13. $x = 2y - 6$
    $x = y + 4$

8-5 Graphing Systems of Linear Equations

FOCUS

Find the point where two lines intersect.

SUN

Have you ever seen a fire started with sunlight and a magnifying glass? The magnifying glass redirects the sunrays (which are lines) so that they meet at a point, called the focal point. A piece of paper or dried leaves placed at this point will ignite from the heat of the sunrays.

UNDERSTANDING THE MAIN IDEAS

Systems with a solution

To find the point where two lines meet, you can carefully graph the lines on the same axes and estimate the coordinates of the point where the lines cross. The coordinates of the point of intersection will make the equations of *both* lines true.

Sample 1

Emma and Julia live 30 mi apart. They agree to ride bikes and meet somewhere between their homes. They leave their houses at the same time. Emma rides at the rate of 12 mi/h, while Julia rides at a rate of 8 mi/h. When and where do they meet ?

Sample Response

First, define the control and dependent variables.

control variable: Let t = the time (in hours) the girls spend riding.
dependent variable: Let y = the distance (in miles) from Emma's house to the meeting point.

Since you know each girl's rate of speed and starting position, you can write two linear equations in slope-intercept form.

Sample Response continues on the next page.

Emma's distance from home: $y = 12t$

Julia's distance from Emma's house: $y = -8t + 30$ ◄──── Julia is biking toward Emma's house, so her original distance of 30 mi from Emma's house is decreasing at the rate of 8 mi/h.

Now, graph the two equations on the same set of axes.

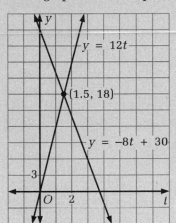

Examining the graph, the lines cross at about $(t, y) = (1.5, 18)$.

Check (✔): Check the coordinates of the intersection point in the two equations.

$y = 12t$	$y = -8t + 30$
$18 \overset{?}{=} 12(1.5)$	$18 \overset{?}{=} -8(1.5) + 30$
$18 = 18$ ✔	$18 \overset{?}{=} -12 + 30$
	$18 = 18$ ✔

After 1.5 h, the girls will meet 18 mi from Emma's house.

For Exercises 1–4, graph the system of equations. Estimate the solution of the system, or write *no solution*.

1. $2x + y = 0$
   $x - y = 6$

2. $y = -x + 7$
   $y = x - 3$

3. $2x - y = 1$
   $3x + y = -6$

4. $y = 3x + 5$
   $y = 3x - 1$

5. Two trains are 420 mi apart and travel toward each other on parallel tracks. One train travels at 80 mi/h, while the other travels at 60 mi/h. How long will it take them to pass each other?

6. Andrea babysits on weekends. One of her customers, the Jacksons, offers to pay her $10 plus $1.50 per hour. Another customer, the Lydons, will pay her $4 per hour. What advice would you give her to help her decide which job to take?

Systems with no solution

Sometimes a system of linear equations has no solution. This happens when the graphs of the equations are parallel lines. Parallel lines have the same slope.

Sample 2

Does this system of equations have a solution?

$$2x + y = 7$$
$$5y = 5 - 10x$$

Sample Response

Rewrite the equations in slope-intercept form.

$$2x + y = 7$$
$$-2x + 2x + y = -2x + 7$$
$$y = -2x + 7$$

$$5y = 5 - 10x$$
$$\frac{5y}{5} = \frac{5 - 10x}{5}$$
$$y = -2x + 1$$

The slopes are the same, –2, but the vertical intercepts are different, 7 and 1.

Since the lines have the same slope but different vertical intercepts, they are parallel and never intersect. Therefore, there is no solution of this system. The graph at the right confirms this result.

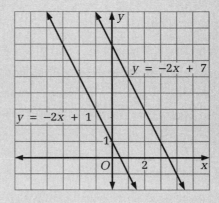

For Exercises 7–10, rewrite each equation in slope-intercept form. Then tell whether each system of equations has a *solution* or *no solution*.

7. $2x + 5y = 10$
$5x + 2y = 10$

8. $2x = -7y + 28$
$4x + 14y = 0$

9. $x - y = 5$
$2y = 2x + 3$

10. $x - 12y = 9$
$3x + 36y = 27$

Review **PREVIEW**

Write an equation for each line. *(Section 8-4)*

11. The slope is $-\frac{3}{8}$ and the point $(5, -4)$ is on the line.

12. The points $(3, -8)$ and $(3, 1)$ are on the line.

Tell whether 4 is a solution of each inequality. Write *Yes* or *No*. Then solve and graph each inequality. *(Section 5-4)*

13. $-3x + 15 > 9$ **14.** $2(x - 1) \leq 0$ **15.** $-2 \geq x - 8$

Graphing Linear Inequalities

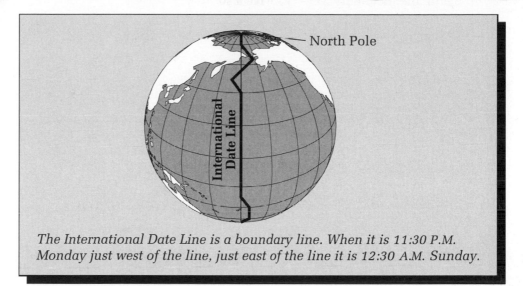

— North Pole

International Date Line

The International Date Line is a boundary line. When it is 11:30 P.M. Monday just west of the line, just east of the line it is 12:30 A.M. Sunday.

KEY TERMS

EXAMPLE / ILLUSTRATION

Linear inequality (p. 456) an inequality whose graph on the coordinate plane is a region whose edge is a line	The graph of the linear inequality $y \geq \frac{2}{3}x - 3$ is shown below. 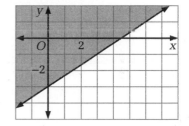
Boundary line (p. 456) the line on the edge of a graph of a linear inequality	The boundary line of the graph above is the line $y = \frac{2}{3}x - 3$.
Solution region (p. 456) the region on the coordinate plane whose points make the inequality true	The solution region shown in the graph above is the boundary line and the shaded region.

UNDERSTANDING THE MAIN IDEAS

A linear inequality looks like a linear equation except that one of the inequality symbols ($<$, $>$, $\leq$, $\geq$) takes the place of the equals sign.

To obtain the equation of the boundary line of the graph of an inequality, change the inequality symbol to an equals sign. To graph an inequality, first graph the boundary line (dashed for $>$ and $<$, or solid for $\geq$ and $\leq$). Then shade the side of the line whose points make the inequality true.

Sample Response

First graph the boundary line $2x - y = 6$. The boundary line is drawn as a solid line, because the inequality symbol is $\geq$ (greater than *and* equal). Rewriting $2x - y = 6$ as $2x = y + 6$ and then as $y = 2x - 6$ (slope-intercept form) reveals that the slope of the boundary line is 2 and the vertical intercept is –6.

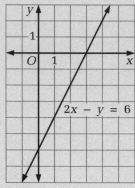

$2x - y = 6$

To decide which region to shade, select two points, one on either side of the boundary line, and test the coordinates in the inequality.

Since the boundary line does not pass through the origin, the point $(0, 0)$ is a good choice for one of the test points (the zeros simplify the computations). A point on either axis on the other side of the boundary line, such as $(4, 0)$, is a good choice for the other test point.

$$2x - y \geq 6$$
$$2(0) - 0 \overset{?}{\geq} 6$$
$$0 - 0 \overset{?}{\geq} 6$$
$$0 \not\geq 6$$

$\longleftrightarrow$

$$2x - y \geq 6$$
$$2(4) - 0 \overset{?}{\geq} 6$$
$$8 - 0 \overset{?}{\geq} 6$$
$$8 \geq 6$$

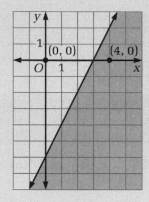

$(0, 0)$ $(4, 0)$

Thus, the region containing the point $(4, 0)$ should be shaded. The completed graph of $2x - y \geq 6$ is shown at the right.

Graph each inequality.

1. $y < -x + 10$

2. $x + y \leq 14$

3. $-3y < x - 12$

4. $-8y + 16 \leq 40$

Sample 2

Write an inequality for the graph shown at the right.

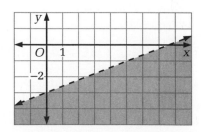

First, write the equation for the boundary line.

Looking at the graph, the vertical intercept is −3. The slope can be computed using the points $(0, -3)$ and $(5, -1)$, which are on the line.

$$m = \frac{\text{change in } y}{\text{change in } x} = \frac{-1 - (-3)}{5 - 0} = \frac{-1 + 3}{5} = \frac{2}{5}$$

Using the slope-intercept form of an equation, the equation of the boundary line is $y = \frac{2}{5}x - 3$.

Since the line is dashed, you know that the inequality symbol is either $>$ or $<$. Since the region below the boundary line is shaded, the inequality is $y < \frac{2}{5}x - 3$.

Write an inequality for each graph.

5.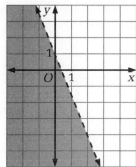

6.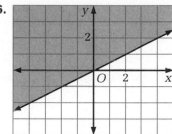

Review **PREVIEW**

For Exercises 7–9, without graphing, tell whether each system has a solution or no solution. *(Section 8-5)*

7. $y = \frac{2}{3}x - 5$

  $y = \frac{2}{3}x + 7$

8. $4x - 7y = 28$

  $4x - 7y = -14$

9. $2x - 5y = 15$

  $y = -\frac{2}{5}x + 3$

10. The school nurse selected 50 health forms at random from the forms on the 715 children enrolled in the school. Of the 50 forms, 12 were not filled out completely. About how many of the school's health forms are incomplete? *(Section 6-2)*

11. A grab bag of 18 toys for a children's party contains 8 horns, 7 secret decoder rings, and 3 tops. A child selects a toy at random from the bag. What is the probability that the toy is *not* a secret decoder ring? *(Section 6-2)*

Graph each inequality on a number line. *(Section 3-3)*

12. $-5 < x \le 3$

13. $0 \le x \le 12$

Systems of Linear Inequalities

Solve problems by
writing and
graphing systems of
inequalities.

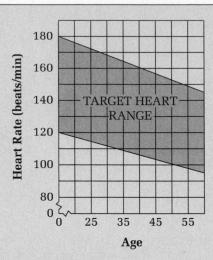

In this graph, shading is used to indicate correct pulse rates for aerobic
exercise. If the point corresponding to your age and pulse rate is in the
shaded region, you know your level of exertion is appropriate.

KEY TERMS

EXAMPLE / ILLUSTRATION

KEY TERMS	EXAMPLE / ILLUSTRATION
System of inequalities (p. 464) two or more inequalities involving the same variables	$y \leq 2x + 1$ $y > 4$

Solution of a system of inequalities (p. 464)
    the coordinates of the points which make all the
    inequalities in a system of inequalities true
	Every point in the doubly-
	shaded region and along the
	solid boundary line in the
	graph below is a solution of the
	system of inequalities above.
	
	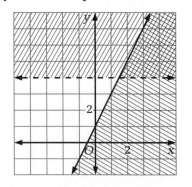

UNDERSTANDING THE MAIN IDEAS

To find the solutions to a system of two linear inequalities, graph both
inequalities on the same set of axes. The points that are solutions of the
system are those points that are located in the doubly-shaded region of
the graph.

Sample

For an upcoming production, the Drama Club is charging $2 for a child ticket and $4 for an adult ticket. There are 400 seats in the theater. The club hopes to sell more than $1000 worth of tickets.

a. Write and graph a system of inequalities to model the situation.

b. Use the graph to tell how many child tickets the club will need to sell if they sell exactly 200 adult tickets.

Sample Response

a. Let x = the number of adult tickets sold.
Let y = the number of child tickets sold.

Since there are 400 seats in the theater, no more than 400 tickets can be sold. That is,

total number of tickets ≤ 400

$$x + y \leq 400$$

Since the club hopes that ticket sales will bring in more than $1000,

ticket sales > 1000

$4x + 2y > 1000$ ◄—— Each adult ticket brings in $4, each child ticket brings in $2.

The system of inequalities is $x + y \leq 400$ and $4x + 2y > 1000$. Now, graph both inequalities on the same set of axes.

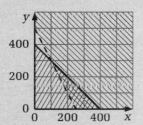 ◄—— *Caution:* Only the first quadrant is used because x and y cannot be negative — there are no negative ticket sales.

The doubly-shaded region of the graph represents the solutions of the system of inequalities (the dashed boundary is not part of the solution).

b. Draw a vertical line segment on the graph of part (a) at $x = 200$ as shown in the graph at the right. These are the solutions of the system where the number of adult tickets is 200. The y-values on this segment go from 101 to 200. (Notice that $y = 100$ is *not* included in these values.)

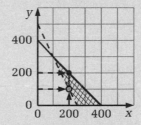

If they sell exactly 200 adult tickets, the Drama Club must sell at least 101 child tickets, but no more than 200.

For Exercises 1–3, refer to the Sample.

1. Use the graph in part (a) to tell whether the club can reach its $1000 goal selling the following combinations of tickets.
   a. 100 adult tickets and 150 child tickets
   b. 300 adult tickets and 100 child tickets
   c. 50 adult tickets and 300 child tickets

INTEGRATED MATHEMATICS 1 Study Guide **205**

2. What is the greatest number of adult tickets that can be sold if the Drama Club is to meet its $1000 goal? the greatest number of child tickets?

3. The Drama Club decides to sell adult tickets for $5 each and child tickets for $1 each. Redraw the graph to model this situation.

For Exercises 4–7, use the graph to tell whether each ordered pair is a solution of the system shown in the graph. Write *Yes* or *No*.

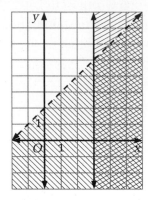

4. $(0, 0)$

5. $(-1, 2)$

6. $(5, -2)$

7. $(3, 0)$

For Exercises 8 and 9, graph each system of inequalities.

8. $y > \frac{1}{4}x - 1$

$y \geq -3x + 5$

9. $x + 2y \leq 5$

$2x + y \geq 5$

10. Eliza Phipps knits hats and mittens to sell at the winter bazaar. A pair of mittens takes her 2 hours to knit. A hat takes her 3 hours. In the months before the bazaar, she will be able to spend up to 240 hours knitting. Hats are usually better sellers, so she plans to make at least as many hats as pairs of mittens.

  a. Write and graph a system of inequalities to model this situation. Let x represent the number of pairs of mittens she will knit. Let y represent the number of hats.

  b. Give three solutions to this situation.

Review **PREVIEW**

Graph each inequality.   *(Section 8-6)*

11. $y \geq -5$

12. $3x + 2y < 18$

13. $y > \frac{4}{3}x - 3$

Find each unknown measure.   *(Section 6-7)*

14.

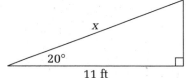

15.

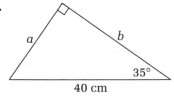

Estimate each square root within the range of two integers.   *(Section 2-9)*

16. $\sqrt{72}$

17. $\sqrt{128}$

18. $\sqrt{238}$

19. $\sqrt{0.75}$

Unit Check-Up	Complete these exercises for a review of Unit 8. If you have difficulty with a particular problem, review the indicated section.

For Exercises 1 and 2, do these things. *(Section 8-1)*

  a. Find the slope and the vertical intercept of each graph.

  b. Write an equation for each line.

  c. Tell whether each graph is an example of *linear growth* or *linear decay*.

1.
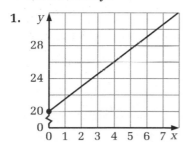

2.
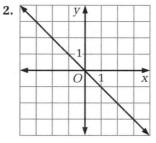

3. Annette starts with a package of 500 sheets of composition paper. She uses 10 sheets per day for her schoolwork. *(Section 8-1)*

  a. Model the situation with a graph.

  b. Find the slope and the vertical intercept of the line, and explain how they are related to the original situation.

  c. Model the situation with an equation.

  d. When will she have 400 sheets left?

For Exercises 4 and 5, do these things. *(Section 8-2)*

  a. Find the intercepts of the graph of the equation.

  b. Rewrite the equation in slope-intercept form.

  c. Graph the equation.

  4. $10x + 6y = 30$ **5.** $5x - 8y = 80$

6. At the Fine Arts Club bake sale, brownies sell for 50 cents each and cookies sell for 15 cents each. The club made a total of $33.45 on sales of cookies and brownies. *(Section 8-2)*

  a. Make a table of possible numbers of brownies and cookies sold. Let b = the number of brownies and c = the number of cookies.

  b. Model the situation with an equation.

  c. Graph the equation. Put the number of brownies on the horizontal axis.

  d. Explain why your graph should or should not cross either axis.

Graph each equation and find the slope of each line. *(Section 8-3)*

  7. $y = 5$ **8.** $2x + 10 = 0$

For Exercises 9–11, write an equation for each line. *(Section 8-4)*

  9. The slope is $-\frac{4}{9}$ and the point (18, 2) is on the line.

  10. The points (4, 8) and (−2, −6) are on the line.

  11. The horizontal intercept is −4 and the vertical intercept is 1.

12. In a thunderstorm, a few seconds elapse between the time you see a flash of lightning and the time you hear the thunder. (This is because sound does not travel as quickly as light.) This relationship can be used to determine the distance to the location where the lightning occurred. The table below gives some examples of this relationship. *(Section 8-4)*

time lag in s (t)	12	24	48
distance to lightning in mi (d)	2.5	5	10

    a. Model this data with an equation for d in terms of t.

    b. Use your model to approximate your distance from a lightning bolt if 15 s pass between the time you see the lightning and the time you hear the thunder.

For Exercises 13 and 14, use a graph to estimate the solution to the system of equations. *(Section 8-5)*

13. $y = 3x - 11$
    $2x + 3y = 0$

14. $y = x - 8$
    $x - 5y = -20$

Graph each inequality. *(Section 8-6)*

15. $3x + 2y \le 18$

16. $x > 6$

For Exercises 17 and 18, graph each system of inequalities. *(Section 8-7)*

17. $x + y \ge 9$
    $x - y \le 3$

18. $y < -2x - 2$
    $y > x + 6$

19. A pouch contains some nickels and dimes. The total value of the coins is at least $1.15. There are no more than 19 coins. *(Section 8-7)*

    a. Write a system of inequalities to model this situation. Let n = the number of nickels and let d = the number of dimes.

    b. Graph the system of inequalities.

    c. What is the greatest number of dimes that could possibly be in the pouch? the least number of dimes?

Spiral Review
Units 1–8

1. Find the square roots of 196.

2. Estimate $\sqrt{110}$ within a range of two integers.

3. Convert 0.04 m³ to cubic centimeters.

For Exercises 4 and 5, find the area of each figure.

4.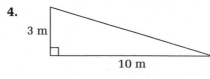

    3 m

    10 m

5.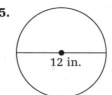

    12 in.

For Exercises 6–8, players spin the spinner at the right once. Find the theoretical probability for winning each amount.

6. less than 50¢

7. more than $2.50

8. 30¢

FOCUS

Investigate and use
the relationship
among the lengths
of the sides of a
right triangle and
recognize different
kinds of reasoning.

Before the new expressway from
downtown to the airport was
constructed, the trip from
downtown required a drive of
8 miles north and 7 miles west.
Taxi fares are \$1.25 for the first
$\frac{1}{4}$ mile and 20¢ for each

additional $\frac{1}{4}$ mile. You can use
the Pythagorean theorem to find
out how much you save in taxi
fares by taking the expressway.

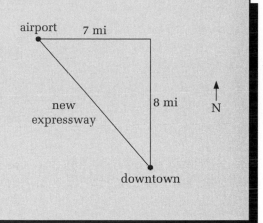

KEY TERMS

EXAMPLE / ILLUSTRATION

Inductive reasoning (p. 479)
   a process of making a general conjecture based on several
   particular examples

The sketches below show that a
triangle cannot be drawn that
has two right angles.

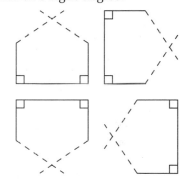

Deductive reasoning (p. 479)
   a process of proving a general conclusion by using facts,
   definitions, and accepted properties

The sum of the measures of the
angles of a triangle is 180°. If
both $\angle A$ and $\angle C$ in $\triangle ABC$ are
right angles, then $\angle B$ must
measure 0°. But this is not
possible. Therefore, by
deductive reasoning, a triangle
has at most one right angle.

UNDERSTANDING THE MAIN IDEAS

The Pythagorean theorem

In any right triangle, the square of the length of the hypotenuse is
equal to the sum of the squares of the lengths of the legs. In the
diagram, $AB^2 = BC^2 + AC^2$. It is common practice to label the
length of the hypotenuse as c and the length of the legs as a and b,
so the formula for the Pythagorean theorem is often stated as
$c^2 = a^2 + b^2$.

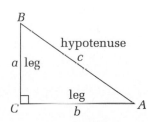

Sample 1

What is the length of the stairway shown in the diagram below?

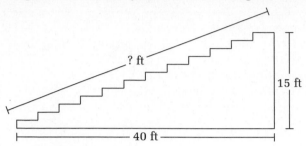

? ft

15 ft

40 ft

Sample Response

The length of the stairway represents the hypotenuse of a right triangle with legs of length 15 ft and 40 ft.

$c^2 = a^2 + b^2$ ← Use the Pythagorean theorem.
$c^2 = (15)^2 + (40)^2$ ← Substitute 15 and 40 for a and b.
$c^2 = 225 + 1600$
$c^2 = 1825$

$c = \sqrt{1825}$ ← Undo the squaring.
$c \approx 42.7$ ← Use a calculator to find the positive square root.

The length of the stairway is about 42.7 ft.

---

1. Which statements are true about right triangle ABC?

   a. $a^2 = b^2 + c^2$ **b.** $a^2 = c^2 - b^2$

   c. $c^2 = a^2 - b^2$ **d.** $a^2 + b^2 = c^2$

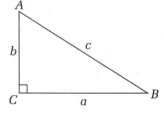

Find the missing length in each right triangle.

2.

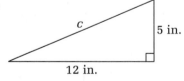

c

5 in.

12 in.

3.

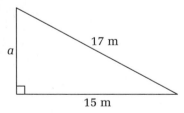

a

17 m

15 m

4.

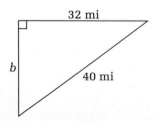

32 mi

b

40 mi

5.

40 ft

c

9 ft

Inductive and deductive reasoning

When you notice that a certain relationship is true in several specific examples and then decide that the relationship will always be true, you are using *inductive reasoning*. When you use known facts and definitions, along with assumed relationships, to show that something is true, then you are using *deductive reasoning*.

Sample 2

Suppose you look at the following chart in which the prime numbers are boxed and decide that *every* prime number greater than 2 is an odd number. What kind of reasoning are you using?

1	2	3	4	5	6	7	8	9	10
11	12	13	14	15	16	17	18	19	20
21	22	23	24	25	26	27	28	29	30
31	32	33	34	35	36	37	38	39	40
41	42	43	44	45	46	47	48	49	50

Sample Response

The reasoning is inductive, since the general conclusion that all prime numbers greater than 2 are odd is based on a group of specific examples.

Sample 3

Use deductive reasoning to prove that every prime number greater than 2 is an odd number.

Sample Response

A prime number is defined as a number that has exactly two factors, the number itself and 1. Every even number greater than 2 has at least three factors, the number itself and the numbers 1 and 2. Therefore, no even number greater than 2 can be a prime number. Thus, every prime number greater than 2 is an odd number.

6. Tyrone drew several pairs of intersecting lines and decided that the measures of pairs of opposite angles are always equal.

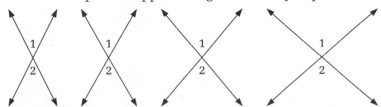

Did Tyrone use inductive or deductive reasoning?

7. Give a deductive proof which shows that Tyrone's conjecture is correct. (*Hint:* Label the angle between $\angle 1$ and $\angle 2$ as $\angle X$. Then use the idea that the sum of the measures of supplementary angles is 180°.)

Review **PREVIEW**

Graph each system. *(Sections 8-5, 8-7)*

8. $y = 3x$
$y = -2x - 5$

9. $3x + 2y \leq 3$
$y > -1$

For Exercises 10–13, find the square roots of each number. *(Section 2-9)*

10. 0.16 **11.** $\dfrac{4}{49}$ **12.** 81 **13.** 289

14. The area of a square is 225 in.^{2}. Find the length of a side of the square. *(Section 2-9)*

Investigating Properties of Square Roots

Simplify and
multiply square
roots and solve
equations like
$2x^2 = 36$.

The target at the right has an overall
diameter of 20 in. Suppose you want the
inner circle to be of a size such that if a
dart hits the target it is just as likely to
land in the shaded area as it is to land
in the inner circle. You can write an
equation involving x^2 to determine the
required radius of the inner circle.

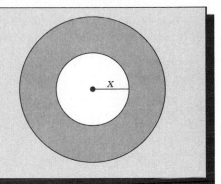

KEY TERMS

EXAMPLE / ILLUSTRATION

Radical form (p. 487)
an expression for the value of the square root of a number
that contains the √ (radical) symbol

The radical form $\sqrt{75}$ can be
simplified to $5\sqrt{3}$.

UNDERSTANDING THE MAIN IDEAS

Simplifying and multiplying square roots

Square roots of numbers can be multiplied and simplified by using the
following product properties of square roots.

For nonnegative numbers a and b:

$$\sqrt{ab} = \sqrt{a} \cdot \sqrt{b} \qquad \sqrt{a} \cdot \sqrt{b} = \sqrt{ab} \qquad \sqrt{a} \cdot \sqrt{a} = a$$

Sample 1

Simplify $\sqrt{48}$.

Sample Response

Method 1

$\sqrt{48} = \sqrt{4 \cdot 12}$ ← 4 is a perfect-square factor of 48; write 48 as the product of 4 and 12.

$= \sqrt{4} \cdot \sqrt{12}$ ← Use the property $\sqrt{ab} = \sqrt{a} \cdot \sqrt{b}$.

$= 2\sqrt{12}$ ← Write $\sqrt{4}$ as 2; $2\sqrt{12}$ means the same as $2 \cdot \sqrt{12}$.

$= 2\sqrt{4 \cdot 3}$ ← 4 is a perfect-square factor of 12.

$= 2\sqrt{4} \cdot \sqrt{3}$ ← Use the property $\sqrt{ab} = \sqrt{a} \cdot \sqrt{b}$ again.

$= 2 \cdot 2 \cdot \sqrt{3}$ ← Write $\sqrt{4}$ as 2.

$= 4\sqrt{3}$

Sample Response continues on the next page.

Method 2

$$\sqrt{48} = \sqrt{16 \cdot 3} \quad \longleftarrow \quad \text{16 is a perfect-square factor of 48.}$$
$$= \sqrt{16} \cdot \sqrt{3} \quad \longleftarrow \quad \text{Use the property } \sqrt{ab} = \sqrt{a} \cdot \sqrt{b}.$$
$$= 4\sqrt{3} \quad \longleftarrow \quad \text{Write } \sqrt{16} \text{ as 4.}$$

Sample 2

Simplify $\sqrt{32} \cdot 2\sqrt{2}$.

Sample Response

$$\sqrt{32} \cdot 2\sqrt{2} = 2 \cdot \sqrt{32} \cdot \sqrt{2} \quad \longleftarrow \quad \text{Group the radical factors.}$$
$$= 2 \cdot \sqrt{32 \cdot 2} \quad \longleftarrow \quad \text{Use the property } \sqrt{a} \cdot \sqrt{b} = \sqrt{ab}.$$
$$= 2 \cdot \sqrt{64}$$
$$= 2 \cdot 8 \quad \longleftarrow \quad \text{Write } \sqrt{64} \text{ as 8.}$$
$$= 16$$

Simplify.

1. $\sqrt{200}$ **2.** $\sqrt{99}$ **3.** $\sqrt{20} \cdot 5\sqrt{2}$ **4.** $2\sqrt{6} \cdot 2\sqrt{10}$

Solving equations like $2x^2 = 36$

To solve an equation involving x^2, such as $2x^2 = 36$, first get the x^2-term by itself on one side of the equation. After dividing both sides by the coefficient of x^2, you undo the squaring. Keep in mind that such equations have two solutions, one positive and one negative, although only the positive solution may make sense in the given situation.

Sample 3

Find the length of the diagonal of the rectangle in terms of x. Simplify your answer.

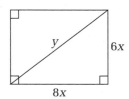

Sample Response

$$(8x)^2 + (6x)^2 = y^2 \quad \longleftarrow \quad \text{Use the Pythagorean theorem.}$$
$$64x^2 + 36x^2 = y^2 \quad \longleftarrow \quad \text{Square the 8 and the 6 as well as the } x\text{'s.}$$
$$100x^2 = y^2 \quad \longleftarrow \quad \text{Combine like terms.}$$
$$\sqrt{100x^2} = y \quad \longleftarrow \quad \text{Undo the squaring; since } y \text{ is a length,}$$
$$\text{use only the positive square root.}$$
$$\sqrt{100} \cdot \sqrt{x^2} = y \quad \longleftarrow \quad \text{Use the property } \sqrt{ab} = \sqrt{a} \cdot \sqrt{b}.$$
$$10x = y \quad \longleftarrow \quad \text{Write } \sqrt{100} \text{ as 10; write } \sqrt{x^2} \text{ as } x.$$

The length of the diagonal is $10x$.

For Exercises 5–7, solve for x.

5. $3x^2 = 36$ **6.** $157 = 3.14x^2$ **7.** $4^2 + 5^2 = x^2$

8. Find the length of the diagonal of a square in radical form.
Let $s = $ the length of a side of the square.

Review **PREVIEW**

In Exercises 9–12, find the missing length in each right triangle.
(Section 9-1)

9.

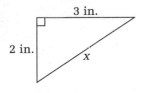

10.

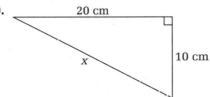

11.

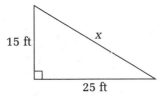

12.

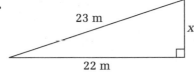

13. The vertices of a triangle are $A(-2, -1)$, $B(1, 3)$, and $C(4, 0)$. Draw a dilation of $\triangle ABC$ with center $A(-2, -1)$ and scale factor 3.   *(Section 6-6)*

Solve.   *(Sections 5-2, 5-6)*

14. $0 = \dfrac{3}{4}x$ **15.** $5 - 5x = 0$ **16.** $2x + 30 = 0$

If-Then Statements and Converses

FOCUS

Write if-then statements and their converses and determine whether they are true or false.

The following are examples of IF...THEN statements that might be used in a BASIC program on a computer.

IF A ∧ 2 + B ∧ 2 = C ∧ 2 THEN PRINT "RT TRI"

IF B ∧ 2 − 4 * A * C >= 0 THEN GO TO SQR(D)

IF X > 10 THEN END

For each of these statements, when the IF clause is true, the THEN part will be carried out. When the IF clause is not true, the computer proceeds to the next statement in the program. Can you describe what happens when the IF clause of each statement is true?

KEY TERMS

EXAMPLE / ILLUSTRATION

KEY TERMS	EXAMPLE / ILLUSTRATION
If-then statements (p. 492) statements containing an *if* clause and a *then* clause	If a figure is a square, then it is a rectangle.
Conditional statements (p. 492) if-then statements	The conditional statement "All squares are rectangles." is equivalent to the if-then statement "If a figure is a square, then it is a rectangle."
Hypothesis (p. 492) the *if* part of a conditional statement	The hypothesis of the if-then statement above is "A figure is a square."
Conclusion (p. 492) the *then* part of a conditional statement	The conclusion of the if-then statement above is "It is a rectangle."
Converse (p. 494) a statement formed by interchanging the *if* and *then* clauses of a conditional statement	The converse of the if-then statement "If a figure is a square, then it is a rectangle." is "If a figure is a rectangle, then it is a square." (*Note:* This converse statement is false.)

UNDERSTANDING THE MAIN IDEAS

If-then statements and their converses

If-then statements are common in mathematics and in everyday life. If-then statements have two parts, a hypothesis, which is the *if* part, and a conclusion, which is the *then* part. An if-then statement can be either true or false. You can show that a conditional statement is false by giving a counterexample in which the hypothesis is satisfied, but the conclusion is not true. The converse of an if-then statement is formed by interchanging the hypothesis and the conclusion. The converse must be checked independently to determine whether it is true or false.

Sample 1

Identify the hypothesis and conclusion of each conditional statement.
a. If you are a registered voter, then you are 18 years old.
b. If a number is odd, then its square is odd.

Sample Response

a. hypothesis: You are a registered voter.   conclusion: You are 18 years old.
b. hypothesis: A number is odd.   conclusion: Its square is odd.

Sample 2

Use the two statements given in Sample 1.
a. Tell whether each statement is *True* or *False*. If the statement is false, give a counterexample.
b. Write the converse of each statement. Tell whether the converse is *True* or *False*. If it is false, give a counterexample.

Sample Response

a. Statement (a) is false; a registered voter can be any age over 18 also.
   Statement (b) is true.

b. The converse of statement (a) is "If you are 18 years old, then you are a registered voter." The converse is false, since only about 70% of the people over 18 are registered to vote. Any one of the other 30% provide a counterexample.

   The converse of statement (b) is "If the square of a number is odd, then the number is an odd number." The converse is true.

For Exercises 1–6, do these things.
  a. Identify the hypothesis and the conclusion of each statement.
  b. Tell whether the statement is *True* or *False*. If it is false, give a counterexample.
  c. Write the converse of the statement.
  d. Tell whether the converse is *True* or *False*. If it is false, give a counterexample.

1. If the product of two numbers is positive, then both numbers are positive.

2. If a figure is a rectangle, it is a parallelogram.

3. If $3x + 5 = 11$, then $x = 2$.

4. If it is impossible for an event to happen, then the probability of the event is 0.

5. If a number is divisible by 8, then it is divisible by 4.

6. The sum of two numbers is a negative number if both numbers are negative.

Two important converses

From arithmetic, you know that the product of any number and zero is zero. This property of numbers can be stated as:

If $a = 0$ or $b = 0$, then $ab = 0$.

The converse of this conditional statement is true, and is useful for solving equations. The converse is called the *zero-product property*:

If $ab = 0$, then $a = 0$ or $b = 0$.

Another useful converse is the converse of the Pythagorean theorem. Recall that the Pythagorean theorem can be stated as:

If $\triangle ABC$ is a right triangle, then $c^2 = a^2 + b^2$.

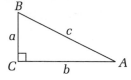

The converse of the Pythagorean theorem is true and can be used to determine if a triangle is a right triangle when you know the lengths of its sides. In $\triangle ABC$ if $a^2 + b^2 = c^2$, then $\triangle ABC$ is a right triangle.

Sample 3

Solve $3x(x - 2) = 0$.

Sample Response

$3x(x - 2) = 0$

$3x = 0$ or $x - 2 = 0$ ⟵ Use the zero-product property.

First solve $3x = 0$:

$3x = 0$

$\dfrac{3x}{3} = \dfrac{0}{3}$

$x = 0$

Now solve $x - 2 = 0$:

$x - 2 = 0$

$x - 2 + 2 = 0 + 2$ ⟵ Add 2 to both sides.

$x = 2$

The solutions are $x = 0$ and $x = 2$.

Solve.

7. $m(2m - 3) = 0$ **8.** $a(a - 5) = 0$ **9.** $3s(2 - s) = 0$

Sample 4

Is $\triangle ABC$ a right triangle?

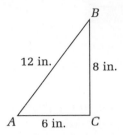

Sample Response

If $\triangle ABC$ is a right triangle, then the hypotenuse is the longest side, $\overline{AB}$.
Use the converse of the Pythagorean theorem:

$c^2 \overset{?}{=} a^2 + b^2$

$12^2 \overset{?}{=} 8^2 + 6^2$ ← Substitute 12 for c, and 8 and 6 for a and b.

$144 \overset{?}{=} 64 + 36$

$144 \neq 100$

Since $c^2 \neq a^2 + b^2$, $\triangle ABC$ is *not* a right triangle.

In Exercises 10 and 11, the lengths of the sides of a triangle are given. Is the triangle a right triangle? Use the converse of the Pythagorean theorem to justify your answer.

10. 8 ft, 14 ft, 17 ft

11. 40 km, 9 km, 41 km

Review

Simplify. *(Section 9-2)*

12. $\sqrt{162}$

13. $2\sqrt{6} \cdot \sqrt{8}$

14. $5\sqrt{10} \cdot 3\sqrt{15}$

A die is rolled. Find each probability. *(Section 6-2)*

15. $P\left(\boxed{\,\cdot\,} \text{ or } \boxed{\,\cdot\,\cdot}\right)$

16. $P(\text{number} \leq 6)$

17. $P\left(\text{not } \boxed{\,\cdot\cdot\,\cdot\cdot}\right)$

9-4 Geometric Probability

FOCUS

Use lengths and areas to determine theoretical geometric probabilities.

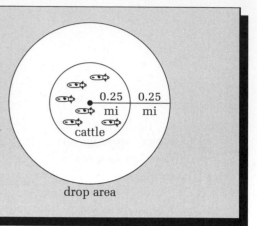

Bales of hay are to be dropped from an airplane by parachute to cattle stranded by a blizzard. The cattle are clustered together within the inner circle of the drop area shown at the right. The probability that a bale of hay will land within the circular region where the cattle are located can be found by comparing the area of the small circle to the area of the large circle.

drop area

KEY TERMS

Geometric probability (p. 502)
   probability based on areas and lengths

EXAMPLE / ILLUSTRATION

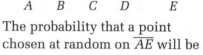

The probability that a point chosen at random on $\overline{AE}$ will be on $\overline{BC}$ is $\dfrac{\text{length of } \overline{BC}}{\text{length of } \overline{AE}} = \dfrac{2}{9}$.

UNDERSTANDING THE MAIN IDEAS

Theoretical geometric probability

You can use what you know about probability as the ratio of successful outcomes to possible outcomes to find probabilities related to areas and lengths of geometric figures.

Sample I

Actors trying out for roles in a play are randomly assigned 20-min time slots between the hours of 1:00 P.M. and 4:00 P.M. What is the probability that an actor will be assigned the time slot from 2:20 P.M. to 2:40 P.M.?

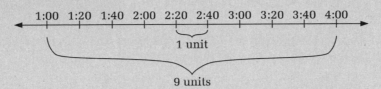
Sample 2

In the situation about the stranded cattle described on the previous page, what is the probability that a bale of hay will land within the region where the cattle are clustered?

Sample Response

Make a sketch. Use the formula $A = \pi r^2$ to find the areas of the two circles. The probability is the ratio of the two areas.

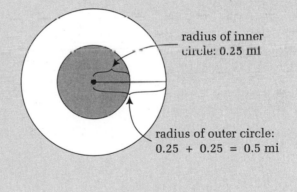

radius of inner circle: 0.25 mi

radius of outer circle: 0.25 + 0.25 = 0.5 mi

$$\text{probability} = \frac{\text{area of inner circle}}{\text{area of outer circle}}$$

$$= \frac{\pi(0.25)^2}{\pi(0.5)^2}$$

$$= \frac{0.0625}{0.25}$$

$$= \frac{1}{4}$$

For each bale of hay, the probability of landing within the region where the cattle are clustered is $\frac{1}{4}$.

1. Which would be greater, the probability that a point chosen at random from each square is in the shaded region in square **A** or in the shaded region in square **B**?

   A.

   B.

2. Mita does her homework between 4:30 P.M. and 6:00 P.M. each day. She usually spends 30 min completing her math assignment. If she receives a phone call during her homework time, what is the probability that she will be working on math?

3. What is the probability that a mosquito flying at random against this screen will enter through the triangular tear in the screen?

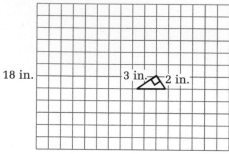

18 in.

3 in. 2 in.

24 in.

4. The numbers in a calculator display are formed by lighting up various segments of the array shown at the right. If you enter a digit at random, what is the probability that segment *d* will be lit? (*Hint:* Check your calculator to see which segments are lit for each digit.)

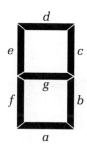

d

e   *c*

g

f   *b*

a

Review **PREVIEW**

5. a. Write the converse of the statement "If $\sqrt{12} = x$, then $12 = x^2$."

b. Tell whether the converse is *True* or *False*. If it is false, find a counterexample. *(Section 9-3)*

6. Suppose a figure is a regular triangle. What are three things you know about the figure? *(Sections 2-5, 5-7, 6-5)*

Give each formula. *(Sections 5-7, 7-6)*

7. area of a trapezoid

8. area of a circle

9-5 Surface Area of Space Figures

FOCUS

Find the surface area of prisms, cylinders, and pyramids.

A store manager is planning to shrink-wrap packages of three VCR tapes for a special sale. The manager wants to know how much plastic material is needed to shrink-wrap 100 packages of tapes. The manager will need to find the surface area of a stack of three tapes in order to know how much plastic is needed per package.

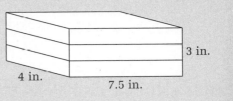

3 in.

4 in. 7.5 in.

KEY TERMS

EXAMPLE / ILLUSTRATION

KEY TERMS	EXAMPLE / ILLUSTRATION
Prism (p. 507) a space figure with two congruent, parallel polygons called bases (The other sides of the prism are called faces.)	
Bases of a prism (p. 507) the two congruent, parallel polygonal sides of a prism	The bases of the prism shown above are the two congruent triangular sides.
Faces of a prism (p. 507) the sides of a prism that are not bases	The faces of the prism shown above are the three rectangular sides.
Cylinder (p. 508) a space figure with a curved surface and two congruent, parallel bases that are circles	
Pyramid (p. 509) a space figure with a polygon as its one base and triangular faces	
Regular pyramid (p. 509) a pyramid whose base is a regular polygon and whose other faces are congruent isosceles triangles	
Height of a regular pyramid (p. 510) the length of the perpendicular segment from the vertex to the center of the base	height

Slant height of a regular pyramid (p. 510)
the height of any one of the congruent triangular faces of a regular pyramid

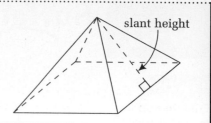
slant height

UNDERSTANDING THE MAIN IDEAS

Surface area of a prism

The surface area of a prism is found by using the formula

Surface Area (S.A.) = area of two bases + areas of faces.

Since the bases are congruent, both bases have the same area. If the bases are triangles, the prism has three rectangular faces; if the bases are rectangles, the prism has four rectangular faces; and so on. Surface area is measured in square units.

Sample 1

All the sides of this trapezoidal prism are to be covered in red felt. How many square yards of felt are needed?

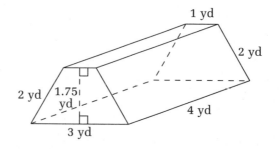

Sample Response

Use the formula S.A. = area of two bases + area of faces.

Step 1 Find the area of the two bases.

The bases are congruent trapezoids with bases 1 yd and 3 yd long, and height 1.75 yd. Use the formula for the area of a trapezoid to find the area of each congruent base.

$A = \frac{1}{2}(b_1 + b_2)h$

$= \frac{1}{2}(1 + 3)1.75$ ⟵── Substitute for b_1, b_2, and h.

$= 3.5$

Now, multiply by 2 to find the area of both bases: $2 \times 3.5 = 7$ yd^2.

Step 2 Find the area of the faces.

There are four rectangular faces.

Two of the faces are 4 yd-by-2 yd rectangles: $A = 2(4 \times 2) = 16$ yd^2.
One of the other faces is a 1 yd-by-4 yd rectangle: $A = 1 \times 4 = 4$ yd^2.
The remaining face is a 3 yd-by-4 yd rectangle: $A = 3 \times 4 = 12$ yd^2.

Now, add to find the total area of all four faces: $16 + 4 + 12 = 32$ yd^2.

Sample Response continues on the next page.

Sample Response continues on the next page.

Step 3 Find the total area.

Substitute the results from steps 1 and 2 into the formula
S.A. = area of two bases + area of faces.

S.A. = 7 + 32 = 39 yd²

A total of 39 yd² of felt are needed to cover the prism.

Identify each type of prism and find its surface area.

1.
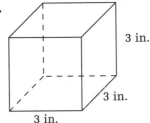

3 in.

3 in.

3 in.

2.
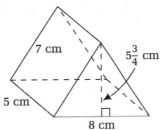

7 cm

$5\frac{3}{4}$ cm

5 cm

8 cm

Surface area of a cylinder

The surface area of a cylinder is found by using the formula

   Surface Area = area of two circular bases + area of curved surface
         S.A. = $2\pi r^2 + 2\pi rh$.

In the formula, the expression for the area of the curved surface is found by noting that the curved surface could be "flattened out" to form a rectangle with length equal to the circumference of the circular base, $2\pi r$, and width equal to the height of the cylinder, h. As for prisms, the surface area of a cylinder is measured in square units.

Sample 2

Find the surface area of the half cylinder shown below.

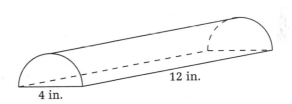

12 in.

4 in.

Sample Response

Step 1 Find the area of the curved surface and the two half-circle bases.

Use the formula for the surface area of a cylinder. Because you are finding the surface area of a half cylinder, divide both sides of the formula by 2.

$$\frac{S.A.}{2} = \frac{2\pi r^2 + 2\pi rh}{2}$$

$$= \pi r^2 + \pi rh$$

Since the diameter of the half cylinder is 4 in., the radius is 4 ÷ 2 = 2 in.

$$\frac{S.A.}{2} = \pi(2)^2 + \pi(2)(12) \quad \longleftarrow \text{ Substitute 2 for } r \text{ and 12 for } h.$$

$$= 4\pi + 24\pi$$

$$= 28\pi$$

$$\approx 88 \text{ in.}^2$$

Sample Response continues on the next page.

INTEGRATED MATHEMATICS 1 **Study Guide**

Step 2 Find the area of the flat surface.

The flat surface is a 4 in.-by-12 in. rectangle.

$A = 4 \times 12$

$\quad = 48 \text{ in.}^2$

Step 3 Find the total area.

Add the areas found in steps 1 and 2.

S.A. $\approx 88 + 48 \approx 136 \text{ in.}^2$

The surface area of the half cylinder is about 136 in.^{2}.

Find the surface area of each cylinder or half cylinder.

3.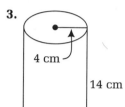

4.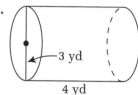

5.

Surface area of a pyramid

The surface area of a pyramid is found by using the formula

S.A. = area of base + area of faces.

In a regular pyramid, all the faces are congruent isosceles triangles, so you need only find the area of one face and then multiply by the number of faces to find the total area of the faces. As for prisms and cylinders, surface area is measured in square units.

Sample 3

Find the surface area of this regular triangular pyramid.

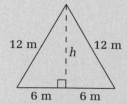

Sample Response

Use the formula S.A. = area of base + area of faces.

Step 1 Find the area of the base.

Since the pyramid is a regular triangular pyramid, the base is an equilateral triangle. First, you need to find the height of the base. (*Note:* The height of an equilateral triangle divides the side to which it is drawn in half, as shown in the figure.)

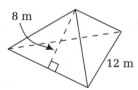

Sample Response continues on the next page.

By the Pythagorean theorem,

$$6^2 + h^2 = 12^2$$
$$36 + h^2 = 144$$
$$h^2 = 108$$
$$h \approx 10.4 \text{ m}$$

Now use the formula for the area of a triangle to find the area of the base.

$$A = \frac{1}{2}bh$$

$\approx \frac{1}{2}(12)(10.4)$ ◄──── Substitute 12 for b and 10.4 for h.

$\approx 62.4 \text{ m}^2$

Step 2 Find the area of the faces.

The base and height of each of the three congruent triangular faces are 12 m and 8 m, respectively. Use the formula for the area of a triangle to find the area of each congruent face.

$$A = \frac{1}{2}bh$$

$= \frac{1}{2}(12)(8)$ ◄──── Substitute 12 for b and 8 for h.

$= 48 \text{ m}^2$

Now multiply by 3 to find the area of all three faces.
$$A = 3 \times 48 = 144 \text{ m}^2$$

Step 3 Find the total area.
Add the areas found in steps 1 and 2.
S.A. $\approx 62.4 + 144 \approx 206.4 \text{ m}^2$

The surface area of the regular triangular pyramid is about 206.4 m².

Find the surface area of each regular pyramid.

6.

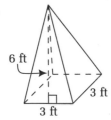

6 ft

3 ft

3 ft

7.

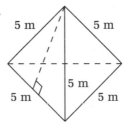

5 m   5 m

5 m

5 m   5 m

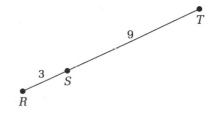

Review **PREVIEW**

For Exercises 8–10, suppose a point on $\overline{RT}$ is picked at random. Find the probability that the point is on each segment named. *(Section 9-4)*

8. $\overline{ST}$ **9.** $\overline{RS}$ **10.** $\overline{RT}$

11. Sketch a parallelogram. To find the area of your parallelogram, what dimensions do you need to know? *(Section 5-7)*

Find the volume of each box. *(Toolbox Skill 19)*

12. a box with length 12 in., width 7 in., and height 10 in.

13. a box with length 6 cm, width 6 cm, and height 5 cm

   INTEGRATED MATHEMATICS 1 **Study Guide**   **227**

Volumes of Prisms and Cylinders

FOCUS

Find the volume
of prisms and
cylinders.

The volume of the prism shown at the right is 1000 cm³, which is equivalent to 1 liter. How could you determine the diameter of a 1-liter cylindrical container that is 10 cm tall?

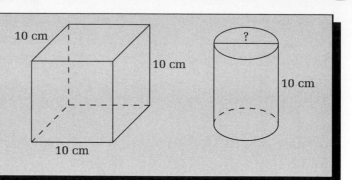

UNDERSTANDING THE MAIN IDEAS

Volume of a prism

The volume of a prism is found by
multiplying the area of the base by
the height of the prism.

Volume of a prism = area of base × height

$$V = Bh$$

Volume is measured in cubic units.

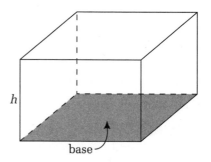

Sample 1

Find the volume of the triangular prism
shown at the right.

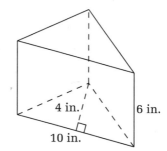

Sample Response

Use the formula $V = Bh$.

Step 1 Find the area of the base.

Since the base is a triangle, use the formula for the area of a triangle.

$A = \frac{1}{2}bh$

$= \frac{1}{2}(10)(4)$ ⟵ Substitute 10 for b and 4 for h.

$= 20$ in.²

The area of the base of the prism is 20 in.².

Sample Response continues on the next page.

Step 2 Find the volume of the prism.

$V = Bh$ Substitute 20 for B and 6 for h. (*Caution:* In
   $= (20)(6)$ ←   the volume formula, use the height of the
   $= 120$ in.^{3} prism, *not* the height of the triangular base.)

The volume of the prism is 120 in.^{3}.

Find the volume of each prism.

1.

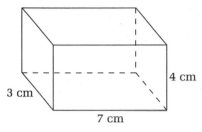

2.

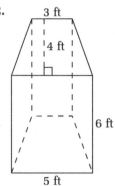

Sample 2

The volume of the trapezoidal
prism shown at the right is 1944 ft^3.
Find the height, h, of the prism.

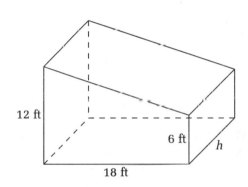

Sample Response

Use the formula $V = Bh$.

Step 1 Find the base area, B.

The dimensions of the
trapezoidal bases are given.
Use the formula for
the area of a trapezoid.

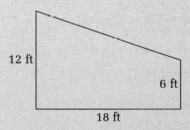

$A = \frac{1}{2}(b_1 + b_2)h$ ←   The variable h in this formula is the height
                  of the base, *not* the height of the prism.

   $= \frac{1}{2}(12 + 6)18$ ←   Substitute 12 for b_1, 6 for b_2, and 18 for h.

   $= \frac{1}{2}(18)18$

   $= 162$ ft^2

Sample Response continues on the next page.

    INTEGRATED MATHEMATICS 1 **Study Guide** **229**

Step 2 Substitute the known values in the volume formula.

$$V = Bh$$
$$1944 = 162h \quad \longleftarrow \text{ Substitute 1944 for } V \text{ and 162 for } B.$$
$$\frac{1944}{162} = \frac{162h}{162}$$
$$12 = h$$

The height of the prism is 12 ft.

Find the missing dimension h.

3.

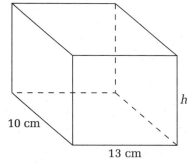

10 cm

13 cm

Volume $= 1430 \text{ cm}^3$

4.

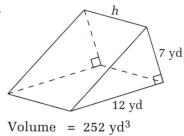

h

7 yd

12 yd

Volume $= 252 \text{ yd}^3$

Volume of a cylinder

The volume of a cylinder can also be found by using the formula $V = Bh$. For a cylinder, the value of B is the area of *one* of the circular bases, πr^2. As for a prism, the volume of a cylinder is measured in cubic units.

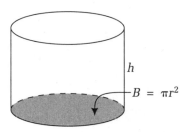

h

$B = \pi r^2$

Sample 3

Find the volume of the cylinder shown at the right.

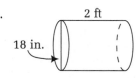

2 ft

18 in.

Sample Response

Use the formula $V = Bh$.

Step 1 Change all dimensions to inches: $h = 24$ in.

Step 2 Find the area of the base.

Use the formula for the area of a circle to find the area of a base. Since the diameter of the circular base is 18 in., the radius is $18 \div 2 = 9$ in.

$$A = \pi r^2$$
$$= \pi(9)^2 \quad \longleftarrow \text{ Substitute 9 for } r.$$
$$= \pi(81)$$
$$\approx 254.5 \text{ in.}^2$$

Sample Response continues on the next page.

> **Step 3** Find the volume of the cylinder.
>
> $V = Bh$
> $\approx 254.5(24)$ ⟵ Substitute 254.5 for B and 24 for h.
> ≈ 6108.0 in.^{3}
>
> The volume of the cylinder is about 6108.0 in.^{3}.

Find the volume of each cylinder.

5.

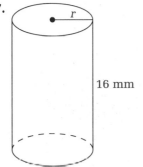

1.4 m

3 m

6.

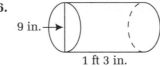

9 in.→

1 ft 3 in.

Find the missing dimension.

7.

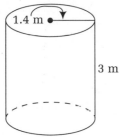

r

16 mm

Volume $\approx$ 1256.6 mm^3

8.

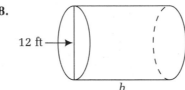

12 ft→

h

Volume $\approx$ 1809.6 ft^3

Review **PREVIEW**

For Exercises 9 and 10, identify each space figure and find the surface area. *(Section 9-5)*

9.

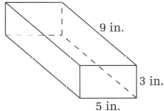

9 in.

3 in.

5 in.

10.

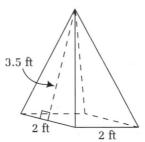

3.5 ft

2 ft   2 ft

11. Convert 60 mi/h to feet per second. *(Section 7-5)*

12. The height and the length of a side of the base of the regular square pyramid at the right are labeled. Find the slant height, s, of the pyramid. *(Sections 9-1, 9-5)*

13. Two points on a line are (−3, 1) and (0, 7). Write an equation for the line. *(Section 8-4)*

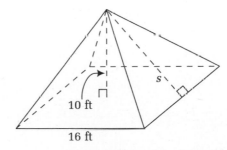

s

10 ft

16 ft

Volumes of Pyramids and Cones

Find the volume of pyramids and cones.

When surf-fishing in the ocean from the beach, a fisherman uses special pyramid-shaped weights on his line to keep the waves from dragging his bait back to shore. He must choose a weight whose size and shape are appropriate for the surf conditions. The companies that manufacture these weights use the formula for the volume of a pyramid to determine the amount of metal needed to produce each weight.

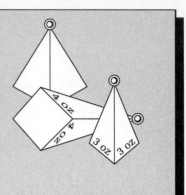

KEY TERMS

EXAMPLE / ILLUSTRATION

Cone (p. 524)
a space figure with one circular base and a vertex

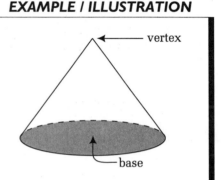

vertex

base

UNDERSTANDING THE MAIN IDEAS

Volume of a pyramid

The volume of a pyramid is $\frac{1}{3}$ the volume of a prism that has the same base area and the same height.

Volume of a pyramid $= \frac{1}{3} \times$ area of base $\times$ height of the pyramid

$$V = \frac{1}{3}Bh$$

The volume is measured in cubic units.

Sample 1

A pyramid has a square base 240 in. long on each side and a height of 160 in. Find the volume of the pyramid.

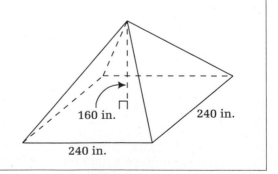

160 in.

240 in.

240 in.

Use the formula $V = \frac{1}{3}Bh$.

Step 1 Find B, the area of the square base.
Use the formula for the area of a square.

$A = s^2$
   $= (240)^2$ ⟵ Substitute 240 for s.
   $= 57,600$ in.^{2}

Step 2 Find the volume.

$V = \frac{1}{3}Bh$

   $= \frac{1}{3}(57,600)(160)$ ⟵ Substitute 57,600 for B and 160 for h.

   $= 3,072,000$ in.^{3}

The volume of the pyramid is $3,072,000$ in.^{3}.

Find the volume of each pyramid.

1.
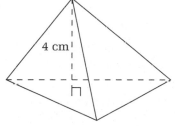

4 cm

$B = 6.02$ cm^2

2.
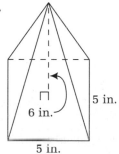

5 in.

6 in.

5 in.

Volume of a cone

The volume of a cone is $\frac{1}{3}$ the volume of a cylinder that has the same base area and the same height.

   Volume of a cone $= \frac{1}{3} \times$ area of base $\times$ height of cone

               $V = \frac{1}{3}Bh$

The volume is measured in cubic units.

Sample 2

Find the volume of this cone-shaped drinking cup.

7 cm

7 cm

Use the formula for the volume of a cone.

Step 1 Find B, the area of the circular base.

Use the formula for the area of a circle. Since the diameter of the circular base is 7 cm, the radius is $7 \div 2 = 3.5$ cm.

$A = \pi r^2$
$\quad = \pi(3.5)^2$ ⟵ Substitute 3.5 for r.
$\quad \approx 38.5$ cm^2

Step 2 Find the volume.

$V = \frac{1}{3}Bh$

$\quad \approx \frac{1}{3}(38.5)7$ ⟵ Substitute 38.5 for B and 7 for h.

$\quad \approx 89.8$ cm^3

The volume of the drinking cup is about 89.8 cm^3.

Find the volume of each cone.

3.
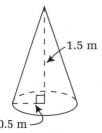
1.5 m
0.5 m

4.
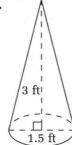
3 ft
1.5 ft

Review **PREVIEW**

Name the space figure and find the volume. *(Section 9-6)*

5.
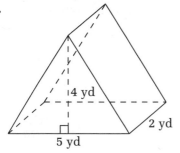
4 yd
2 yd
5 yd

6.
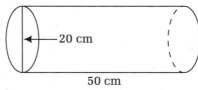
20 cm
50 cm

For Exercises 7–9, polygon *ABCDEF* ~ polygon *PQRSTU*. *(Section 6-5)*

7. What is the scale factor between the polygons?

8. Find BC.

9. Find ST.

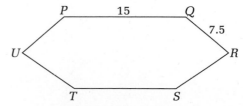

A 6 B
F   C
E 5 D

P   15   Q
                    7.5
U   R
T   S

10. Solve the proportion $\dfrac{x^2}{9} = \dfrac{64}{81}$.

(Sections 6-3, 9-2)

Similar Figures: Area and Volume

FOCUS

Use ratios of corresponding lengths, areas, and volumes in similar figures.

The top container shown at the right holds 1 pint of frozen yogurt. The bottom container holds 1 quart of frozen yogurt. Notice that the dimensions of the containers are not doubled in order to double the volume. (Recall that 1 quart = 2 pints.) Instead, they are multiplied by a factor equal to the cube root of 2, $\sqrt[3]{2}$, which is about 1.26.

5 cm

10 cm

10 cm

6.3 cm

12.6 cm

12.6 cm

KEY TERMS

Similar space figures (p. 532)
    figures that have the same shape but not necessarily the same size

EXAMPLE / ILLUSTRATION

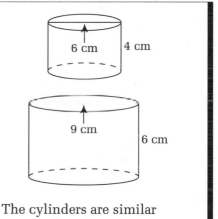

6 cm   4 cm

9 cm   6 cm

The cylinders are similar because $\frac{6}{9} = \frac{4}{6}$.

UNDERSTANDING THE MAIN IDEAS

Areas of similar polygons

When the ratio of corresponding side lengths for two similar polygons is $a : b$, then the ratio of their areas is $a^2 : b^2$.

The ratio of corresponding side lengths for the similar rectangles shown at the right is $\frac{5}{10} = \frac{4}{8} = \frac{1}{2}$. The ratio of their areas is $\frac{20}{80} = \frac{1}{4} = \frac{1^2}{2^2}$. (Notice that doubling the dimensions multiplies the area by $2^2 = 4$.)

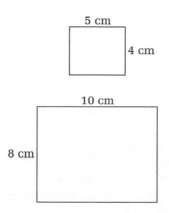

5 cm

4 cm

10 cm

8 cm

Sample 1

Parallelogram $PQRS$ ~ parallelogram $WXYZ$.

a. Find the ratio of the areas of the
two parallelograms.

b. If the area of parallelogram $PQRS$
is 50 in.^{2}, what is the area of
parallelogram $WXYZ$?

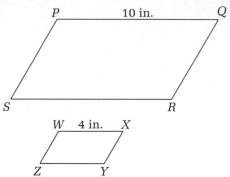

Sample Response

a. Ratio of lengths of corresponding sides: $\dfrac{PQ}{WX} = \dfrac{10}{4} = \dfrac{5}{2}$

The ratio of the areas is found by squaring the terms of the ratio of
corresponding side lengths.

Ratio of areas: $\dfrac{5^2}{2^2} = \dfrac{25}{4}$

b. Use the ratio of areas from part (a) and the area of parallelogram
$PQRS$ to find the area of parallelogram $WXYZ$. Let $x =$ the area of
parallelogram $WXYZ$.

$\dfrac{\text{area of parallelogram } PQRS}{\text{area of parallelogram } WXYZ} \colon \dfrac{50}{x} = \dfrac{25}{4}$ ⟵ *Caution:* Be sure to keep the corresponding terms of the ratios in the correct order.

Solve the proportion for x.

$$\dfrac{50}{x} = \dfrac{25}{4}$$
$25x = 4(50)$ ⟵ Use cross products.
$25x = 200$
$$\dfrac{25x}{25} = \dfrac{200}{25}$$
$x = 8$

The area of parallelogram $WXYZ$ is 8 in.^{2}.

**Find the ratio of the areas of each pair of similar figures. Then find the
missing area.**

1.
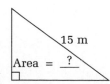

10 m
Area
= 24 m^2

15 m
Area = __?__

2.
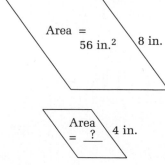

Area =
56 in.^{2} 8 in.

Area
= __?__   4 in.

3.
Area =
24 cm^2

6 cm

Area = __?__

15 cm

Volumes of similar space figures

When the ratio of corresponding lengths for two similar space figures is $a : b$, then the ratio of their volumes is $a^3 : b^3$.

The ratio of corresponding lengths for the cubes (all cubes are similar) shown at the right is $\frac{7}{14} = \frac{1}{2}$. The ratio of their volumes is $\frac{7^3}{14^3} = \frac{343}{2744} = \frac{1}{8} = \frac{1^3}{2^3}$. (Notice that doubling the dimensions multiplies the volume by $2^3 = 8$.)

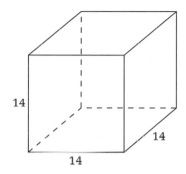

Sample 2

The two cylinders shown at the right are similar.

a. Find the ratio of the volumes of the two cylinders.

b. If the volume of cylinder A is 2π in.^{3}, what is the volume of cylinder B?

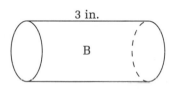

Sample Response

a. Ratio of corresponding lengths: $\frac{2}{3}$

The ratio of the volumes is found by cubing the terms of the ratio of corresponding lengths.

Ratio of volumes: $\frac{2^3}{3^3} = \frac{8}{27}$

b. Use the ratio of volumes from part (a) and the volume of cylinder A to find the volume of cylinder B. Let $x =$ the volume of cylinder B.

$\dfrac{\text{volume of cylinder A}}{\text{volume of cylinder B}} : \dfrac{2\pi}{x} = \dfrac{8}{27}$ ← *Caution:* Be sure to keep the corresponding terms of the ratios in the correct order.

$\dfrac{2\pi}{x} = \dfrac{8}{27}$

$8x = 54\pi$ ← Use cross products.

$\dfrac{8x}{8} = \dfrac{54\pi}{8}$

$x = 6.75\pi$

The volume of cylinder B is 6.75π in.^{3}.

Find the ratio of the volumes of each pair of similar space figures. Then
find the missing volume. In Exercises 5 and 6, leave your answers
in terms of π.

4.

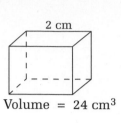

2 cm

4 cm

Volume = 24 cm³

Volume = __?__

5.

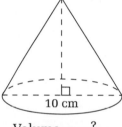

6 ft

5 ft

Volume = 54π ft³

Volume = __?__

6.

10 cm

4 cm

Volume = 8π cm³

Volume = __?__

7.

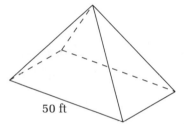

20 ft

50 ft

Volume = __?__

Volume = 25,000 ft³

Review **PREVIEW**

8. Find the volume of a square pyramid with height
18 cm and base length 22 cm. *(Section 9-7)*

9. a. What are the coordinates of the vertices
of pentagon *RSTUV*? *(Section 4-2)*

b. What is the line of symmetry? *(Section 1-7)*

c. Translate pentagon *RSTUV* 3 units to the left
and 2 units down. What are the coordinates of
the image *R'S'T'U'V'*? *(Section 4-3)*

d. Rotate pentagon *RSTUV* 90° counterclockwise
about the origin. What are the coordinates of the
vertices of the image *R"S"T"U"V"*?
(Section 4-4)

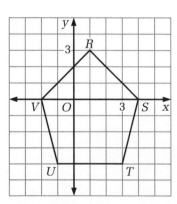

Unit Check-Up

Complete these exercises for a review of Unit 9. If you have difficulty with a particular problem, review the indicated section.

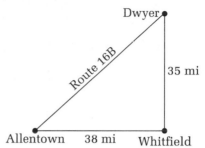

1. Use the map at the right. Whitfield is due east of Allentown and due south of Dwyer. What is the distance, to the nearest tenth of a mile, from Dwyer to Allentown along Route 16B? *(Section 9-1)*

2. Reggie uses the following reasoning to decide that the sum of two even numbers is always even.

   Let the two even numbers be $2m$ and $2n$. Their sum is $2m + 2n$. By the distributive property, $2m + 2n = 2(m + n)$. But $2(m + n)$ is always an even number because it has 2 as a factor. Therefore, the sum of two even numbers is always even.

   Is Reggie using inductive or deductive reasoning? *(Section 9-1)*

3. Simplify $\sqrt{112}$. *(Section 9-2)*

4. Solve $3x^2 = 72$. *(Section 9-2)*

Use the following if-then statement for Exercises 5–8:

If a triangle is a right triangle, then it has two acute angles. *(Section 9-3)*

5. Identify the hypothesis and the conclusion of the statement.

6. Tell whether the statement is *True* or *False*. If it is false, give a counterexample.

7. Write the converse of the statement.

8. Tell whether the converse is *True* or *False*. If it is false, give a counterexample.

9. Between 4:00 P.M. and 7:00 P.M., Kim bags groceries at the supermarket. She has one half-hour break during this period. The break can occur anytime after 4:30. What is the probability that Kim's break will be between 5:30 and 6:00. *(Section 9-4)*

10. **Open-ended** Design a spinner with red, blue, and green sections in which the probability that the spinner will land on blue is $\frac{4}{9}$. *(Section 9-4)*

11. Identify the space figure shown at the right and find its surface area. *(Section 9-5)*

12. The surface area of a cylinder is about 942.5 cm^2. The radius of its base is 10 cm. Find the height of the cylinder. *(Section 9-5)*

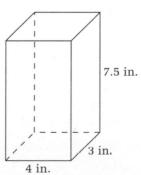

13. Find the volume of a cylinder with height 20 cm and diameter 16 cm. *(Section 9-6)*

14. **Writing** Describe the steps you would take to find the volume of the space figure shown at the right. *(Section 9-6)*

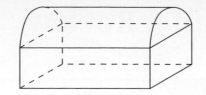

15. Find the volume of a square pyramid whose base measures 3 in. on a side and whose height is 5 in. *(Section 9-7)*

16. Find the volume of a cone with height 9 cm and radius 5 cm. *(Section 9-7)*

17. The ratio of the radii of two similar cylinders is 2 : 5. What is the ratio of their volumes? *(Section 9-8)*

Spiral Review

Units 1–9

Find the coordinates of each vertex of △*PQR* after each translation.

1. 3 units up

2. 2 units right

3. 1 unit left and 2 units up

4. 5 units right and 4 units down

Draw all lines of symmetry for each figure or write *no symmetry*.

5.   6.   7.

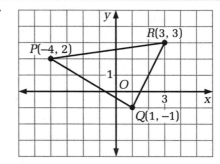
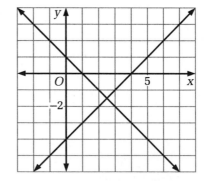

Estimate the solution of the system from the graph. Then find the exact solution.

8. $y = x - 1$
   $y = -x + 3$

9. $x - y = 4$
   $x + y = 1$

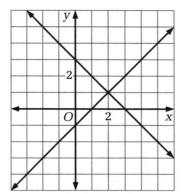

For Exercises 10–12, write each product as a power of 10.

10. $10^{12} \cdot 10^4$ 11. $10^5 \cdot 10^5$ 12. $10^3 \cdot 10^{20}$

13. Complete this conjecture about multiplying powers of 10:
    $10^a \cdot 10^b = 10^?$.

14. Give the converse of the following if-then statement.
    If $a = 0$ or $b = 0$, then $ab = 0$.

15. Is the converse you wrote for Exercise 14 *True* or *False*?

Reflections

Recognize and draw the mirror image of an object.

At this point in the game of billiards shown at the right, the purpose of the next shot is to hit the cue ball C in such a way that it makes no contact with ball A but hits ball B, sending ball B in the direction of the pocket in the lower right corner. The

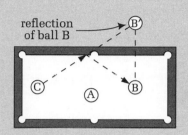

reflection of ball B

diagram shows how to use a cushion shot in which the cue ball C hits the side of the table and bounces back to hit ball B. The idea of reflection in a line helps you find the point along the side of the table at which you must aim. The reflection of ball B outside the table, with the edge of the cushion as the line of reflection, is used to locate this point. When cue ball C hits the cushion at the proper point, it rebounds off the cushion at an angle toward ball B.

KEY TERMS

EXAMPLE / ILLUSTRATION

Reflection (p. 548) a transformation that produces a mirror image of a figure	$\triangle A'B'C'$ is a reflection of $\triangle ABC$.
Line of reflection (p. 548) the line over which a figure is reflected	line of reflection
Orientation (p. 548) the direction, either clockwise or counterclockwise, in which the points on a figure are ordered (In a reflection, the orientation is reversed.)	clockwise orientation counterclockwise orientation

x-axis (p. 550) the horizontal axis in the coordinate plane	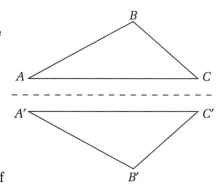
y-axis (p. 550) the vertical axis in the coordinate plane	

UNDERSTANDING THE MAIN IDEAS

Reflections

A reflection of a figure is a mirror image of the figure. The figure and its image are congruent ($\triangle ABC \cong \triangle A'B'C'$) and are located on opposite sides of the line of reflection. Each point on the image (such as point B') is the same distance from the line of reflection as the corresponding point (B) on the original figure. The orientation of the image (A'–B'–C' is counterclockwise) is in the opposite direction from the orientation of the original figure (A–B–C is clockwise).

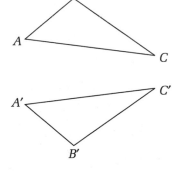

Sample 1

$\triangle A'B'C'$ is the reflection image of $\triangle ABC$. Copy the triangles, draw the line of reflection, and name three segments that are divided in half by the line of reflection. Describe the orientation of each triangle.

Sample Response

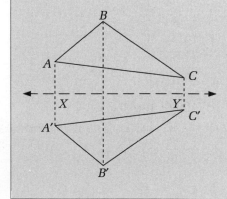

$\overleftrightarrow{XY}$ is the line of reflection; $\overline{AA'}$, $\overline{BB'}$, and $\overline{CC'}$ are divided in half by $\overleftrightarrow{XY}$.

$\triangle ABC$ has clockwise orientation; $\triangle A'B'C'$ has counterclockwise orientation.

**In Exercises 1–4, tell whether each transformation is a reflection.
If it is not, tell why not.**

1.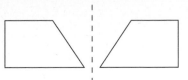

2.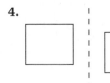

3.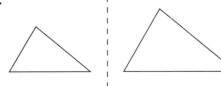

4.

Reflections on a coordinate plane

When a polygon on a coordinate plane is reflected over the *x*-axis or
the *y*-axis, the coordinates of the vertices of the polygon are useful when
drawing the image of the original polygon.

Sample 2

Copy quadrilateral *WXYZ* on graph
paper. Indicate the *x*- and *y*-axes and
give the coordinates of the vertices.
Then reflect quadrilateral *WXYZ* over
the *y*-axis. Write the coordinates of the
vertices of quadrilateral *W′X′Y′Z′* and
describe the orientation of quadrilateral
WXYZ and its image.

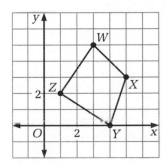

Sample Response

The orientation of
quadrilateral *WXYZ* is
clockwise; the orientation
of quadrilateral *W′X′Y′Z′*
is counterclockwise.

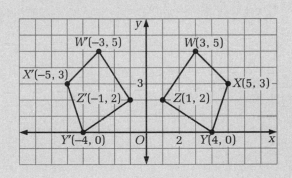

*INTEGRATED MATHEMATICS 1 **Study Guide*** **243**

Copy each figure and reflect it over the indicated line.
Describe the orientation of the original figure and its image.

5. *x*-axis

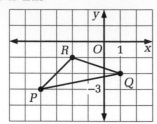

6. *y*-axis

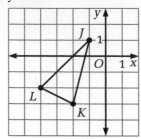

7. *y*-axis

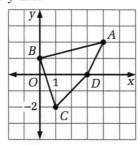

8. *x*-axis

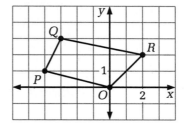

Review **PREVIEW**

9. Find the ratio of the volumes of a cone with radius 8 cm and a similar cone with radius 18 cm.   *(Section 9-8)*

10. The ratio of the diameter of two similar cylinders is 5 : 2. The volume of the larger cylinder is 750π cm³. What is the volume of the smaller cylinder?   *(Section 9-8)*

Graph each equation.   *(Section 8-3)*

11. $y = -2$ **12.** $x = 3$ **13.** $y = 1$ **14.** $x = -4$

10-2 Transforming Parabolas

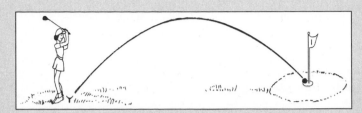

FOCUS

Translate and reflect the graph of $y = x^2$.

Suppose a golfer hits a golf ball off the tee at a 45° angle and at a velocity of 30 yd/s. Then the distance x that the ball travels from the tee and the height y of the ball can be found by using the equation $y = -0.004x^2 + x$. To find the distance the ball will travel, you can solve the equation $0 = -0.004x^2 + x$. The nonzero value of x that satisfies this equation is the maximum distance the ball will travel from the tee.

KEY TERMS

EXAMPLE / ILLUSTRATION

Parabola (p. 555)
the graph of an equation such as $y = x^2$, $y = (x + k)^2$, or $y = x^2 + k$

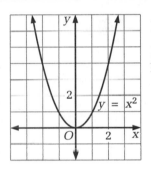

Vertex of a parabola (p. 555)
the point of a parabola that lies on the line of symmetry of the parabola

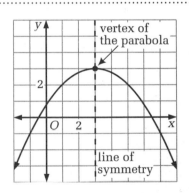

UNDERSTANDING THE MAIN IDEAS

Graphing and translating $y = x^2$ and $y = -x^2$

The graph of $y = x^2$ is a parabola that opens upward, while the graph of $y = -x^2$ is a parabola that opens downward. The graphs of $y = x^2 + k$ and $y = -x^2 + k$ are vertical translations of the graphs of $y = x^2$ and $y = -x^2$, respectively. The graphs of $y = (x + k)^2$ and $y = -(x + k)^2$ are horizontal translations of the original graphs, respectively.

Sample 1

Tell how to translate the graph of $y = -x^2$ in order to produce the graph
of each equation.

a. $y = -x^2 + 1$ **b.** $y = -x^2 - 1$
c. $y = -(x + 1)^2$ **d.** $y = -(x - 1)^2$

Sample Response

a. $y = -x^2 + 1$

1 is *added* to $-x^2$.
Translate the graph of
$y = -x^2$ *up* 1 unit.

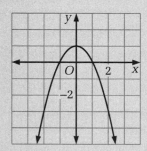

b. $y = -x^2 - 1$

1 is *subtracted* from $-x^2$.
Translate the graph of
$y = -x^2$ *down* 1 unit.

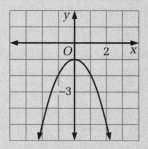

c. $y = -(x + 1)^2$

1 is *added* to x.
Translate the graph of
$y = -x^2$ *to the left* 1 unit.

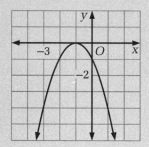

d. $y = -(x - 1)^2$

1 is *subtracted* from x.
Translate the graph of
$y = -x^2$ *to the right* 1 unit.

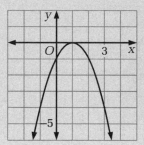

**Match each equation in Exercises 1–4 with the translation of $y = -x^2$
that produces it.**

1. $y = -x^2 + 5$ **A.** to the right 5 units

2. $y = -(x + 5)^2$ **B.** down 5 units

3. $y = -(x - 5)^2$ **C.** up 5 units

4. $y = -x^2 - 5$ **D.** to the left 5 units

In Exercises 5–7, match each function with its graph below.

5. $y = -x^2 + 2$ **6.** $y = (x + 2)^2$ **7.** $y = -(x - 2)^2$

A. 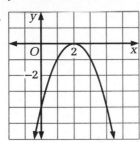   **B.** 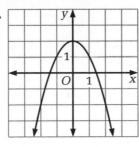   **C.**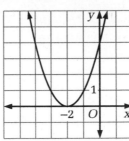

Vertex and axis of symmetry of a parabola

The graphs of $y = x^2$ and $y = -x^2$ are both parabolas that have the origin $(0, 0)$ as their vertex and the y-axis (the line $x = 0$) as their line of symmetry. Vertical translations of these graphs do *not* change the line of symmetry, but they do change the y-coordinate of the vertex. Horizontal translations change both the line of symmetry and the x-coordinate of the vertex.

Sample 2

For the graph of each equation, write the equation of the line of symmetry and the coordinates of the vertex.

a. $y = -x^2 + 3$ **b.** $y = -(x - 4)^2$

Sample Response

a. $y = -x^2 + 3$

Translate the graph of $y = -x^2$ 3 units up.

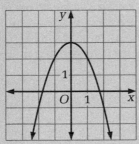

The vertex moves up 3 units from $(0, 0)$ to $(0, 3)$. The line of symmetry is still $x = 0$.

b. $y = -(x - 4)^2$

Translate the graph of $y = -x^2$ to the right 4 units.

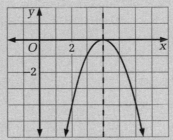

The line of symmetry and the vertex move to the right 4 units. The line of symmetry is $x = 4$, and the vertex is $(4, 0)$.

For the graph of each function, do these things.

  a. Write the equation of the line of symmetry.

  b. Find the coordinates of the vertex.

8. $y = (x + 8)^2$ **9.** $y = -x^2 - 5$ **10.** $y = -(x - 10)^2$

   *INTEGRATED MATHEMATICS 1 **Study Guide** 247*

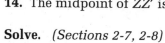
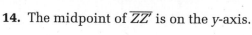
$\triangle X'Y'Z'$ is the reflection image of $\triangle XYZ$.
Tell whether each statement is *True* or
False. If false, rewrite the statement so
that it is true. *(Section 10-1)*

11. The *x*-axis is the line of reflection.

12. $\triangle X'Y'Z'$ is congruent to $\triangle XYZ$.

13. $\triangle X'Y'Z'$ has the same orientation as $\triangle XYZ$.

14. The midpoint of $\overline{ZZ'}$ is on the *y*-axis.

Solve. *(Sections 2-7, 2-8)*

15. $6x - 30 = 0$ **16.** $17 - 2x = 17$ **17.** $4x + 24 = 0$

Use the zero-product property to solve each equation. *(Section 9-3)*

18. $8s = 0$ **19.** $5p(p - 2) = 0$ **20.** $2x(x + 3) = 0$

Factors and Intercepts

Use a table of values to sketch a parabola, and use algebra to find the coordinates of the points where a parabola crosses the axes.

The water in the first fountain shown below is directed upward at an angle of 45°. For any given water pressure, the 45° angle gives a maximum horizontal range for the spray. In the second fountain, the water is directed upward at an angle of 60°. The 60° angle gives a greater height for the spray, but shortens the horizontal range. Parabolic equations can be used to determine the heights and distances for different angles.

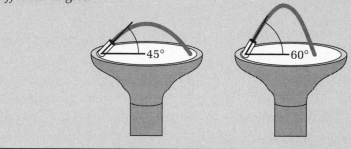

KEY TERMS

x-intercept (p. 563)
the x-coordinate of the point at which a graph intersects the x-axis

y-intercept (p. 563)
the y-coordinate of the point at which a graph intersects the y-axis

EXAMPLE / ILLUSTRATION

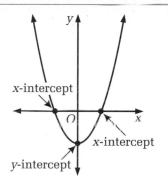

UNDERSTANDING THE MAIN IDEAS

Intercepts of a graph

The x-intercepts of a graph are the x-coordinates of the points where the y-coordinate is 0. The y-intercept is the y-coordinate of the point where the x-coordinate is 0. The intercepts can be found from a table of x- and y-values, from a graph, or by solving the equation of the graph.

> ### Sample 1
>
> Graph $y = (x - 2)(x + 1)$. Give the x- and y-intercepts.

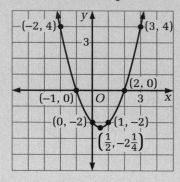
Sample 2

Use algebra to find the intercepts of the graph of $y = (2 - x)(3 + x)$.

Sample Response

Step 1 Find the x-intercepts.

The graph crosses the x-axis where $y = 0$.

$y = (2 - x)(3 + x)$

$0 = (2 - x)(3 + x)$ ⟵ Substitute 0 for y.

Use the zero-product property:

$2 - x = 0$ or $3 + x = 0$ ⟵ If $ab = 0$, then either $a = 0$ or $b = 0$.

$2 - x + x = 0 + x$ $3 + x - 3 = 0 - 3$

$2 = x$ $x = -3$

The x-intercepts are 2 and -3.

Step 2 Find the y-intercept.

The graph crosses the y-axis where $x = 0$.

$y = (2 - x)(3 + x)$

$y = (2 - 0)(3 + 0)$ ⟵ Substitute 0 for x each time it occurs.

$y = (2)(3)$

$y = 6$

The y-intercept is 6.

Make a table of values and graph each parabola. Give the x- and y-intercepts.

1. $y = x(x + 1)$

2. $y = (1 - x)(2 + x)$

Without graphing, find the x- and y-intercepts of the graph of each equation.

3. $y = (x + 6)x$

4. $y = x(x - 5)$

5. $y = (x - 3)(x - 6)$

6. $y = (x + 7)(x - 8)$

7. $y = (2x - 1)(x + 4)$

8. $y = (3x + 6)(x - 2)$

Review PREVIEW

Tell how to translate the graph of $y = x^2$ in order to produce the graph of each function. *(Section 10-2)*

9. $y = x^2 + 5$

10. $y = x^2 - 9$

11. $y = (x + 4)^2$

Write each expression as a power of ten. *(Section 1-3)*

12. $10^3 \times 10^3$

13. $10^{-5} \times 10^8$

14. $\dfrac{10^{12}}{10^2}$

15. $\dfrac{10^3}{10^9}$

10-4 Working with Powers

Use shortcuts for
simplifying powers.

*A frequently-used unit of data storage in a computer is the kilobyte (K).
One kilobyte is 2^{10}, or 1024 bytes. The byte is a sequence of 2^3, or 8 bits.
The bit is the smallest unit of data in the computer. Thus, a kilobyte is
$2^{10} \cdot 2^3 = 1024 \times 8 = 8192 = 2^{10+3}$ bits. Early personal computers
often had 256 kilobytes of memory. Since $256 = 2^8$, this is equivalent to
$2^8 \cdot 2^{10} = 2^{8+10} = 262{,}144$ bytes, or $2{,}097{,}152 = 2^{21}$ bits. More recent
personal computers have several megabytes (MB) of memory. A megabyte
is 2^{20}, or, $1{,}048{,}576$ bytes. How many bits of storage is 1 megabyte?*

UNDERSTANDING THE MAIN IDEAS

Finding the product of powers

To find the product of powers that have the same base, add the
exponents. In symbols, for a given base a, $a^m \cdot a^n = a^{m+n}$.
It is important to remember that the powers must have the same
base for this rule to apply.

Sample 1

Simplify.

a. $b \cdot b^3$ **b.** $x^5y \cdot xy^5$ **c.** $(-a^3)(2a)$

Sample Response

a. $b \cdot b^3 = b^1 \cdot b^3$ ⟵ Rewrite b as b^1.

$\qquad = b^{1+3}$ ⟵ Use the product of powers rule.

$\qquad = b^4$

b. $x^5y \cdot xy^5 = (x^5 \cdot x) \cdot (y \cdot y^5)$ ⟵ Group powers of x and powers of y.

$\qquad = (x^5 \cdot x^1) \cdot (y^1 \cdot y^5)$ ⟵ Rewrite x as x^1 and y as y^1.

$\qquad = x^{5+1} \cdot y^{1+5}$ ⟵ Use the product of powers rule for powers with the same base.

$\qquad = x^6y^6$

c. $(-a^3)(2a) = (-1a^3)(2a^1)$ ⟵ Rewrite $-a^3$ as $-1a^3$ and $2a$ as $2a^1$.

$\qquad = (-1 \cdot 2) \cdot (a^3 \cdot a^1)$ ⟵ Group numbers and powers of a.

$\qquad = -2 \cdot a^{3+1}$ ⟵ Use the product of powers rule.

$\qquad = -2a^4$

Simplify.

1. $b^2 \cdot b^8$ **2.** $x^2 \cdot 2x$ **3.** $(-y^3)(6y^4)$ **4.** $(4ab^2)(a^3b^3)$

Finding the power of a power

To find a power of a power, multiply the exponents. In symbols,
$(a^m)^n = a^{m \cdot n}$.

> ### Sample 2
>
> Simplify $(c^3)^6$.
>
> ### Sample Response
>
> $(c^3)^6 = c^{3 \cdot 6}$ ⟵ Use the power of a power rule.
> $ = c^{18}$

Simplify.

5. $(x^2)^4$ **6.** $(y^2)^9$ **7.** $(k^5)^5$ **8.** $(p^3)^3$

Finding the power of a product

To find the power of a product, find that power of each factor and then multiply. In symbols, $(ab)^n = a^n \cdot b^n$.

> ### Sample 3
>
> Simplify.
> **a.** $(-2x)^4$ **b.** $(3m^2n^5)^3$
>
> ### Sample Response
>
> **a.** $(-2x)^4 = (-2)^4 \cdot x^4$ ⟵ Use the power of a product rule.
> $ = 16x^4$ ⟵ Use the power of a power rule.
> **b.** $(3m^2n^5)^3 = 3^3 \cdot (m^2)^3 \cdot (n^5)^3$ ⟵ Use the power of a product rule.
> $ = 27m^6n^{15}$ ⟵ Use the power of a power rule.

Simplify.

9. $(-a^3)^4$ **10.** $(6y^2)^5$ **11.** $(-3x^2y)^3$ **12.** $(7a^2b^3c^4)^2$

Review PREVIEW

For Exercises 13 and 14, find the x- and y-intercepts of the graph of each function. *(Section 10-3)*

13. $y = (x - 1)(x + 3)$ **14.** $y = (x - 2)(x + 2)$

15. a. Suppose 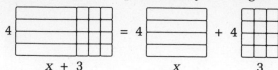 represents x and ☐ represents 1.
Write a statement represented by the diagram below.

4 ▢▢▢ = 4 ▢▢ + 4 ▢▢
$x + 3$ x 3

b. Draw a diagram similar to the one in part (a) to represent the statement
$3(x + 5) = 3x + 3 \cdot 5$. *(Section 5-3)*

Use the distributive property to rewrite each expression. *(Sections 1-5, 5-2)*

16. $4(y + 5)$ **17.** $3(2x - 8)$ **18.** $-2(x - 9)$ **19.** $(x + y)5$

10-5 Factored Form and *x*-Intercepts

FOCUS

Factor and expand algebraic expressions, and use factoring to find the *x*-intercepts of parabolas.

An art project involves designing and making a hooked rug. The canvas is a rectangle, 36 in. by 60 in. The rug is to have a uniform black border. There is enough black yarn to fill in 500 in.² of the canvas. To find the maximum width for the black border, you need to solve the equation $500 = 4x^2 + 2(60 - 2x)x + 2(36 - 2x)x$ or $500 = 192x - 4x^2$.

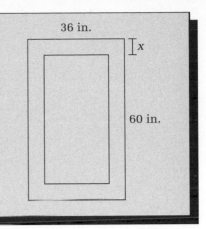

36 in.

x

60 in.

KEY TERMS

EXAMPLE / ILLUSTRATION

Factored form (p. 577)
an expression written as the product of its factors

The expression $2x(x - 6)$ is in factored form.

Expanded form (p. 577)
the expression obtained by multiplying the terms of the factored form of an expression

The expression $2x^2 - 12x$ is in expanded form.

Binomial (p. 578)
an expression involving the sum or difference of two unlike terms

The expression $2x^2 - 12x$ is a binomial.

Monomial (p. 578)
a number, a variable, or a product of numbers and variables

The terms $2x^2$ and $-12x$ are monomials.

Factored completely (p. 578)
an expression written in factored form such that no factor can itself be factored again

The expression $2x(x - 6)$ is factored completely; neither $2(x^2 - 6x)$ nor $x(2x - 12)$ is factored completely.

UNDERSTANDING THE MAIN IDEAS

Expanding and factoring expressions

Algebraic expressions that are expressed as products can be expanded by doing the indicated multiplication. Conversely, algebraic expressions in expanded form can be rewritten as products by factoring. Area models can be used to show how to factor and expand expressions geometrically. The distributive property can be used to perform factoring and expanding algebraically.

Sample 1

Expand $x(x + 4)$.

Sample Response

Method 1: Expand using algebra tiles.

Area $= x \cdot (x + 4) = x^2 + 4x$

Method 2: Expand algebraically.

$x(x + 4) = x \cdot x + x \cdot 4$ ⟵ Use the distributive property.
$\qquad\qquad = x^2 + 4x$

Expand each expression.

1. $-x(x + 6)$ **2.** $(3 + x)x$ **3.** $-2x(2x - 4)$

Sample 2

Factor $x^2 - 3x$.

Sample Response

Method 1: Factor using algebra tiles.

Area $= x^2 - 3x = x^2 + (-3x)$
$\qquad\qquad\quad = x(x - 3)$

Method 2: Factor algebraically.

$x^2 - 3x = x \cdot x - 3 \cdot x$ ⟵ Rewrite each term as a product.
$\qquad\quad = x(x - 3)$ ⟵ Use the distributive property in reverse.

Factor each expression.

4. $x^2 + 8x$ **5.** $16x - 2x^2$ **6.** $2x^2 + 5x$

Finding x-intercepts

Previously, you used equations written in factored form to find the x-intercepts of their graphs. If the equation is given in expanded form, factoring the expanded expression will help you find the x-intercepts.

Sample 3

The graph of $y = 8x - 2x^2$ is a parabola. Find the x-intercepts of the graph.

Sample Response

Step 1 Factor the expression $8x - 2x^2$ completely.

$8x - 2x^2$

$8 \cdot x - 2 \cdot x \cdot x$ ←— Rewrite each term as a product.

$4 \cdot 2 \cdot x - 2 \cdot x \cdot x$ ←— Find the greatest common factor of the numbers.

$2x(4 - x)$ ←— Factor out $2x$, the greatest common factor.

Step 2 Use the factored form to find x when $y = 0$.

Write the original equation in factored form.

$y = 2x(4 - x)$

$0 = 2x(4 - x)$ ←— Substitute 0 for y.

$0 = 2x$ or $4 - x = 0$ ←— Use the zero-product property.

$0 = x$ or $4 - x + x = 0 + x$

$x = 0$ or $x = 4$

The x-intercepts of the parabola are 0 and 4.

For Exercises 7–9, do these things:
  a. Factor one side of each equation completely.
  b. Find the x-intercepts of the graph of each equation.

7. $y = x^2 - 3x$ **8.** $y = 6x - x^2$ **9.** $y = 3x^2 + 9x$

Review **PREVIEW**

Simplify. *(Sections 2-6, 10-4)*

10. $y^3 \cdot 2y^2$ **11.** $2x^2(-3x^4)$ **12.** $(2pq)^2$ **13.** $(4b^3)^2$

14. $x^2 + 2x + 7 + x$ **15.** $x^2 - 6x + 8x - 5$ **16.** $x^2 - 3x - 7x + 10$

For the graph of each equation, name the line of symmetry and the coordinates of the vertex. *(Section 10-2)*

17. $y = x^2 + 7$ **18.** $y = x^2 - 25$ **19.** $y = (x + 8)^2$

    INTEGRATED MATHEMATICS 1 **Study Guide**

Multiply two binomials, and use a formula to find the line of symmetry of a parabola.

The rockets in a fireworks display follow paths that are parabolas. The rocket shown follows a path described by the equation

$$y = 4x - \frac{1}{128}x^2,$$

where x is the horizontal distance in feet from the launch point and y is the height in feet above the ground. The rocket is designed to explode at its highest point, which is at the vertex of the parabola. To find the coordinates of the vertex, you need to first find the equation of the line of symmetry.

path of rocket

KEY TERMS

Trinomial (p. 584)
    an expression with three monomial terms

EXAMPLE / ILLUSTRATION

The expression $3x^2 + 6x - 5$ is a trinomial.

UNDERSTANDING THE MAIN IDEAS

Multiplying binomials

You can find the product of two binomials by using algebra tiles or by using the distributive property.

Sample 1

Expand $(x + 4)(x + 3)$.

Sample Response

Method 1: Expand using algebra tiles.

Build a rectangle with the dimensions $x + 4$ and $x + 3$.

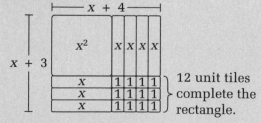

12 unit tiles complete the rectangle.

Sample Response continues on the next page.

Express the area of the rectangle as the product of its length and widths:

$A = (x + 4)(x + 3)$

Now express the area of the rectangle as the sum of the areas of the tiles:

$A = (x + 4)(x + 3) = x^2 + 7x + 12$

Method 2: Expand algebraically.

$(x + 4)(x + 3) = (x + 4)x + (x + 4)3$ ⟵ Use the distributive property.
$= x^2 + 4x + 3x + 12$ ⟵ Use the distributive property.
$= x^2 + 7x + 12$ ⟵ Combine like terms.

Expand each product.

1. $(x - 3)(x + 4)$ **2.** $(2x + 1)(x - 1)$ **3.** $(4x - 3)(2x - 2)$

Line of symmetry, vertex, and y-intercepts of a parabola

A parabola whose equation is of the form $y = ax^2 + bx + c$ opens upward if $a > 0$ and downward if $a < 0$. The line of symmetry for a parabola of this type is the vertical line with equation $x = -\frac{b}{2a}$. The vertex of the parabola is on the line of symmetry. The y-intercept is the point where the graph intersects the y-axis, that is, where $x = 0$.

Sample 2

Without graphing, find each feature of the graph of $y = x^2 - 2x - 8$.
a. the equation of the line of symmetry
b. the coordinates of the vertex
c. the y-intercept

Sample Response

a. Use the formula for the line of symmetry.

$x = -\frac{b}{2a}$

$= -\frac{(-2)}{2 \cdot 1}$ ⟵ Substitute -2 for b and 1 for a.

$= 1$

The equation of the line of symmetry is $x = 1$.

b. The vertex is on the line of symmetry, $x = 1$, found in part (a).
Substitute 1 for x in the equation to find the y-coordinate.

$y = x^2 - 2x - 8$
$= (1)^2 - 2(1) - 8$ ⟵ Substitute 1 for x.
$= 1 - 2 - 8$
$= -9$

The coordinates of the vertex are $(1, -9)$.

c. The y-intercept is the value of y when $x = 0$.

$y = x^2 - 2x - 8$
$= (0)^2 - 2(0) - 8$ ⟵ Substitute 0 for each x.
$= -8$

The y-intercept is -8.

Without graphing, find each feature of the graph of each equation in Exercises 4–6.

  a. the equation of the line of symmetry

  b. the coordinates of the vertex

  c. the y-intercept

  4. $y = x^2 + 5x - 6$ **5.** $y = x^2 + 10x + 25$ **6.** $y = x^2 - 9$

Review **PREVIEW**

For Exercises 7–10, expand each product. *(Section 10-5)*

  7. $x(3x + 2)$ **8.** $(x - 7)x$ **9.** $-5x(2x + 2)$ **10.** $3x(4x - 2)$

11. Factor the right side of the equation $y = 20x - 5x^2$. Then find the x-intercept(s) and y-intercept of the graph of the equation. *(Section 10-5)*

12. Find the x-intercepts of the graph of $y = (x - 7)(x + 10)$. *(Section 10-5)*

Write all pairs of factors for each number. *(Toolbox Skill 7)*

  13. 18   **14.** 23   **15.** 32   **16.** 48

10-7 Using Factors to Sketch $y = x^2 + bx + c$

FOCUS

Factor trinomials
and sketch the
graph of a
parabola.

Business analysts consider overhead, production costs, and pricing factors when developing profit equations for businesses. An example of such an equation might be $y = -132 + 28x - x^2$, where y is the profit and x is the number of units produced. By analyzing this equation and its graph (shown at the right), the business can determine the number of units produced which will maximize profits.

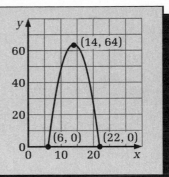

UNDERSTANDING THE MAIN IDEAS

When a trinomial is given in the expanded form $x^2 + bx + c$, you can use the relationship between the integers b and c to help you write the trinomial in factored form. The following diagram illustrates the relationship.

These two integers must have a
product of c and a sum of b.

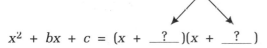

$$x^2 + bx + c = (x + \underline{\ ?\ })(x + \underline{\ ?\ })$$

If two integers cannot be found whose product is c and whose sum is b, then the trinomial $x^2 + bx + c$ cannot be factored.

Sample 1

Factor $x^2 - x - 6$.

Sample Response

$$x^2 - x - 6 = (x + \underline{\ ?\ })(x + \underline{\ ?\ })$$

Find a pair of integers whose product is –6 and whose sum is –1. The integers must have different signs because their product is negative.

Write all possible pairs whose product is –6.

  –1 and 6   1 and –6   –2 and 3   2 and –3

Find the sums of these pairs of integers, looking for the pair having a sum of –1.

  –1 + 6 = 5   1 + (–6) = –5   –2 + 3 = 1   2 + (–3) = –1

The integers 2 and –3 have both a product of –6 and a sum of –1.
Therefore,

$$x^2 - x - 6 = (x + 2)(x + (-3))$$
$$= (x + 2)(x - 3)$$

Sample 2

Factor $x^2 + 12x - 35$.

Sample Response

$x^2 + 12x - 35 = (x + \underline{})(x + \underline{})$

Find a pair of integers whose product is -35 and whose sum is 12.
The integers must have different signs because their product is negative.

Write all possible pairs whose product is -35.

   1 and -35 -1 and 35   5 and -7 -5 and 7

Find the sums of these pairs of integers.

   $1 + (-35) = -34$ $-1 + 35 = 34$ $5 + (-7) = -2$ $-5 + 7 = 2$

None of the pairs of integers has a sum of 12. Therefore, the trinomial cannot be factored.

Factor each trinomial that can be factored using integers. If a trinomial cannot be factored, write *not possible*.

1. $x^2 + 10x + 24$ **2.** $x^2 + 2x - 63$ **3.** $x^2 - 3x - 8$

Sketching the graph of $y = x^2 + bx + c$

You can make a reasonably accurate sketch of a parabola by determining the line of symmetry, the coordinates of the vertex, and the x- and y-intercepts of the graph from the equation of the parabola.

Sample 3

Use the vertex, the intercepts, and symmetry to sketch the graph of $y = x^2 - 2x - 3$.

Sample Response

Step 1 Find the equation of the line of symmetry.

$x = \dfrac{-b}{2a}$ ⟵ Use the formula for the line of symmetry.

$x = \dfrac{-(-2)}{2 \cdot 1}$ ⟵ Substitute 1 for a and -2 for b.

$x = 1$

The equation of the line of symmetry is $x = 1$.

Sample Response continues on the next page.

Step 2 Find the coordinates of the vertex.

From the line of symmetry found in part (a), the x-coordinate of the vertex is 1.

$y = (1)^2 - 2(1) - 3$ ⟵ Substitute 1 for x in the equation.
$y = -4$

The coordinates of the vertex are $(1, -4)$. Locate the vertex on the graph.

Step 3 Find the intercepts.

a. Find the y-intercept.

$y = (0)^2 - 2(0) - 3$ ⟵ Substitute 0 for x in the equation.
$y = -3$

The y-intercept is -3.

b. Find the x-intercepts.

Factor the right side of the equation.

$y = x^2 - 2x - 3$
$y = (x - 3)(x + 1)$ ⟵ The product of -3 and 1 is -3; the sum of -3 and 1 is -2.
$0 = (x - 3)(x + 1)$ ⟵ Substitute 0 for y.
$x - 3 = 0$ or $x + 1 = 0$ ⟵ Use the zero-product property.
$x = 3$ or $x = -1$

The x-intercepts are 3 and -1.

Step 4 Use the vertex, intercepts, and symmetry to sketch the parabola.

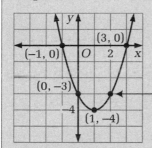

By symmetry, the point $(2, -3)$ is on the parabola.

Use the line of symmetry, the vertex, and the intercepts to sketch the graph of each equation.

4. $y = x^2 - 6x + 8$ **5.** $y = x^2 + 2x - 3$ **6.** $y = x^2 - 2x - 8$

Review **PREVIEW**

Expand each product. *(Section 10-6)*

7. $(x - 3)(x - 7)$ **8.** $(x + 4)(x - 5)$ **9.** $(x + 8)(x - 5)$

Solve each equation. *(Sections 2-8, 9-2)*

10. $8x + 4 = 2$ **11.** $x^2 = 169$ **12.** $x^2 = 48$

Evaluate each expression when $a = 1$, $b = 4$, $c = -2$, and $d = 16$.
(Section 2-2)

13. $b^2 - 4ac$ **14.** $-\dfrac{b}{2a}$ **15.** $-b + \sqrt{d}$

Solve problems
about situations
modeled by
parabolas.

The path of the water from this fire hose is described by the equation $y = -\frac{1}{40}x^2 + 2x + 0.5$, where x is the horizontal distance in meters from the nozzle and y is the height in meters of the water stream above the ground. Suppose the fire is on the fifth floor of a highrise building. To determine whether the water will reach the fifth-floor fire, you need to find the coordinates of the vertex of the graph of the equation $y = -\frac{1}{40}x^2 + 2x + 0.5$.

KEY TERMS

EXAMPLE / ILLUSTRATION

Quadratic equation (p. 599)
an equation that can be written in the form
$0 = ax^2 + bx + c$, where a, b, and c are
numbers and $a \neq 0$

The equation
$0 = 6x^2 - 12x + 2$
is a quadratic equation.

Quadratic formula (p. 601)
the formula $x = -\frac{b}{2a} \pm \frac{\sqrt{b^2 - 4ac}}{2a}$
used to find the solutions of a quadratic equation

To find the solutions of the
equation above, substitute
$a = 6$, $b = -12$, and $c = 2$
into the quadratic formula.

$$x = \frac{-(-12)}{2(6)} \pm \frac{\sqrt{(-12)^2 - 4(6)(2)}}{2(6)}$$

The solutions are
$x = 1 + \frac{\sqrt{6}}{3}$ and $x = 1 - \frac{\sqrt{6}}{3}$.

UNDERSTANDING THE MAIN IDEAS

Solving $0 = ax^2 + bx + c$ by graphing

The solutions of $0 = ax^2 + bx + c$ are the x-intercepts of the graph of the equation $y = ax^2 + bx + c$. Thus, one way of solving the equation is by drawing an accurate graph. If the graph does not cross the x-axis at points that correspond to integral units on the grid, the solutions you get from analyzing the graph will be approximations.

Sample 1

Solve $10x^2 - 5x - 50 = 0$ by graphing.

Graph the quadratic function $y = 10x^2 - 5x - 50$.

Step 1 Make a table of values.

x	−3	−2	−1	0	1	2	3
y	55	0	−35	−50	−45	−20	25

Step 2 Use the table to draw a graph.

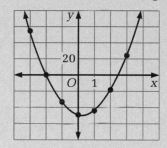

Step 3 Read the x-intercepts from the graph.

The intercepts are at −2 and 2.5, so the solutions of
$10x^2 - 5x - 50 = 0$ are $x = -2$ and $x = 2.5$.

Check (✔): Substitute −2 and 2.5 in the original equation.

$$10(-2)^2 - 5(-2) - 50 \stackrel{?}{=} 0 \qquad 10(2.5)^2 - 5(2.5) - 50 \stackrel{?}{=} 0$$
$$40 + 10 - 50 = 0 ✔ \qquad 62.5 - 12.5 - 50 = 0 ✔$$

Sketch a graph to solve each quadratic equation.

   1. $0 = x^2 - 2x - 3$ **2.** $0 = x^2 - 6.5x + 9$ **3.** $0 = x^2 + 2x - 2$

Using the quadratic formula to solve $0 = ax^2 + bx + c$

The quadratic formula gives the exact solutions to any equation
$0 = ax^2 + bx + c$ by using the values of a, b, and c. Often the
solutions involve square roots of numbers that are not perfect
squares. In such cases, you can approximate the solutions or
give the exact solutions in square root form.

Sample 2

Use the quadratic formula to solve $2x^2 + 5x = 25$.

Step 1 Write the equation in the form $ax^2 + bx + c = 0$ and determine the
values of a, b, and c.

$$2x^2 + 5x = 25$$
$$2x^2 + 5x - 25 = 25 - 25$$
$$2x^2 + 5x - 25 = 0$$

Thus, $a = 2$, $b = 5$, and $c = -25$.

Sample Response continues on the next page.

Step 2 Use the quadratic formula.

$$x = \frac{-b}{2a} \pm \frac{\sqrt{b^2 - 4ac}}{2a}$$

$$x = \frac{-5}{2(2)} \pm \frac{\sqrt{5^2 - 4(2)(-25)}}{2(2)}$$ ← Substitute 2 for a, 5 for b, and -25 for c.

$$= -\frac{5}{4} \pm \frac{\sqrt{25 + 200}}{4}$$

$$= -\frac{5}{4} \pm \frac{\sqrt{225}}{4}$$

$$= -\frac{5}{4} \pm \frac{15}{4}$$

The solutions are $x = \frac{10}{4} = 2.5$ and $x = \frac{-20}{4} = -5$.

Check (✔): Substitute 2.5 and -5 in the original equation.

$$2(2.5)^2 + 5(2.5) \stackrel{?}{=} 25 \qquad\qquad 2(-5)^2 + 5(-5) \stackrel{?}{=} 25$$

$$2(6.25) + 12.5 \stackrel{?}{=} 25 \qquad\qquad 2(25) - 25 \stackrel{?}{=} 25$$

$$12.5 + 12.5 \stackrel{?}{=} 25 \qquad\qquad 50 - 25 \stackrel{?}{=} 25$$

$$25 = 25 \text{ ✔} \qquad\qquad 25 = 25 \text{ ✔}$$

Use the quadratic formula to solve each equation.

4. $0 = x^2 - 11x + 18$ **5.** $-2x^2 + 7x - 5 = 0$ **6.** $x^2 - 6 = 0$

Review

For Exercises 7–9, factor each trinomial. *(Section 10-7)*

7. $x^2 + 6x - 55$ **8.** $x^2 - 3x - 28$ **9.** $x^2 + 19x + 84$

10. Use the vertex and the intercepts to sketch the graph of the equation
  $y = x^2 + x - 6$. *(Section 10-7)*

Find the x- and y-intercepts of the graph of each equation.
(Sections 8-2, 10-3)

11. $y = 6x + 3$ **12.** $y = -2.5x$ **13.** $y = x^2 + 4x$

| Unit Check-Up | Complete these exercises for a review of Unit 10. If you have difficulty with a particular problem, review the indicated section. |

Copy each figure and reflect it over the indicated line. Describe the orientation of the original figure and its image. *(Section 10-1)*

1. *y*-axis

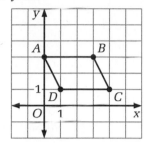

2. *x*-axis

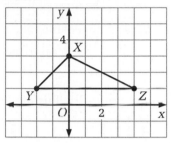

For Exercises 3–5, tell how to translate the graph of $y = x^2$ or $y = -x^2$ to produce the graph of each function. *(Section 10-2)*

3. $y = x^2 - 5$ **4.** $y = -(x - 4)^2$ **5.** $y = -x^2 + 6$

6. *Open-ended* Sketch parabolas that meet the following conditions.
   a. The parabola has no *x*-intercepts.
   b. The *x*- and *y*-intercepts are the same. *(Section 10-3)*

Find the *x*- and *y*-intercepts of the graph of each equation. *(Section 10-3)*

7. $y = (x + 5)(x - 3)$ **8.** $y = (2x - 8)x$

Simplify. *(Section 10-4)*

9. $a^2 \cdot a$ **10.** $c^2 \cdot c^4 \cdot c$ **11.** $(-x^2)(6x^5)$

For Exercises 12–14, do these things.
   a. Factor one side of the equation completely.
   b. Find the intercepts of the graph of each equation. *(Section 10-5)*

12. $y = 8x - 2x^2$ **13.** $y = 3x^2 + 27x$ **14.** $-x^2 - 3x = y$

Without graphing, find each feature of the graph of each equation in Exercises 15–17.
   a. the equation of the line of symmetry
   b. the coordinates of the vertex
   c. the *y*-intercept *(Section 10-6)*

15. $y = 2x^2 + x - 21$ **16.** $y = 16 - x^2$ **17.** $y = x^2 - 12x + 20$

18. *Writing* Describe the steps you would use to factor the trinomial $x^2 + 10x + 24$. *(Section 10-7)*

Factor each trinomial that can be factored using integers. If a trinomial cannot be factored, write *not possible*. *(Section 10-7)*

19. $x^2 + 13x + 36$ **20.** $x^2 - 6x - 40$ **21.** $x^2 + 3x + 5$

Solve each quadratic equation. *(Section 10-8)*

22. $x^2 + 7x = 8$ **23.** $-4x^2 + 2x = -8$ **24.** $20 = x^2 + 5x$

Spiral Review
Units 1–10

Use right triangle *ABC* shown at the right for Exercises 1–6.

1. Find the area of $\triangle ABC$.

2. Find c.

3. What is the tangent ratio for $\angle B$?

4. What is the sine ratio for $\angle A$?

5. What is the cosine ratio for $\angle B$?

6. $\triangle DEF \sim \triangle ABC$ and $DE = 10$. Find EF.

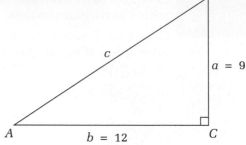

Suppose you roll a fair die. Find each probability.

7. $P\left(\text{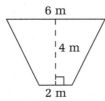}\right)$ 8. $P\left(\text{not } \text{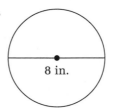}\right)$ 9. $P(\text{number less than 7})$

Use the graph at the right for Exercises 10–13. Give the coordinates of each vertex of $\triangle X'Y'Z'$ after the transformation described in each exercise.

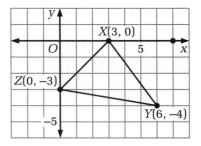

10. a translation 2 units left and 2 units up

11. a rotation of 180° about the origin

12. a reflection in the y-axis

13. a reflection in the x-axis

Solve each system of linear equations.

14. $3x + 2y = 18$
    $y = 3x$

15. $y = x - 5$
    $-4x + y = 10$

16. $y = 7x - 3$
    $y = -5x + 21$

Find the area of each figure.

17.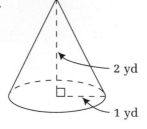

6 m
4 m
2 m

18.

8 in.

19.

2.5 ft
3.5 ft

Find the volume of each figure.

20.

2 yd
1 yd

21.

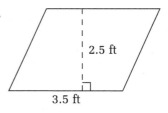

7 in.
10 in.
